FIELDING'S
SELECTIVE
SHOPPING GUIDE
TO EUROPE
1990

FIELDING'S BERMUDA AND THE BAHAMAS 1990
FIELDING'S BUDGET EUROPE 1990
FIELDING'S CARIBBEAN 1990
FIELDING'S EUROPE 1990
FIELDING'S MEXICO 1990
FIELDING'S PEOPLE'S REPUBLIC OF CHINA 1990
FIELDING'S SELECTIVE SHOPPING GUIDE TO EUROPE 1990

FIELDING'S AFRICAN SAFARIS
FIELDING'S ALASKA AND THE YUKON
FIELDING'S CALIFORNIA
FIELDING'S EUROPE WITH CHILDREN
FIELDING'S FAMILY VACATIONS USA
FIELDING'S FAR EAST 2nd revised edition
FIELDING'S HAVENS AND HIDEAWAYS USA
FIELDING'S LEWIS AND CLARK TRAIL
FIELDING'S LITERARY AFRICA
FIELDING'S MOTORING AND CAMPING EUROPE
FIELDING'S SPANISH TRAILS IN THE SOUTHWEST
FIELDING'S WORLDWIDE CRUISES 4th revised edition

FIELDING'S SELECTIVE SHOPPING GUIDE TO EUROPE

1990

JOSEPH AND JUDITH RAFF

FIELDING TRAVEL BOOKS
c/o WILLIAM MORROW & COMPANY, INC.
105 Madison Avenue, New York, N.Y. 10016

ISSN: 0071-487X

ISBN: 0-688-04676-2

ISBN: 0-340-51047-1 (Hodder & Stoughton)

Printed in the United States of America

Thirty-fourth Edition

1 2 3 4 5 6 7 8 9 10

Text design by Marsha Cohen/Parallelogram

Maurice Fievet

Joseph Raff

For 29 years Joe and his wife, Judith, have lived in Europe and crisscrossed their beat annually by car, train, boat, and plane to report on the latest trends and developments for readers of the Fielding guides.

Born in New York, Joe was graduated from the University of North Carolina at Chapel Hill, studied at Harvard, Ohio, and Indiana universities, and then reported for the Associated Press and *Sports Illustrated* before moving overseas to edit the *Rome Daily American*. Since 1961 he has worked on the Fielding guides to Europe.

Travel writing for the Fielding publications requires almost six months of road work each year. Between times Joe is an avid sailor, an ardent tennis enthusiast, and an Alpine skier. He lives on Mallorca.

Maurice Fievet

Judith Raff

Judith shares with Joe the demanding research schedule that goes into the preparation of the Fielding European guides. Her specialty is the evaluation of merchandise and current fashions for the *Selective Shopping Guide,* but still she is involved totally in the gathering, weighing, and reporting on every major field of activity covered in the Fielding guides to Europe.

Born in Philadelphia, she was educated at Connecticut College for Women, the University of North Carolina, and New York University. When there is time for leisure, it is usually answered through downhill skiing, golf, tennis, or sharing the helm on *Spoondrift,* the Raffs's boat.

APPROXIMATE CLOTHING SIZES
(American-Continental)

Women's Clothing

American	6	8	10	12	14	16
Continental						
France	36	38	40	42	44	46
Italy	38	40	42	44	46	48
Rest of Europe	34	36	38	40	42	44

Women's Shoes

American	4	5	6	7	8	9
Continental	35	36	37	38	39	40

Men's Sweaters

American	S	M	L	XL
Continental	48	50	52	54

Men's Shoes

American	8	8½	9½	10½	11½
Continental	41	42	43	44	45

APPROXIMATE CLOTHING SIZES
(American-British)

Women's Clothing

American	8	10	12	14	16
British	10	12	14	16	18

Women's Shoes

American	4	5	6	7	8	9
British	2½	3½	4½	5½	6½	7½

Men's Sweaters

American	S	M	L	XL
British	38	40	42	44

Men's Shoes

American	8	8½	9	9½	10	10½	11	11½	12	13
British	7	7½	8	8½	9	9½	10	10½	11	12

CONTENTS

THE '90 SCENE

While international currencies continue to gyrate relative one to another, the invariable constant in the shopper's equation is that a discerning eye can always spot quality and uniqueness. Even for similar goods, foreign products frequently are priced well below those in North America. In any event, what you'll want to buy will be of European origin. (On a recent check of the items for sale in the JFK duty-free shops, an overwhelming preponderance of stocks were not "Made in USA," but perfumes from France, sunglasses from Italy, Spanish leather, Swiss Army knives, scarves, glassware, pottery, and shelves of merchandise from all over the globe. It makes you wonder what America *does* produce that is desired globally.) France is bursting with designer fashions and beautifully styled and crafted take-aways. Spain and Portugal are once again genuine moneysavers for unique gifts and arts as well as for artisan items. The marketplaces of Scandinavia are still very alluring. England—always popular with tourists—is certainly a good buy, as are Scotland and Ireland. Greece, too, is beckoning as a challenger for trade, while Germany, Austria, and the Benelux nations have distinctive inventories for luxurious moods. Italy continues to shine its spotlight on grace, line and material—eternally major ingredients whether you are shopping for footwear or a Ferrari. Switzerland, of course, remains as solid and as unchanging as an Alp.

But by the time you reach Europe, the capricious monetary world could take another turn and the prices quoted throughout this book—always in U.S. dollars for your convenience—might be off a smidgen. So please don't pillory us if that Spanish mantilla is $31.98 or $31.12 instead of $30.26. (It could also just as easily shake out at $26.50 in today's whizbang flux of currencies.)

Basically, this *Shopping Guide* is composed as a service to our readers. It is a specialized volume directed to a limited audience. It could not exist if it weren't for the fact that while we are doing shopping research all over Europe, we are simultaneously gathering facts and opinions for bestselling books such as *Fielding's Europe* and *Fielding's Economy Europe*. Space is so limited in those other guides that we simply don't have the capacity to elaborate on shopping matters as we would wish to. We can only touch the highlights in those other volumes. This *Shopping Guide* benefits from the enormous outlays we already are spending to be in 17 countries every year on our other investigative legwork. It is a method of "maximizing" our efforts to give shoppers a better deal.

But even with this, it is not enough, and so some of the key shops that we chose and we decided were worthy of inclusion have put a small sum against their advertising budgets to help us tell their stories better and to keep this specialized publication going for our readership. That sum, incidentally, doesn't even begin to cover our out-of-pocket expenses on the road. Moreover, we annually decline to accept numerous shops that try to ''buy'' their way into this book. Our motive here is not so much commercial as it is the continuance of quality reporting about *selective* shopping. If we can guide you to a pleasurable purchase or divert you from an unhappy experience, then the cost of this book will have been retrieved many times over.

THIS SIDE OF THE ATLANTIC

Smart shopping doesn't begin at the counter or showcase. It starts even as you are contemplating where you want to go. And because this book focuses on *selectivity,* we are especially aware of how important it is to save you money on basics. After all, with dollars saved through clever advance planning there will be more dollars available to answer the temptations of the European marketplace.

Furthermore, some countries provide advantages over others. Similarly, if there are certain items on your list, the trip can bring even richer rewards. If you are in the market for some high-ticket prizes (an expensive Swiss watch, a fur coat, or a car, to mention only three examples), your purchase in Europe can more than pay for your round-trip fare and several weeks of touring. The trick is to know what you want beforehand and through the use of this book plan for your acquisitions in advance. Many, many lower-priced items also are better buys in Europe than they are at home.

MAIL ORDERS: AT YOUR SERVICE TODAY AND TOMORROW

Thinking ahead is one sure way to save money. You're going to see a cascade of unusual and alluring shopping items. Naturally, you won't want to lug all of these around with you, and even if you could travel with a camel caravan there will be more treasures that you would like to have in the future—gifts for Christmas, birthdays, weddings, and whimsical moments when you are feeling generous. If you had only bought an extra silk scarf, some placemats, or alabaster egg for that unexpected occasion!

The answer, of course, is Mail Order. It is a very big business in Europe today, so if you are aware of that fact you can visit the best stores, pick up their detailed and colorful catalogs, get an idea firsthand about the quality and uniqueness of their products, and be prepared for any future impulse or need.

As you travel—and hopefully with this book as your partner—you will undoubtedly observe that there are reputable mailorder outfits and gyp joints. We have tried to indicate the houses of integrity in later pages. These fine establishments are described under their individual countries. They will make it very clear to you what all the costs are, insure your goods, pack them meticulously, and utilize the most efficient method for transporting them to you at a price that is reasonable.

Once at home you will have on hand your own file of brochures and catalogs from the pick of your shopping harvest. If you are missing any, you can always write to the store managers whose names and addresses are usually listed in these pages; they will gladly supply you with their publicity. These are as valuable as gilt-edged bonds. They will save you dollars and trouble should you try to find similar products in the United States. Even if you could find them in your local specialty stores, the prices would probably be higher than what you will pay. This is because your Main Street merchant is faced by exactly the same Customs duties you are; to these he must add higher brokerage fees plus the profit margin of his agency, to which he then tacks on his own markup. Hence, your import costs over the years will be lower, your prices overall will be lower, and the variety at your command will be infinitely greater.

Several points to remember:

▪ Some of the comparative clothing sizes listed in the beginning of this book vary significantly from place to place. (We even know of some manufacturers who intentionally put smaller size labels on larger garments in order to flatter their stouter customers.) We recommend that anything that is styled to fit tightly be viewed with caution before ordering it by mail. The better establishments use reliable labels, so you can trust the houses described herein.

▪ Don't forget to inquire whether you can utilize your credit card for mail-order purchases. The better stores provide this service, and you are the one to gain since the charge is rendered in dollars on the day of your purchase. This prevents slippery practices by some merchants who wait until favorable currency conditions jack the prices up in their behalves.

▪ If there is something radically wrong about the purchase you received, don't send it back in an impulsive huff. Instead, explain your complaint to the seller and wait for instructions. Otherwise, before the merchant could claim it, you might force him to pay the often substantial difference in his national customs fees between export merchandise and merchandise for use within his borders. This could complicate the settlement and finally cost you more.

PLANNING AHEAD TO SAVE

Duty-free airport shops have been generous in their advertising budgets, boasting about how you can save bundles if you hold your purchases until you alight at their portals. T'ain't always so. To prevent the chagrin that comes from overpaying, jot down the Stateside prices of favorite items for on-the-spot comparison. Sometimes the town shops are even cheaper than the airport boutiques. While the latter may promote tax-free purchases, they certainly are not non-profit organizations. If you are informed beforehand, the hype will have no effect.

While you were shopping for your transatlantic passage, you undoubtedly ran into dozens of ads for cheap-cheaper-cheapest flights to Europe. The offerings are almost endless, but not all of the bargains are in the air. Some are on the ground. **Eurail-pass,** for example. If you are moving extensively from one nation to the next, you can save hundreds of dollars through the *stateside* purchase of such a travel program. There are provisions for first and second class as well as an extra-low-cost **Youth-pass.** Find out further details from your travel agent, who also can issue the cards to you.

If you are not crossing numerous frontiers, then individual nations feature their own **rail plans** (BritRail in the U.K. is one sterling example among many) that can put extra money in your pocket for spending along the route. Many of these include additional transport by **ferries** and **buses** plus rail links from cities to airports. At a time when the taxi fare to an air terminus might equal the purchase of a bottle of French perfume or a quart of champagne for friends back home, here's a fine way to gain some ground economically.

Once you arrive at your destination, many capitals or nations offer **one-to-several-day passes** (Oslo Card, Helsinki Card, England's National Trust, etc.) which provide cut-rate or free entry to their showcase sights plus reduced or no-cost passage on their transportation systems. These are outlined in detail in our companion volume, *Fielding's Europe 1990.*

In the larger metropoli, take the trouble to learn the subway system, underground, *metro,* or *U-bahn.* They are not like New York's grafitti-ridden sweatboxes. In Paris, they ride on rubber wheels and are so silent that two people can speak in a normal voice. In Brussels, they resemble the finest first-class carriages in America—well, actually, they are better. Stations are generally safe, maps are clearly marked, prices are low, and connections are swift. The savings over taxi fares are vast.

Auto purchases: If you are in the market for a car (especially something like a BMW, Mercedes, Jaguar, etc.) you can order it in advance, enjoy use of it around Europe, send it home, and come out with an overall profit after all expenses are paid. The saving on a quality vehicle could be close to $4000 or even more. A California reader purchased a Mercedes for $19,000, paid shipping and customs totaling $1500, and another $5000 for conversion to U.S. standards. The market value for the same car in San Mateo (his home) was $34,000! The reader cautions, however, that conversion to DOT/EPA specifications is a key feature. He recommends that U.S. mechanics do the job because European alterations sometimes are not accepted by U.S. authorities. Check first to see if your U.S. dealer has a European delivery service and conversion warranty. You might save a lot and have fun in the bargain.

Telephones: It's useful to know that what you can save potentially on transatlantic phone calls can go a long, long way toward additional purchases abroad. Many travelers are not aware of the outrageous sums added by many overseas hotels—add-ons ranging from 100% to 450% and more. That sort of supplement can represent quite a big chunk out of your shopping budget. Here are a few actual examples to illustrate the gouging: A $20 7-minute call from Hamburg to Rochester, NY was billed at $110 by one hotel. A $39 call from Italy to the U.S. had a $117 surcharge tacked on. A call from Barcelona to Oakland, CA (standard tariff $120) was upped to more than $500!

But there are methods for avoiding such heavy billings. AT&T pioneered **Teleplan,** a program whereby participating hotels agree to limit surcharges to one U.S. dollar or its equivalent for all USADIRECT and AT&T Card calls. The list of hotels and hotel chains offering AT&T Teleplan is constantly growing and changing. Current Teleplan participants include all Inter-Europe Hotels, the Irish Hotel Federation, the Ledra Hotel of Cyprus and all Holiday Inn Asia/Pacific hotels.

Another method for minimizing hotel surcharges and for cutting calling expenses is USADIRECT. AT&T introduced USADIRECT service to Europe in 1985 in order to provide U.S. travelers with an inexpensive, fast and easy way to call home from overseas. With USADIRECT you just dial an access number from any phone in the country to reach an AT&T operator in the U.S. who completes your call. The USADIRECT access numbers are usually toll-free or, in some countries, may be charged as local calls. Just charge your calls to an AT&T Card or call collect. The USADIRECT access numbers for Europe include Austria (022–903–011), Belgium (11–0010), Denmark (0430–0010), Finland (9800–100–10), France (19–0011), Germany (0130–0010), Italy (172–1011), Netherlands (06–022–9111), Norway (050–12–011), Sweden (020–795–611), Switzerland (046–05–0011), and the United Kingdom (0800–89–0011).

What to do if USADIRECT service or Teleplan is not available? Phone your party in the U.S. and quickly ask that they call you back. (Since calls are charged on a time basis, even a high surcharge is bearable when the call is for less than a minute.) A second method is to use an AT&T Card so that the charges are billed to your U.S. number at the American rate (even if the call emanated from Europe). A third way is to phone from a local telephone office where the charges are at the official rate only.

With AT&T USADIRECT service and AT&T Teleplan or if you ''shop'' wisely and knowingly before you call, you could save a bundle on what you spend to keep in touch with the folks back home.

For more information on international calling while you're in the U.S., dial 1–800–874–4000.

ONCE YOU'VE ARRIVED

There are some important differences between shopping customs in Europe and in America. The lore even varies from the north to the south of the Continent and on either side of the English Channel. Let's look at a few examples and some basic tips:

■ In the central or southern lands where the siesta still prevails, most stores lock their doors at lunchtime—an inevitable annoyance to travelers-in-a-hurry. Individual shopping hours are listed throughout this text.

■ Arriving in a town only to discover it's a fiesta and shops are shut can be frustrating, so check our section (at the beginning of each country chapter) on Public Holidays, and try to plan accordingly.

■ Before departure, jot down the complete clothing sizes of family members and favored friends. Otherwise, you might unexpectedly bump into *just* the gift they'd like—and be forced to pass it up.

■ Remember the basics: (1) though the dollar has declined fractionally in comparison with some currencies, we are going to lead you to the *best* buys (not always the cheapest), since we believe that you are going to Europe to find the extraordinary rather than the commonplace shopping choices, (2) you can gain extra advantage through your duty-free allowance, (3) you can save significant import costs on dutiable items, (4) Europe provides infinitely more variety than your markets at home can display for foreign merchandise, and (5) usually you can go right to the source to buy rather than purchase items made (and sometimes poorly) under license or which are fraudulent. (More about counterfeiting top-line goods at the end of this chapter.)

▪ Never try to horse-trade in establishments such as those we recommend, because the prices are fixed. In Flea Markets, antique shops, second-rate souvenir traps, and the like, however, haggle your head off, for savings up to 50%. Sometimes, if you are willing to pay cash, stores will give a discount equivalent to what they have to pay as a percentage to credit card companies.

▪ Go alone on your buying rounds, without a professional courier; their commission could be your discount. An exception is our *Guidelines* pilot scheme in Madrid (see ''Spain''), which is a reader service rather than a tourist gouge.

▪ If you are going the made-to-measure route, refuse last-minute acceptance of any garment at your hotel, airport, or departure point. *Get ALL of your fittings (2 is chancy so 3 should be minimum) before leaving.*

▪ Continental methods of packing for U.S. shipment can sometimes turn your hair white. Use your own expediter, your hotel concierge, or get a guarantee of safe arrival or free replacement from the dealer if you are in doubt.

▪ *Always print,* not handwrite, your name and address—especially on mail orders.

▪ The Treasury Department has ordained that you may neither leave nor enter the U.S. with $10,000 or more in cash and/or traveler's checks unless you officially register the sum with a Customs Officer (Form 4790). Furthermore, if this much money has been mailed to you in any single chunk along the road, you must notify the Commissioner of Customs, Currency Transportation Reports, Washington, DC 20229. Solution? Rely on credit cards or, every time you go broke while you're out of the country, write yourself a check for $9999.99.

▪ If your mind has been made up prior to departure to acquire any large item abroad, a shrewd way to protect yourself is to get a letter of credit from your bank. You tell your banker to take care in advance of the currency registration and let him know what's to be shipped. As soon as the seller is ready to send the merchandise, he forwards to the bank a description of the number of cartons or packages involved, plus a bill of lading. In this way, the vendor is not paid until he has presented a stamped receipt that your purchase is actually on its way. And ALWAYS arrange that it is amply insured.

■ In certain cases the fees collected by forwarding agents, warehouses, etc., can make your $50 article cost $80 by delivery time at your house. Best solution always: Carry it by hand. Next best: Ship it by *parcel post,* if the dimensions will pass—*not* through a shop or broker. If none of these works, then be sure to get an *all-inclusive transport quotation* before buying. (Many of the top shops in this book do that automatically.) Incidentally, transatlantic air-cargo rates might be lots cheaper than you think. Not only is it wise to transport all of your over-ocean suitcases either in this category or as *unaccompanied baggage* (which often rides the same airplane as you do and could save a small fortune!), but you ought to investigate these tariffs at any airline office with regard to your particularly fragile or unwieldy purchases.

■ The actual time-in-transit from the Continent is short, but red tape or dockside pileups might delay delivery to your front door. Thus, if your purchase doesn't arrive within your projected span, don't fly up the chimney in a fury. Give it time. It's almost sure to get there safely, but later than you'd been promised.

■ The law allows you to bring in up to $400 worth of merchandise per person (retail rather than wholesale value) without paying a cent. Only one carton of foreign cigarettes and 100 cigars (not Cuban) qualifies for inclusion in this exemption. In addition, there is a flat 10% duty on the next $1,000 of purchases and above that $1400 total the standard tables of levies are applied. Families residing in one household may pool their flat 10% benefits, even with babes in arms; if they constitute a quartet, as an example, they are allowed 4 x $1000 or $4000 under this arrangement. You may also send an unlimited number of under-$50 (fair retail price) gifts from abroad to U.S. friends. Your free importation of wines and booze (subject totally to individual *state* laws) is fixed at 1 quart per individual 21 years of age or older.

Duty-free items: Antiques produced more than 100 years before your date of entry; original paintings, drawings, and sculptures of any age; books, prints, lithographs, maps over 20 years old.

Limitations: Certain trademarked cameras, perfumes, watches, musical instruments, tape recorders and jewelry, usually held to total of one to three items of each brand (list available in any Customs office).

Toughly restricted or prohibited: Foreign fruits, meats, vegetables, all goods made from endangered species of animals (see below), absinthe, liqueur chocolates, most foods unless ingredients are plainly printed on their labels, firearms, ammunition, wildlife, lottery tickets, and narcotics. While items that voyagers are caught in failing to declare are still seized, undervalued ones may now be purchased if penalties equal to their full values are paid. Everything must be for your personal (not commercial) use. SAVE YOUR SALES SLIPS. For further official information, a 32-page booklet called *Know Before You Go: Customs Hints for Returning U.S. Residents* and a less valuable eight-pager called *GSP & The Traveler* plus *Trademark Information*, *Importing a Car*, and *Pets, Wildlife, U.S. Customs* are available free of charge. You may either pick them up at any Customs office or obtain them by mail from the U.S. Customs Service,

Box 7407, Washington, DC 20044. Last, for specific data about duties on any particular object or objects not listed in these publications, send your inquiry to the Public Information Division, U.S. Customs Service, 2100 K St., Washington, DC 20229.

▪ Economy tip: As stated above, gifts costing less than $50 (fair retail value) may be mailed from overseas by you *or by the shop* (limit: 1 parcel per day receivable by the same person) on a duty-free basis. Mark them ''Unsolicited Gift—Value Under $50''—but don't cheat, because they're liable to be confiscated. No effect on your legal exemption, so go to it!

▪ Jewelry purchased overseas: Correct appraisal of jewelry is such an enormously specialized science, so loaded with pitfalls, that if you should desire to have it done on your return from your trip, find a member of the authoritative, ultra-exclusive Gemological Society of America to evaluate it for you or, failing that, a member of the American Gem Society.

▪ Stringent legislation has now been passed by the United States and Canadian governments that (1) bans the import of all merchandise that originates from more than 400 endangered species of animals, (2) obligates their Customs officials to seize it upon attempted entry and later to destroy it, and (3) gives them the option of slapping *criminal* charges against the offender when they are not convinced that the traveler has made the purchase in innocence or in ignorance of the law. Random examples are furs of the spotted cat family (leopard, cheetah, tiger, ocelot) or of seal, alligator or crocodile products (some varieties are okay), vicuna products, whalebone (including scrimshaw), ivory and tortoiseshell. Most European retailers are already aware of this curb and will warn you about it; others aren't, and still others won't. Although crocodile handbags are widely regarded as an accepted status symbol abroad, scorn is beginning to stir against ladies who parade leopard or similar coats. If you possess any of these things and decide to take them in your wardrobe for your journey, you might have a devil of a time convincing the inspectors on your return that they were in your possession before these tough measures were passed.

   ▪ Counterfeiting swindles are common—just as they are in Manhattan or Sausalito. Bogus Rolex, Cartier, Piaget, and Baume & Mercier watches are being manufactured by the thousands in Milan, Hong Kong, and elsewhere; then peddlers market them on the streets, often as "stolen" goods that can be had "for as little as $100!" The movements are the cheapest grade. The forgers imitate the watch face, the name, the copyrighted trademark, and the band. Sometimes they even print copies of the guarantee forms. Since, as an example, a Piaget electronic quartz original costs about $10,000 while these are run off the illicit production line for between $20 and $25 apiece, how long could these phonies be expected to function? An extension of this sham is the appearance of an array of articles—"West German" jogging shoes, pen-and-pencil sets, apparel, cassette tapes, handbags, "perfumes," drugs, so-called mink and a multitude of exotic furs, glassware, and a number of others even to chemical hog-fatteners and Walt Disney films—that bear precise duplicates of the labels and trademarks of famous companies but that are copies made in fly-by-night factories. Levi Strauss security agents found $50,000 worth of fake "Levis" from Israel and Paraguay in warehouses in the Netherlands and Switzerland—prompting the rueful remark by the firm's Italian manager that "these miserable jeans are our biggest competitor." Bright-yellow boxes of inferior copycat film labeled "Kossek" or "Kolak" are appearing in lowergrade camera stores. Shoddy canvas items falsely bearing the Dior name are infesting the Mediterranean area. You can buy a "Louis Vuitton" bag from a folding-table merchant on Rome's Via del Corso or on a number of other "respectable" boulevards elsewhere that falls apart with bewildering rapidity. In other words the same flimflams that occur on our shores also occur abroad. This is why we again urge that you patronize only the shops that are recommended in this book.

AUSTRIA

SHOPPING HOURS

Vienna: Weekdays from 8, 8:30 or 9 a.m.–6 p.m.; shuttered Sat. at midday. *Other cities:* same openings; closing hours variable.

PUBLIC HOLIDAYS

Jan. 1, Jan. 6, Easter Mon., May 1, Ascension Day, Whitmonday, Corpus Christi, Aug. 15, Oct. 26 (Austrian National Day), Nov. 1, Dec. 8, Dec. 25–26.

MAIL ORDERS

Very few shops in Austria issue catalogs or brochures. We have assembled several noteworthy exceptions. **A. E. Koechert** (outstanding Viennese-style jewelry), and **Resi Hammerer** (glamorously chic Loden and sports apparel) are 100% reliable and vastly experienced in international and intercontinental shipping. The Imperial Hotel offers a mouth-melting piece of publicity for its marvelous **Imperial Torte,** the finest Austria produces and now available for gift airmailing worldwide and express if time is short. **Michaela Frey Team** (exclusive enamel jewelry) will always dispatch leaflets depicting their latest lines free of charge.

Near Innsbruck at *Wattens,* **Swarovski,** the silver crystal people, provide a vast volume of their versatility that can be packed, shipped, and insured. In *Salzburg,* at **Slezak,** Proprietress Mrs. Dorli Gehmacher personally oversees the selection of top-quality leather goods and accessories. **Sigrist** will send, free of charge, material describing the glass, porcelain and silver they stock. If *any* item or classification mentioned in these stores should catch your eye and spark your serious interest, write to the director along the lines we have suggested in ''Mail Orders: At Your Service.''

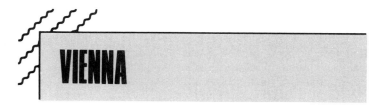

SHOPPING AREAS

The City Fathers have created pedestrian malls that are lined with benches, transplanted trees, and lighting patterns. These traffic-free islands of serenity include **Karntnerstrasse** (the main shopping street), **Graben, Kohlmarkt,** and **Naglergasse;** several more are in the outlying precincts. They are a delight. **Mariahilferstrasse** is a less-expensive venue.

THINGS TO BUY

Petit point, Viennese-style precious jewelry, enamel jewelry, sweaters, regional clothing, leather goods, Viennese handicrafts, porcelain, crystal, Imperial Torte, antiques, *objets d'art,* furniture, stamps, clocks, a potpourri at the Dorotheum Auction.

TAX REFUND FOR PURCHASES

Foreign travelers who make any purchases of 1000 schillings or more per shop may claim a refund of the Value Added Tax which had been automatically levied on every item. Special forms, (U 34), to be presented upon request for inspection when leaving the country, must be filled in at the store. Since this VAT bite constitutes a substantial percent of what you have paid, your savings (up to 25% in some cases) through this exemption can be hefty.

Antiques: At last count there were around 700 art and antique dealers. Always haggle—and always expect to beat them down about 10%. The best browsing is around the **Dorotheum Auction** (see below). **Johann Kern** (Kohlmarkt 7) seemed especially promising; **Wolfgang Siedler** (Himmelpfortgasse 13–15)—expert appraiser for the Court of Justice—also looked good, as did **Herbert Asenbaum** (Karntnerstrasse 28) and **August Siedler** (Kohlmarkt 3). **Hofgalerie Dr. Wolfgang Hofstatter** (Spiegelgasse 14) and his brother **Paul Reinhold Hofstatter** (Braunerstrasse 12) are well known for wood carvings and statues of the 12th to 17th centuries.

Art Galleries: The 4 best-known are **Am Graben** (Graben 7), **Peithner-Lichtenfels** (Seilergasse 16), **Wuerthle** (Weihburggasse 9), and **Manfred Scheer** (Getreidemarkt 10 and 16). The first features 19th-century art nouveau, while the others highlight more contemporary works.

Auction House: Finally, don't miss the historic, internationally famous **Dorotheum Auction** (Dorotheergasse 17, Tel: 515600). Large sales occur in March, April, and May, but since the dates vary, it's best to write ahead for details about these. However, there are several auctions taking place each afternoon and, best of all, purchases can now be made over the counter as in regular stores. They also highlight different specialties each month. What goes under the hammer runs the gamut from art to furniture to stamps to clothing to silver to jewelry to clocks to car parts and bric-a-brac—20% of it unclaimed from its pawn-shop division; items as low as 50¢, with 70% under $300; catalogs in German; no sales tax if shipped abroad. Here's what to do: (1) Visit first for pre-inspection; (2) Note from tags on items desired number for identification, reserve price, and amount of tax; (3) Allow for this tax plus the 10% house commission; (4) Set your top bid in your head and *don't go over it in the excitement of the competition;* (5) Raise hand for attention and start action at lower figure if nobody else does; (6) Stop action similarly if a few seconds are necessary for calculation; (7) Purchase awarded after final 3 calls; (8) Pay for and pick up or forward your buys.

For those who don't speak German, house bidders are available for a small fee; check with your hotel concierge for what is scheduled. There is usually something going on all the time. Open Mon.–Fri., 10 a.m.–6 p.m. and Sat., 8:30 a.m.–noon. Fast, lively, great savings, great fun!

Austrian Handicrafts: **Osterreichische Werkstatten** (Karntnerstrasse 6) offers the highest quality and most interesting variety we have found in the capital. A perennial favorite is the classic, age-old *Weinheber* (wine siphon), set neck down so that upward pressure from your glass activates the valve. They will be happy to check the mechanism with water while you watch.

Books: **Buchhandlung in der Hofburg** (Hofburgpassage 6) is very close to the entrance to the Imperial Palace. Dr. Gerhard Muller has carefully stocked his shelves with most of the historical and pictorial tomes that would interest visitors and serve as rewarding souvenirs.

Candles: **Metzger** (Stephansplatz 7, across street side of Cathedral), founded in 1685, displays a legion from birthday-cake size to massive, ornate models. For streamlined modern candles try the small shop of **Marious Retti** (Kohlmarkt 10).

Clothing (Conventional):   **E. Braun & Co.** (Graben 8) and **W. F. Adlmuller** (Karntnerstrasse 41) are the Viennese homes of these Europe-wide chains. **Popp und Kretschmer** (Karntnerstrasse 51) is loaded with high-fashion clothing, bags, belts, leather goods, and other accessories.

Confection: Here's one way to have your cake and eat it too! **The Imperial Torte** has a heritage going back to its earliest fan, Emperor Franz Joseph. But it has never been over-commercialized like other Viennese pastry and in our collective opinion, this writing team has never sampled anything better. Created by the chefs of the capital's most prestigious hotel, the Imperial (formerly a palace), it is purchasable from the hotel itself when you are visiting or—if you do as we often do—it can be ordered by airmail. Beautifully packaged in small size (a pinch under a pound) or large (a smidgen over 2 lbs.), the royal presentation makes an impressive gift. Delivery time globally is well within the month-long shelf life of the rich chocolate treat and we have enjoyed ours well beyond the marginal date, even deepfreezing pieces and serving them in perfect condition several months later. Since currencies fluctuate, let's quote Austrian shillings: Small 260 AS takeaway, large 420 AS; add 35 AS for the attractive wooden box for the swift overseas shipment plus postal charges of roughly 175 AS for the Small; 265 AS for the Large. There's an express service available, too. It's much simpler to charge it to a major credit card by sending your order to Hotel Imperial Wien, Karntner Ring 16, A-1015 Wien. If your sweet tooth can't wait the telephone number is (222) 50110-0 and in the USA you can place an order by dialing tollfree (800) 242–0420. Delicious!

Crystal and Porcelain: **Lobmeyr** (Karntnerstrasse 26 and branch in Salzburg), is a distinguished house with a vast array of finest crystal tablesets, gleaming mirrors, Hungarian Herend china, classic and modern artistic engravings, gift articles, and other *belles tournures.* It has an outstanding museum as well. **Wiener Porzellanmanufaktur Augarten** (Stock-Im-Eisenplatz 3, Mariahilferstrasse 99, and the Scholoss Augarten) features beautiful Spanish Riding School figurines and elegant dinner settings. **Rasper & Sohne** (Graben 15) has a large establishment in this general category which incorporates a charming "Drop In Boutique" and many unusual items for the home. This company also operates in several other Austrian cities. **E. Bakalowits' Sohne** (Spiegelgasse 3) is the famous chandelier designer which did most of the fixtures for the Opera House, the Town Hall, and the Atomic Commission.

Cutlery: **Deckenbacher & Blumner** (Karntnerstrasse 21-23 and Mariahilferstrasse 70) takes rightful pride in its carving sets, matched sets of 6 knives, extra-fancy carving sets with matched knives, corkscrews, cigar cutters, and similar items, all with beautiful stag handles.

Department Stores and Shopping Centers: **Steffl** (Karntnerstrasse, opposite the Ambassador Hotel) sells a galaxy of merchandise from Scotch tape to that extra suitcase, at normal local prices. It's best of its ilk. The **Palais Ferstel** (Freyung), renowned for its architecture, has become the nucleus of a new and exclusive complex of shops. While there, stop in at the Cafe Central (Herrengasse 14), which has been a literary meeting place for years. This, too, is an integral part of Viennese life.

Down Quilts: **Gans** (Brandstatte 1, behind St. Stephans Cathedral) is a wide-awake company which has been making nights happier ever since 1882. By daylight, their craftsmanship and aesthetic qualities will be immediately apparent, too.

Enamel Jewelry: For 40 years the **Michaela Frey Team** (Gumpendorferstr. 81, 6th district; Tel: 5971160) has been the star performer in the traditional art of enamelling. It's an open secret, however. An open house, too, since you can watch the craftsmen and -women at their delicate trade. Its nucleus of 10 graduate artists from the Vienna Academy of Arts here is creating beautiful pieces of lustrous enamel jewelry which are unique in the world. For ladies: perfectly matching sets of necklaces, bracelets, rings, earrings, brooches and belts in tremendous varieties, to be combined with beautiful silk scarves and shawls. For children: charming sets of bracelets, rings, brooches, necklaces and tiny earrings. The wide range of prices run from $15–$250. The head office and huge showroom-boutique are only a 3-minute walk from the leading Mariahilferstrasse shopping area; no noon closing weekdays; open Sat. until noon. Visitors can always watch a video-clip about the manufacturing process (in the language of choice) which is very informative. See also under *Paris*.

Embroidery: **Zur Schwabischen Jungfrau** (Graben 26) has set tables and made beds in discriminating households since 1720. Of special interest are the table linens which coordinate with the porcelain designs of such factories as Augarten (Prince Eugene and Vienna Rose patterns), Miessen, and Herend. Machine-embroidered place mats run around $25 a piece, while hand-worked ones are $55 each. They are the ultimate in refinement and delicacy. **Ludwig Nowotny** (Petersplatz–Freisingergasse 4) has been producing the patterns and materials needed for fine art needlework since 1818. They have Gobelins for chairs, benches, and cushions; other reproductions from museums and chateaux; petit-point designs for handbags. They can help you match the level of your own ability to create masterpieces with thread.

Florist: **Sadtler** (Opernring 13) is tops.

Gifts: **House of Presents** (Karntner Ring 3, next to the Hotel Bristol) has an interesting array.

Hats: **Collins-Hute** (in the subterranean crossover by the Hotel Bristol) stocks the typical Tyrolean type for men at a price range of $27 and upward.

Jewelry: **A. E. Koechert** (Neuer Markt 15, across from the taxi entrance of the Hotel Krantz-Ambassador) is worth the time of anyone who likes extraordinarily fine brooches, rings, clips, bracelets, necklaces, and original creations in the renowned Viennese style. Austrian handwork in precious metals and gems not only has its distinctive flavor, but labor costs are so low that only Portugal can offer such comparatively modest price levels in this specialty. This particular shop, founded in 1814 by the great-great-grandfather of the present proprietor, was designated by successive Emperors as Crown Jewelers to the Imperial Court— an honor which involved, among other things, the stewardship and maintenance of the fabulous Royal Treasure Chamber, still a major sightseeing attraction at the Imperial Palace. Their connection with the Royal Family brought members of other reigning houses to the Koecherts—and many a diadem or necklace worn for majestic European occasions came from the first floor of this baroque establishment, where Austria's best goldsmiths continue their wizardry. Dazzlingly opulent pieces are available to the millionaire trade, but for travelers like us who haven't much to spend, Koechert also shines with equal radiance. Their selection of exclusively designed clips and other items in the forms of flowers, dogs, sunbursts, fish, and ferns made of cut crystal, precious stones, and brilliants runs from $300 to $400. There's an intangible quality and spirit in them which makes them as characteristically Viennese as gold filigree carving is characteristically Portuguese. This ethereal, special, different beauty is impossible for us to describe; all we know is that we love it and that you won't find it elsewhere. The gentlemanly Dr. Dietrich Koechert will take personal care of you. A treasure house.

Knitted Shirts, Jackets, and Sweaters: **Sykora & Tochter** (Plankengasse 4).

Leather Goods: **Madler** (Graben 17 near Kohlmarkt and St. Stephen's Cathedral and another branch at Mariahilferstrasse 24 outside but near the ''Ring'') has *no* connection whatsoever with the famous Zurich firm. They stock a wide range of suitcases, small luggage, carry-on bags, handbags, vanity cases, brief-cases, and scores of gift items. The workmanship is excellent; the styling has flair; the price range is appealing.

Markets: The **Flea Market** is held behind the Naschmarkt (Wienzeile) every Sat. morning.

Petit-point: **Maria Stransky** (Hofburgpassage 2) is a vital part of the wonderful world of Vienna. Even its address is linked to splendors of a gracious age, it being located in the historic Hofburg or Imperial Palace. If you are versed in this highly specialized art, here you will find a needleworker's Valhalla; if you are not, then the helpful staff will take the time to explain the elaboration, background, and creativity in such skills. Ingrid Vytlacil is an expert in this field, so let her lead you across the shelves filled with purses, eyeglass cases, bags, pictures, plus brooches, pendants, and other signets of connoisseurship. Since this establishment has been a Viennese fixture for more than eight decades, it has a monopoly on the finest fingers in the region. And it is a mark of pride that *only* articles from the Maria Stransky studio are sold here. Just try to imagine the options offered: 900, 1600, 2500, and 3000 stitches to the square inch. The latter techniques occupy more than 15 hours per inch, no specialist being able to concentrate with a magnifying glass for more than 3 hours at a time. Now *that's* quality!

Regional Clothing: For over 30 years **Resi Hammerer** (Karntnerstrasse 29–31) has been considered the number one *haute couture* fountainhead for arrestingly elegant Austrian creations for women. Two floors of dashing Lodenwear (year-round usage); exclusive materials and models, own workshops, branches in Linz and Bregnez; big mail-order business. The "Lovely Things" at **Liebe Sachen** (Wahringerstr. 151) are designer Brigitte Hernuss' very own. These eye-catching, show-stopping jackets, skirts and ensembles carry the art of Austrian *trachten* into the chicest realms imaginable. They are party clothes *par excellence*. **Lanz** (Karntnerstr. 10) is a long-time favorite with branches around the nation. For menswear also, as well as women's ready-to-wear, **Loden-Plankl** (Michaelerplatz 6) and **Tostmann** (Schottengasse 30) are additional choices.

Stamps: **Numismatica** (Fuhrichgasse 6, behind the Hotel Sacher) is the nation's numismatic nirvana.

Textiles: **Boecker** (Karntnerstrasse) offers a wide selection, plus conventional garments.

Tobacco: **Tabakspezialitaten-Geschaft** (Kohlmarkt 6) has everything.

Toy Soldiers: **Josef Kober** (Graben 14-15) has a large army.

Viennese Handicrafts: **Elfi Muller & Co.** (Karntnerstrasse 53, opposite the Opera House) is a find for Austrian mementos.

If she doesn't happen to have the particular item you might be after, try **Modette** (Karntnerstrasse 12) or **Elysee** (Karntnerstrasse 2) for wearables.

SALZBURG

THINGS TO BUY

Leather goods, lederhosen, handicrafts, regional clothing, engraved glass, sporting equipment, crystal and porcelain, jewelry, silk flowers and dried arrangements, pottery, candles.

Antiques and Art: There's wonderful browsing on Goldgasse. Try **Galerie Salis** (#13) and **M. H. Grotjan** (#15). **Galerie Welz** (Sigmund-Haffner-Gasse) sponsors some of the finest exhibitions and has a wide-ranging library of art books.

Candles: **Peter Nagy** (Getreidegasse, opposite the Goldener Hirsch Hotel) is a master craftsman in wax. Not only does he make Christmas and ceremonial candles, but there are honey, scented, and herb ones too. The last actually have layers of seeds cunningly incorporated into them. Woven baskets of flowers and traditional decorative motifs have been molded in burgundy, green or beige wax and hang on cords to serve as unusual wall ornaments or to dangle from Christmas trees. The variety is endless within the tiny precincts. **Ferdinand Weber** (Getreidegasse 3) also enjoys popularity. He has gingerbread cookies along with beeswax creations.

Chocolate: No visit to Salzburg would be complete without purchasing that souvenir of souvenirs—a box of **Mozartkugeln.** They are available *everywhere*. They are chocolate-covered marzipan spheres which local wags refer to as ''Mozart's Balls,'' wrapped in glitzy paper and bearing the visage of the city's favorite son. They are sold individually as snacks or boxed as gifts for duets, trios, quartets, quintets, or (probably) full symphony orchestras. The packing possibilities are numbing.

Country Fashions and Sporting Goods: **Sport und Waffen E. Dschulnigg KG** (Griesgasse 8), otherwise known locally simply as Dschulnigg, for many years has been one of the most esteemed houses for field-and-stream specialties plus casualwear in Europe. Next to Dschulnigg, a shop for children recently made its debut. Called **Cosi's by Dschulnigg** (Griesgasse 6), it sells an exclusive line of Austrian regional clothing for 4–14-year-old youngsters, all designed by talented Constance Dorn, the Dschulniggs' daughter and brilliant young manageress. In the main store, the loden wardrobe is one of the finest to be found anywhere; this is important since quality varies widely and is not always discernible to the untrained eye. Costumes for both sexes, hand-knitted vests, walking jackets in marvelously colored and durable Austrian boiled wool, a vast variety of apparel for town or country is here to discover. Outdoorsmen and outdoors-women will find meticulously traced sporting guns of every type, equipment for dogs, bows and arrows, and hundreds of accessories not available in North America. Then, too, if you want to arrange your own hunt or sporting activities, Mr. or Mrs. Dschulnigg will handle all of the details happily and aim you in the right direction. Very unusual and top-of-the-line as a shop and as a service.

Crystal and Porcelain: **Sigrist** (Griesgasse 13) has been a celebrated purveyor of tableware and gifts since 1838. The china and glassware are displayed in a vast vaulted and columned ground-floor showroom. Most of Europe's stellar names are represented—Meissen, Dresden, Lladro, Wedgwood, Hutschenreuther, Villeroy & Boch, Baccarat, Lalique, Daum, Saint Louis, Riedel, Waterford, Christofle—to name just a few. If you're overcome by shopping, restoratives are served in a charming cafe upstairs. **Rasper & Sohne** and **E. Bakalowits** have outlets on Mozartplatz, next to each other. Another Viennese firm, **J. & L. Lobmeyr,** is located at Schwarzstrasse 20.

Flowers: They're ubiquitous—and when they're not fresh they are in spectacular dried arrangements incorporating seeds, pods, ribbons, shells, straw, cones, and many other of nature's whatnots. Street sales are common, but the best establishment we've found with the widest selection and the most skillfully composed creations is **Doll** (Getreidegasse 3); actually, you'll find its dollhouse precinct in a tiny columned arcade off this shopping mall. For silk flowers as well as dried posies, go to **Salzburger Blumenstube** (Hof Getreidegasse 25). **Mesgarzadeh** (Greisgasse 4) has antique dolls as well.

Glass Specialist: **Fritz-Reiner Kres** (Sigmund-Haffner-Gasse 14) is where you can watch your fresh purchase being initialed or etched under your own particular commission. This house is especially big on tableware and commemorative pieces such as marriage and baptismal glasses. The "Tree of Life" motif is one of its most popular themes.

Handicrafts: **Salzburger Heimatwerk** (Residenzpl. 9) provides towering appeal not only to shoppers but to sightseers as well. The reason for this is that it resides beneath one of the most popular touristic targets in the entire Salzburg area: *The*

Glockenspiel Tower, which rings out its merry melodies throughout the day. The collection of artisan products is one of the best in Europe and certainly the Salzburger flavor and design flair make it the most colorful anywhere.

Jewelry: **Lahrm** (Universitatsplatz 5 and 16) creates delicacies as frail as dandelion seeds and as evanescent as will-o'-the-wisps—designed, of course, by the personable Mr. Lahrm, who is usually present to show you his distinctive lines. Ask to see his hearts, a specialty. Antique pieces are beautifully presented here as well as they are at the two **Koppenwallner's** shops: **Anton** (Klampferergasse 2) and **Paul** (Alter Markt 7 and Univessitatsplatz 4). The former (like Lahrm's boutique at #16) emphasizes lower cost costume jewelry for the Salzburger attire known as *trachten.* Also in the top league, especially for garnets, is **H. von Rautenberg Nachfolger** (Alter Markt 15). **Elfriede Pfleger,** a personality in the Salzburg music realm, is a prima donna (a real one) when it comes to antique collections from estates and baptismal silverware. You'll find her in the historic Franziskanerkloster, an apt location for such a star performer.

Leather Goods: **Slezak** (Markartplatz 8 plus a branch in the Sheraton Hotel and another in the heart of the Old City next to the famous Cafe Tomaselli) has the highest quality and widest selection we've found just about anywhere in Austria. Ladies' handbags for city, travel, country, and sport; gold-embroidered evening bags and belts; all styles, sizes, and types of leather suitcases; roomy attache and briefcases; Necessaire cases and overnight bags; very first quality sweaters; silk and cotton blouses, skirts, and the famous Geiger brand of jackets and skirts; gloves; tasteful souvenirs and accessories; fine petit point handbags; eyeglass cases; much more. They feature wonderful men's wallets, too. A paradise for mailing gifts to the U.S. Prices? 100% decent. Mrs. Dorli Gehmacher and her staff are exceptionally cordial. On a supraprofessional basis we have esteemed this group as special friends for more than three decades. Second to none nationally in its field for taste and integrity.

Lederhosen and Leather Wearables: **Jahn-Markl** (Residenzplatz 3) always comes up with top quality at low costs—and thanks to Erwin Markl, there's a cozy feeling about this ancient little place.

Market: **Grunmarkt** (Universitatsplatz-Wiener-Philharmoniker-Gasse) is a morning pastime for residents and tourists alike from Mon.–Sat. Snack on a hot *wurst* as you browse.

Recordings: **Sound of Music** (Judengasse 17) and **EMI-Columbia Austria** (Universitatsplatz 15) are both usually among the earliest purveyors of music from the Salzburg Festivals. Each inventory is a magnum opus.

Regional Ceramics: **Guglhupf** (Franz-Josefs-Kai 5) is where you will find the colorful range of Gmundner Keramik artisanware from upper Austria—breakfast and dinner sets, vases and candlesticks. Popular patterns include Dirndl (in pink, blue, or brown), Scattered Flowers, Forget-me-not, Biedemeier, the charming blue-speckled Tupferli Blau, and their oldest design, Green Flame, with matching tablecloths and napkins. **Gruppe H** (Hof Getreidegasse passage) is a showcase for the late master ceramist Gudren Baudisch. Lots of gift ideas here too.

Regional Fashions: The Salzburg area is famous for its very specialized attire *(trachten):* everything from day wear to the most extravagant evening costumes. The lore of the hillsides is expressed in peasant scarves, silver buttons, salmon-pink cravats, buckle shoes, and a host of ingratiating accessories. **Alois**

Wenger u. Co. (Getreidegasse 29) features the operetta stylings that seem to appeal to Everyman and Everywoman in the neighborhood. **Lanz** (just across the *Staatsbrucke,* on the right bank) has a higher quality in the same mentality, while **Madl** (am Grunmarkt, Universitatsplatz 12) would be the fashionable feminine variation on this theme; the latter, in fact, borders on haute couture in the *hochland.* **Ennsmann** (Getreidegasse 31) has a boutique devoted solely to *trachten* accessories of exquisite quality—snowy white blouses, puffed-sleeve sweaters hand-knitted with *naif* motifs on the backs, antique belts and leather bags that have been embroidered with goose-feather thread—all rare and costly.

Shoes: Step out in style (Salzburg variation) with the brand called Trachten Schue Hans Behr, found at **Tagwerker Schue** (Getriedegasse 19).

Wood Carving: **Lackner** (Badergakchen, behind the candle shop of Peter Nagy) is where the souls of all good Austrian whittlers go to rest. Anything from room decoration to an angel to hang over your canary is available. **S. Kopfberger** (Judengasse 14) handles more popular expressions of the same craft, as well as the inevitable music boxes, cribs, and creches.

INNSBRUCK

THINGS TO BUY

Regional clothes, handicrafts, pipes, Austrian jewelry, bells, beeswax candles.

Austrian Jewelry: **Sigrid Jager** (Herzog-Friedrichstrasse 22, in the old city) works with garnets and silver. Every piece is sculptured by hand, and the designs are interesting. Worth a visit.

Bells: **Glockenspiel Grassmayer** has been owned and operated by the same family since its founding in A.D. 1599. That itself is a recommendation.

Candles: **Tiroler Imkergenossenschaft** (Meranerstrasse 2) is a honey for beeswax buffs.

Handicrafts: **Tiroler Heimatwerk** (Meranerstrasse 2) now seems to us a bit dreary. We prefer **Handwerkskunst** on Wilhelm Greilstrasse.

Pipes: There's happy puffing at **Lorenz** (Meinhardstrasse 7) where all types of Tyrolean models are sold. A broad selection of wood carvings is available, too.

Regional (Tyrolean) Apparel: **Lodenbaur** (Brixner Strasse 4) is our unequivocal first choice. Fritz Baur runs this splendid house with keenness, competence, and charm. Very fine indeed, **Lanz,** also good, has a branch in town.

Silver Crystal: **Swarovski,** the greatest manufacturer of artistic glass, has its own factory retail shop in *Wattens,* 10 miles east of Innsbruck, situated next to the famous Swarovski works. Founded in 1895, it now employs about 8000 persons worldwide creating precise and peerless jewelry stones, full lead crystal chandelier pendants, cut gemstones, transfer jewelry and the Silver Crystal gift articles. A visit to Wattens is an impressive experience. You'll find a complete cross section of all sparkling designer products: articles of the popular Silver Crystal range— in the finest full lead—as well as a great variety of costume jewelry and, of course, the successful Swarovski crystal adornments appreciated by women all over the world. The spacious shopping area also includes a large selection of typical Austrian souvenirs. Pause to watch craftsmen demonstrating their skills of glass blowing, engraving, painting, cutting and gem cutting. Initials are engraved free; worldwide mailing is a matter of course. Ask the kind multilingual attendants to explain the generous VAT rebate system. Open May–Sept. Mon.–Sat. 8 a.m.–6 p.m. and Sun. and holidays 8 a.m.–noon. Oct.–Apr. weekdays 8 a.m.–6 p.m. and Sat. 8 a.m.–noon. After shopping enjoy a refreshment in the cozy Cafe Kristall.

ELSEWHERE IN AUSTRIA

Zell am See

This city boasts some of the most beautiful dried flower displays ever purloined from Mother Nature in the shop of **Isabella Bader** (Anton Wallnerstr. 5). This talented and attractive model and designer has great taste and flair. As these items require meticulous work, don't expect them to be inexpensive. Still, some sell for as little as $8 while the more intricate, large combinations range up to $250.

NOTE · · · Watch out for the styling (not quality) of Austrian men's street shoes and suits (women's wear and ski outfits are among the best in the world), all American or imported mass-produced items such as fountain pens, radios, electrical appliances, etc. (monstrous import duties), and the raft of gimcracks marked, for instance, ''Souvenir of Hochland, High in the Edelweiss.'' Finally, you can count on the fact that legions of price tags are upped for the duration of any major festival.

SHOPPING HOURS

Everything operates full blast from 9:30 a.m.–6 p.m. On Fridays almost all establishments remain open until 8, as they do every weekday evening in the capital's City II.

PUBLIC HOLIDAYS

Jan. 1, Easter Mon., May 1, Ascension Day, Whitmonday, July 21 (National Day), Aug. 15, Nov. 1, Nov. 11, Dec. 25.

MAIL ORDERS

Among the establishments that follow, we have had personal experience in mail ordering with only one—**F. Rubbrecht,** the lace people, who will send you a stunning 16-page color catalog for $5; they request payment be made in bills or by check to **F. W. Rubbrecht.** We've always found them consummate in the kindness of their attention and the promptness of their deliveries. Therefore, we have total faith that, if you should wish to follow the procedures described in "This Side of the Atlantic," this venerable landmark (*the* European arbiter of lace) would handle your inquiries with the same fine interest and celerity.

BRUSSELS

SHOPPING AREAS

There are three main districts: (1) downtown around **boulevard Adolphe Max, rue Neuve,** and the **Grand' Place;** (2) midtown in the **Sablon** area especially **rue des Minimes** and **rue de Rollebeek;** and (3) uptown in the fashionable neighborhoods around **avenue Louise, avenue la Toison d'Or,** and **boulevard Waterloo,** including **Porte Namur** and **place Stephanie.**

   Transformations and additions to the Brussels cityscape have notably stepped up the convenience and aesthetics of its shopping milieu. Covered galleries shelter the walker from inclement weather. (The oldest, built in 1846, is the Galeries Saint-Hubert near the Grand' Place.) Rue Neuve has become a pedestrian street. Between Innovation and Bon Marche, there is a huge shopping center called City II (on 3 levels) plus the New BM, a more specialized department store.

THINGS TO BUY

Lace, charms, diamonds, jewelry, glass, firearms, handmade chocolates, antiques, modern pewter, tapestry, custom-made bicycles, special bowling balls, Cuban cigars, model railways, books, Provence products, gourmet provisions, flea-market "discoveries," and especially perfume at the airport duty-free installation upon departure.

SAVINGS ON PURCHASES

VAT is a hefty 19–25%. This is automatically deducted whenever items are mailed abroad. You must be able to show sales receipts from each store where you have shopped for a minimum of 3000 B.Fr. if you are going to carry articles through Customs and gain the tax rebate.

Antiques and Antique Reproductions: **Delplace** (rue de la Namur 30), the country's largest purveyor, is of international repute. **Costermans** (5 Grand Sablon) offers thousands of choices among fire backs, mantelpieces, chandeliers, lanterns, and even furniture. Reports assure us that these people are expert shippers—but we can't know until we're better acquainted. Both are very well respected in the capital. If they don't have what you seek, Place Sablon is clustered with fine specialists, and the **Antique Market** is held in tents here all day on Sat. and until 1 p.m. on Sun.

Arms: For centuries this nation has been world famous for the superb quality of its weapons—especially its shotguns. **Maison du Chasseur & Mahillon Reunis** (ave. Louise 413) is the official FN-Browning agent. It also features hunting and sports clothes. In addition, there is an upstairs gallery called **L'Art Animalier.** A shooting ground near the capitol is operated by these experts. **Armes Binet & Fils** (17 rue Royale) is equally prestigious.

Baked Goods: There are two world-famous purveyors here. One is **Dandoy** (rue au Beurre 31 and rue Charles Buls, both close to the Grand' Place). Among its most popular features are crisp, rich spice cookies called ''speculoos'' and a light, sweet rusk called ''pain a la grecque.'' Their molded types in all sizes make a good gift; large individual ones are $3–12. They ship all over the map. The other is **Wittamer** (Grand Sablon), more a *patisserie,* which is regarded just as highly.

Bicycles: **Eddy Mercks,** the cyling hero of this land, who has won the Tour de France 5 times, will fit you at his home in *Meise* (S'Herenweg 11, Tel: 02.2696272) with a custom-made job. Price? Starting at roughly $9000.

Books: **Smith and Son** (bd. Adolphe Max) stocks a large selection of hardcover titles and more than 2000 paperbacks. **Librairie des Galeries** (Galerie du Roi 2) has an extensive and versatile gathering of art volumes as does **Franco Maria Ricci Ed.** (Sablon Shopping Gardens, 36 place du Grand Sablon). The latter is a name well known to art book connoisseurs for their innovative series; the production is extraordinary.

Bowling Balls (Really!): You will be interested to know that this country claims to make the best bowling balls on the globe. It started with the importation of ivory and teak from the Belgian Congo. Almost any sport shop can supply this bulky excess baggage.

Candles: **Au Dominicain** (rue Dominicain 5) works wonders in wax.

Chocolates: The Belgian queens of these especially distinguished delights are **Wittamer, Neuhaus, Mary, Corne, Nihoul,** and **Godiva.** All have several branches scattered through the city. Fun, fanciful, and fabulously fattening.

Cigars: **Zabia** (rue Lebeau 8-10) carries the full range of Davidoff's world-famous tobacco. Due to the U.S. ban, be careful with Cuban cigars.

Children's Clothing: **Dujardin** (8-10 avenue Louise) is the pinnacle of chic for the younger generation.

Contemporary Craft Work: At **La Main** (209 chaussee de Charleroi) rich veins of talent run through the collection.

Crystal and Porcelain: **Buss** (84–86 rue du Marche-aux-Herbes) is only a few steps away from Belgium's number one attraction, the Grand' Place, and carries the finest names in glassware and china. **Art et Selection** (83 rue du Marche-aux-Herbes, across the street) is a glittering showcase featuring, among other things, exquisite pieces from Val St. Lambert.

Cutlery: **Au Grand Rasoir** (7 rue de l'Hopital, close to the Hotel Amigo) carries the peerless Henckels (''The Twins'') plus Dreizack lines. Fine hunting knives are one of its outstanding specialties. The prices are inexpensive for the superb quality. Proprietor Cielen is extremely helpful.

Department Stores and Covered Galleries: **Innovation** is indisputably the leader. **Marks & Spencer** and **C. & A.** follow. We think that all of the local five-and-tens are cheesy. **Sablon Shopping Gardens,** on the Grand Sablon, is a super-elegant venue, the latest effort of designers of covered shopping space. Besides 30 stores there are 3 restaurants, bubbling fountains, and verdant plants. It's a relaxed atmosphere in which to browse. The art, antiques, and jewelry are high caliber.

Embroidery: **Nephertiti** (57 rue de la Paix) is the domain of Mrs. Seghers who is a genius with her needle. Some of her work incorporates 30 different colors and gold thread. She can match dinner plate designs onto Belgian linen tablecloths.

Gourmet Provisions: No interested visitor to Brussels should miss a slaver through any or all of the following emporiums: **Le Foie Gras Artisanal** (rue Americaine 158, where foie gras is only the beginning), **Le Grand Cerf** (Grand Cerf 22, which is the hobby shop of the fabulous Villa Lorraine restaurant and which features its creations), **Rob** (a super supermarket with 3 branches at Porte de Namur 9, bvd. de la Woluwe 28, Chaussee de Waterloo 1331), **Langhendries** (rue de la Fourche 41, with a stunning gamut of cheeses), and **De Roover** (Chaussee d'Ixelles, also with legendary cheese displays).

Home Furnishings: **Tour de Bebelle** (27 rue de Rollebeek) is where you'll find the exclusive fabrics, wallpapers and tiles designed by Isabelle de Broghrave.

Jewelry: While Brussels is a city of riches and generous expense accounts, there are quite a few houses which cater to the carriage trade with plastic money. But for old-line traditions combined with zesty new ideas and applications, the one that knocks our eyes out-up-and-sideways is **Leysen Freres,** which also happens to be located in one of the most gemlike squares in the capital, at 36 place du Grand Sablon. You'll certainly want to be in this district sightseeing, so have a look at these personal sights too.

Lace: **F. Rubbrecht** (Grand' Place 23), sited in a charming building known as the ''House of the Angel'' since the 16th century, is a lighthouse of quality, fair prices, and reliability among the seas of cheapjack competitors which poisonously flourish in the capital. *Insist* on going here, in spite of what chiseling local concierges, taxi drivers, guides, and envy-ridden similar dealers might tell you about it being ''out of business'' or ''closed.'' Authentic handmade Brussels laces (called ''Luxeuil''), Princess laces, and the largest collection of true antique laces in the nation—unique pieces from private collections—are its 3 pillars. Everything that's in a lacemaker's vocabulary is available here—table linens, home decorations, fashion accessories, wedding veils and christening gowns; worldwide shipment; tax-free export within legal limits. All of Mr. and Mrs. Rubbrecht's designs and motifs are executed by selected and trusted women workers who, generation after generation, have passed along this art. Among the clients of this pacesetter are the Belgian Royal Family, scores of diplomats stationed there and abroad (U.S.A., Brazil, Italy, Korea, Japan, etc. etc.) and dozens of business firms such as Ford, ICI, Shell, and Walt Disney Studios. Lace and fine crystal have had a love affair for centuries. You'll now find as well some of the most splendid pieces of handcrafted Val-Saint-Lambert Belgian Crystal chosen especially to match the glorious inventory of this store. In addition, as a sideline, they are the sole distributors in Belgium of the world-famous collection of bronze miniatures from Bermann in Vienna. The young and delightful Rubbrechts and their competent staff—all 5 of them quintilingual—will give you a friendly welcome. Tops in Europe.

Leather: **Delvaux** (blvd. A. Max 22, ave. de la Toison d'Or 24, and Galerie de la Reine 31) is almost unknown outside Belgium, but for more than 150 years Europeans-who-know have esteemed it as highly as Hermes, Gucci, and Loewe.

Lingerie: **Nina Meert** (5 rue de Florence) combines lace and linen to come up with a beguiling line of nightgowns.

Markets: The **Flea Market,** known both as the **Marche-aux-Puces** and **Vieux Marche,** functions daily 7 a.m. to 2 p.m. in the square of Jeu de Balle. Haggle until you're puce; expect as much as 50% lower than the asking price. This one is a pale imitator of the larger Paris classic, but if you're lucky you'll walk away a winner. The aforementioned **Antique Market** (Place Sablon all day Sat. and to 1 p.m. on Sun.) convenes in green-and-red tents, the official colors of Brussels. The merchandise runs from modest to very expensive things, including silver, porcelain, and furniture. Also bargain, bargain, bargain here, as well as in any store of this class. The bustling **Food Market** operates on Sun. from 8 a.m.–1 p.m. near the South Station. It offers a tremendous variety of produce, fruits, flowers, spices, and imports from the Mediterranean (olives, peppers, more). Quite a sight. There's also a **Bird Market** from 8 a.m.–1 p.m. on Sun. and Mon. in the Grand' Place.

In *Liege,* the historic **Batte Sunday Market** notably outshines its Brussels competitor in color, versatility, and serious interest to buyers. Encyclopedic variety of merchandise; parley just as hard for the same rewards; go earliest possible between 9 a.m. and noon. *Formidable!*

Men's Tailors: **Harry de Vlaminck** (blvd. Waterloo 32), **Bouvy** (ave. Louise 46 and ave. Toison d'Or), and **Rose & Van Geluwe** (36 place du Grand Sablon) are the pick of the pack. All carry exceptionally smart suits and shirts. The first of this trio imports its sportswear from prodigious Brioni of Rome, the third is famous for its made-to-measure garments. All are pricey but outstanding.

Minerals and Fossils: **La Geode** (rue Marche-aux-Herbes 53) is the local pacesetter in this field. The **Rock Shop,** one of the Sky Shops at the airport, has treasures from the deep such as pearls, coral, and shells, as well as those dug out of the earth.

Model Railways: Buffs will be enchanted with **Brand** (rue Marche-aux-Herbes 60), which offers an extensive repertory plus Belgian minivillages and the like.

Mosaic and Jewel-Encrusted Tables: **Chale** (ave. Louise 117) is necessarily up-market. Every piece is unique; each bears the Chale signature with an encrusted ruby serving as its period. Some of his tables are set with prehistoric fossils, opaque stones, mosaics of marcasite, lapis lazuli, and turquoise. Others have inset slices of translucent agate or cornelian that are illuminated from underneath. Smaller items include doorknobs and boxes. Such treasures must command high tariffs.

Paris Fashions: Virtually all of the best Parisian shops and boutiques have branches here.

Perfume: **Brussels Airport Duty and Tax Free Sky Shops** offer tremendous savings—among the most competitive—if you are leaving the Benelux countries. The selection is vast and very up-to-date. In the main Departure Hall the counters are long; the staff know their business; they work quickly and efficiently because it is usually crowded. There are more kiosks further on, too, in the lounges around the departure gates.

Pewter: Have no fears about purchasing MODERN pewter at reputable dealers such as **Postainiers Huttois** (Galeries St. Hubert). The center of the industry is in the village of *Huy*, near *Liege*. The gift shop at the **Wittamer Pastry Center** (place du Grand Sablon) has an attractive selection of ashtrays, goblets, measures, pitchers, plates, and candelabra that is entirely Portuguese. Unless you're a qualified expert, however, our urgent advice is that you don't go out on a limb by acquiring ANTIQUE pewter in this city. Too tricky for us!

Pipes: Belgian briar is superb. **Tabagerie Tete d'Or** (rue Tete d'Or 13) might be called the local Dunhill's, even though the products are not quite up to the inimitable British quality.

Provence Products: **Souleiado** (bvd. de Waterloo 14) is replete with this French-Mediterranean merchandise made up in dresses, scarves, bags, notebooks, diaries, pillowcovers, boxes, tablecloths, tea cozies, and goodness knows what else. The colors are engaging.

Scientific Marine Instruments and Automatic Music Instruments: There is a vast assemblage at **Ascima** (ave. Louise 81). Wonderful for collectors.

Woodcraft: **Michelangeli** (rue Marche aux Herbes 19) is a showcase for the small or often monumental sculpture of Gualverio Michelangeli; he represents the sixth generation of carpentry in his family. The whimsy of the faces, toys, beasties of the zoo and the wild, as well as plump airplanes, trains, and godzillas are perfect for any child—or splinter groups up to 99 years of age.

SHOPPING AREAS

Meir and **De Keyserlei** are the main hubs; streets around the **Grote Markt** abound with galleries and antique shops.

THINGS TO BUY

Diamonds, antiques, copperware, linens, chocolate.

Diamonds: Here in the city which was once the richest in the world and remains one of the busiest maritime ports on this globe, tens of millions of karats in diamonds are traded annually. Their worth? Approximately 6 billion dollars!

Less than a half hour's drive from Brussels there is a small and dazzling enclave called **Diamondland.** Traditionally, and for security reasons, this marketplace of precious gems was "off-limits"—a forbidden zone to all but professional visitors.

Not any longer.

You are invited to come eyeball-to-eyeball with the industry.

The vast showroom, only a few steps from Antwerp's central railway station, is a thriving colony of enterprising craftsmen who have cut 6 out of 10 diamonds you have ever seen in your lifetime. Within the modern edifice at Appelmansstraat 33-A there are polishing benches, design studios, educational demonstrations and jewelry showcases where you can become enlightened and enthralled over the derivation, treatment and presentation of the most cherished stones in the world. Even a person well versed in gemology comes away with a better understanding of the components of diamonds—elements such as color, clarity, karatage, cut, fluorescence and valuation. A visit here is like a privileged trip to the inner sanctum of a heretofore secret profession. The statistics alone are significant: approximately 80% of the labor is devoted to industrial diamonds, 18% to ornamental work, and 2% to investment-grade stones. Whenever you indulge in the purchase of such a luxury you will want to be prepared with as much knowledge as possible. Diamondland can provide the advice of experts; your purchase will be tax-free—a price advantage that could very well cover the cost of your transatlantic flight and enhanced by the fact that it is the perfect carry-home shopping item. Private appointments can be made by telephoning 03/2343612; or you can go to the information center at Diamondland any Monday through Saturday from 9 a.m. to 6 p.m.

Here's the largest exhibition of its type in the world—a multi-faceted reassurance that diamonds are forever.

Markets: **Bird Market** (close to the City Theatre) not only has our feathered friends for sale, but a Noah's Ark of dogs, cats and fish as well, each Sunday from 9 a.m.–1 p.m. **Friday Market** (Vrijdagmarkt) held, naturally, on Friday, and, just to be confusing, on Wednesday mornings, too, gathers together all kinds of used items including a lot of old furniture. **Antique Market** (Lijnwaadmarkt—north side of the Cathedral which is at Groenplaats 21) is in progress every Saturday from Easter to the end of October; antiques and oddments galore. **Rubens Markt** (in the ancient precincts of the Grote Markt) is a once-a-year affair on August 15. It's most colorful since the stallholders sport period costumes.

DENMARK

SHOPPING HOURS

Usually 9:30 a.m.–5:30 p.m., no noon closings; Sat. 9 a.m. to 1 or 2 p.m.; many stay open until 7 or 8 p.m. on Fri.

PUBLIC HOLIDAYS

Jan. 1, Easter Thurs.-Mon., Prayer Day (fourth Fri. after Easter), Ascension Day (40 days after Easter), Pentecost, June 5 (Constitution Day), Dec. 25–26.

MAIL ORDERS

The Danes are blessed with a heaven-sent talent for design— sometimes twinklingly whimsical, nearly always sweepingly graceful and enchantingly original. Their unique approach to line, form, and color sets this little nation apart as one of the prime favorites of visiting and mail-order shophounds. For professionals or hobbyists in this milieu, the annually issued *Design from Scandinavia* is a beautiful oversized magazine that is distributed in more than 100 countries and territories. It contains hundreds of full-color plates of furniture, textiles, handicrafts, interior decorations and much, much, more. You may examine or buy it at New York's Museum of Modern Art. Among our favorites in Copenhagen, **Illums Bolighus** issues a compilation of 80-odd pages of stunningly beautiful and unusual wantables. And, if you're in a hurry, you can phone them at 01 14 19 41. **Hans Hansen Silver** periodically updates brochures of its elegant and exclusive silver and gold collections. These samplers are yours for the asking. **Brodrene Andersen,** Denmark's fashionable answer to Brooks Brothers, limits its Christmas catalog to Danish customers, but its many foreign postal requests are welcomed and expedited. The **Sweater Market** enjoys a gigantic postal volume. Although **Bang & Olufsen** does not handle mail orders, their handsome catalog is free for the asking—very useful as backgrounding before you visit the Copenhagen store.

HOW TO BUY A FUR

Extensive research on this subject has revealed the following expert advice which all potential buyers should utilize before making any final selection:

1. Make certain that you are dealing with a reliable furrier whose information you can trust. Hosts and hosts of ladies who consider themselves shrewd in getting discount ''bargains'' at wholesale houses in reality *lose* money in the inferior products they are sold through their innocence.

2. Check the pelts for freshness. This is easier than any customer might think. If the hair shows any indication of dryness, this garment has been too long at the shop.

3. The feel of the fur must be soft and pliable. It must be dense with strong guardhairs. This is especially necessary in foxes, as poor grades very quickly shed.

4. The weight is determined by the thickness of the leather. Wild fur taken at prime season has thin leather and a thick fur. In speaking of minks, the males are much larger, hence the leather is thicker; therefore, a coat made from these pelts will necessar-

ily weigh more. Thus, as a broad basic rule, the less the leather, the better the apparel. *Important: A fine quality fur will ALWAYS be soft and lightweight.*

5. Any natural fur must be clear in its color. The secret throughout this category is the presence of what is known in the trade as the "bluish cast." Brown fades into a lighter reddish tone; gray becomes beige/yellow; others take on different tints eventually. Here is why the "bluish cast" in the original is so important. As further examples, a dark mink must be dark grayish brown, not reddish; a gray mink must be bluish, not yellowish; a blue fox must be gray, not brown.

6. It is normal to find small price differences in what might appear to be similar styles. But if there's a sizable gap, you can rest assured that there is also a sizable difference in the class of the fur and in its workmanship.

7. Inspect the edges of the coat carefully to verify that there is no splitting so that you can see the leather through the hairs. Look with equal closeness at the closing over the shoulders. These are places which very clearly will indicate the good or shoddy nature of its work. Also establish that there is a nice turnback (the facing) on the front, sleeves, and hem. Here is another positive indicator whether it is a worthy candidate or not.

8. Coats put together from separate undersize pieces are most definitely not advised. Among other things, they commonly split at their seams.

9. As you will read later, most countries, including the U.S.A., have ratified the Washington Convention, which prohibits the importation of endangered species such as leopard, tiger, cheetah, lion, snow leopard, and others. America has gone further in banning all sea mammals except the Alaska fur seal, with a general embargo against all other fur seals, hair seals, rock seals, bladder seals, and members of this family. The wearer risks instant confiscation. Any dependable furrier will give you full details.

COPENHAGEN

SHOPPING AREAS

Stroget is a pedestrian street ¾ mile long. It links the Radhus-pladsen and Kongens Nytorv. Down its length are 5 streets: Frederiksberggade, Nygade, Vimmelskaftet, Amagertorv, and Ostergade. Parallel to the Stroget on one side are Farvergade, Kompagnistraede, and Laederstraede and on the other side the Latin Quarter around the university. Nearby **Fiolstraede** and **Kobmagergade** are where locals often stroll.

THINGS TO BUY

Arts and crafts, home furnishings, silver, ceramics, crystal, mink, porcelain, sweaters, fabrics, fine wearing apparel, hi-fi equipment, pipes, watches, amber, books, toys, innumerable small items with Danish charm. As previously stated, scores of North Americans consider Danish shopping the finest on the Continent. Most of the merchandise is outstandingly tasteful in the special national way—and prices, in spite of the "MOMS" jackups, are *still* eminently decent for the values which are offered.

ADDED VALUE TAX

The highly controversial "MOMS"—a 22% (actually 18.03% of the retail price) "value increment" tax increase on goods—is effective on a national scale *within* the country. But there are loopholes for the foreign visitor. Now, all residents of non-E.E.C. nations (a.k.a. ''third countries'') may hand-carry as many articles as desired out of the country as long as the *total* amount purchased in *each* shop is worth 600 Dkr. or more and be eligible for the tax rebate. Merchants who display a red Tax-Free sticker are part of the program and will supply you with the correct form and explain the method of getting the customs' stamp at Kastrup airport, where you mail the export invoice. Later the tax, minus a small handling charge, is refunded to you either through your own bank or sent by check to you. An alternate procedure has been introduced that permits immediate reimbursement to departing airline passengers at Den Danske Bank at Copenhagen Airport. If you are flying out of the country from there ask your merchant about the special form needed for this operation. Don't fail to have your forms stamped at the frontier of the country if you leave by any other means. You'll want to gain the saving. These documents are returned to the company where you made your purchase and they reimburse you directly. Goods that are shipped *directly to your home or to anywhere outside its borders* qualify for the substantial discount.

Airport Shopping: See our special report at the end of this chapter concerning duty-free purchases for outward bound travelers; there's an improved and streamlined procedure used by the shops in this complex for the tax deduction process.

Antiques: Kompagnistraede and Laederstraede, continuations of the same thruway, are the nidus. Fiolstraede also contains a cluster of shops. **Royal Copenhagen Antiques** (Bredgade 11) is truly definitive for the Danish design which has had such international impact over scores of years. Here's a splendid exhibition of R-C and Bing & Grondahl porcelain, Holmegaard glass, Michelsen and Georg Jensen silver. The last even boasts its own museum on the premises. Nearby, **Branners Bibliofile Antik-variat** (Bredgade 10) features (when available) the hand-painted, hand-lettered Book of Hours. Woodcuts, incunabula, seascapes, engravings by Old Masters, and other printed rarities fill out the stock. **Art Deco** (St. Strandstraede 19) is aptly named, and, if you're into that period, have a word with Gunnar Marek.

Arts and Crafts: **Dansk Kunst Hardwerk** (Amagertorv) spreads out over two floors. There is a preponderance of pottery in a gallery-like setting.

Art Galleries: Jacob Asbaek and his charming wife have converted their own 17th-century mansion into the quaint and enticing **Galerie Asbaek** (Ny Adelgade 8). Sculptures, paintings, drawings, and prints by leading international artists are cunningly placed in this unusual milieu. Even their garden is used for display. Hours: Mon. to Fri. 11 a.m.–6 p.m.; Sat. 11 a.m.–4 p.m.; Sun., by appointment only. Very effective and exciting. **Court Gallery** (Ostergade 24) is also among the handful of the best known and most highly regarded. **Gallery Jerome** (Hovedvagtsgade 2), although small, is making it big now. The emphasis is on modern works by a stable of international names—heavily weighted toward Danish painters and Cobra. Outside of town, in the village of Holte (near to the enchanting Sollerod Kro), is the newish **Gallerie Æblegarden** (Sollerodvej 15, Tel.: 02.80.33.50). Their prints and lithographs come through Christies in London, but aside from that phase, there are constantly changing shows of modern paintings. Here's a bonus for you when you're touring the countryside.

Art Auction Houses: **Arne Brunn Rasmussen** (Bredgade 33) specializes in the sales of both antique and modern furniture, glass, and bric-a-brac, as well as old paintings. **Kunsthallens Auktioner** (Kobmagergade 11) places fine paintings of various periods on its block. Both will supply evaluations and take tax-free orders from visitors.

Bookbinder: **Bogbind Henning Jensen,** tucked behind Bjorn Wiinblad Hus in Pistolstraede, are small, dedicated practitioners of this fast-vanishing art.

Books: Denmark is one of the handiest countries in which to restock your supplies of stateside books and magazines. **Boghallen** in Politikens Hus (Town Hall Square), **G.E.C.** (Gad Pedestrian Mall), and **Arnold Busck** (Kobmagergade near Runderarn) offer the most versatile assemblages in English.

Boutiques: **Bee Cee** (Ostergade 24; branches at Hotel Scandinavia and Copenhagen Airport) stands for the ubiquitous Birger Christensen—and by now you should know that this name means q-u-a-l-i-t-y. The spirit throughout is so gay and youthful that the chic buyer of any age finds it irresistibly a la mode. Here you will find the finest selection of fashion imaginable: Eye-arresting sportswear, casual clothes, accessories, blouses, labels such as Sonia Rykiel, Claude Montana, Castelbajac, Missoni, and Giorgio Armani. It has Danish originals plus imports from Italy, France (at prices usually the same as you'd pay there), England, and the other Scandinavian countries. In its Hotel Scandinavia boutique there are male and female Danish hand-knitted sweaters (your own pattern also custom-woven by elderly homebodies) from $100 to $125. Manageress Miss Tove Lutzen (or Ellen Petak at the airport shop) and her English-speaking staff are alert to the latest fashion trends. Walking through this level you enter the **Chanel** establishment, an independent house which appears to be a duplicate of the Parisian site on rue Cambon. If you continue your shopping stroll, the **Bee Cee Fur Collection** also occupies a loaded chamber in the same Pistol Street armory. Here the ammunition is fur-lined raincoats, as well as their sports furs, and more. Within the enclave is **Kenzo,** the Japanese clothing designer, his shop being a Danish duplicate of the Kenzo masterpiece at Place Victoire in Paris. The expanded downstairs is devoted to his menswear—and be sure to try on the distinctive Kenzo Jeans, fellas. The modern **Caroll Tricot Boutique,** (Ostergade 26) first-cousin to the ones poppin' up in France, England and America is nearby.

Children's Togs: **Createx Jeunesse** (Gronnegade 32) pampers newborns to 18-year-olds. Helle Buchardt Jorgensen has an eye for color and style—she buys Italian, French and Dutch designs to fill her cupboards so you'll find the Cacharel, Daniel Hechter, Lacoste, New Man, Petit Bateau and Oilily labels in these elfin quarters. Every item from layettes to jogging sets reveals great flair.

Chocolate: **Anthon Berg** (Ostergade 1) is a brand name of quality in these latitudes.

Clothing: Ever hear of a legend called Brooks Brothers? Well, if the airline ticket in your pocket didn't prove otherwise, you could believe that you were in that revered American institution the moment you step into **Brodrene Andersen** (Ostergade 7-9) in the heart of Copenhagen's Old Town. This Danish house has been a stitch in time for well over a century, stylishly attiring the Establishment fraternity—including, we might add, the Royal Danish Court since its more recent princes were in knee pants. Andersen's richly conservative, paneled interior exudes masculine character—and so does its debonair clothing. Many of its materials are purchased on London's stately Savile Row—the sort that even make women look twice (and then usually with envy). General Manager Jorgen Nexoe-Larsen (3rd generation), your impeccable host, opens a sesame of sartorial treasures—suits and jackets from Zegna, Valentino, Cerruti, Boss and Chester

Barrie plus Aquascutum classics, and 100% hand-tailored outfits. A big range of leisure wear is also available from famous
names as Henry Cotton's, Polo Ralph Lauren, Gant, and Lacoste. And don't despair, ladies: You can turn waiting time to
profit in Andersen's well-stocked women's department, where
there are troves of lovely sweaters, slacks, and skirts from Les
Copains, Bogner, Hermes, and van Laack. The purchase tax may
also be avoided by dispatching all goods to your home. In addition to Director Nexoe-Larsen, who would happily solve your
problems, Mrs. Brandt in the Ladies' Department, and Mr. Gul-
lov also speak perfect English and are also the souls of kindness.
Princely—and that's only half of it!

Creative Jewelry: **Gerda Lynggaard** (Niels Hemmingsens
Gade 20) has built her dashing fame in the realm of feminine
accessories ornamented with anything from coconut shell to polished silver; it has the richness of nacre, pearl, amber, and ebony,
refined textures of rare African woods, the burnished glow of
metal, the boldness of bone or cord or leather or whatever she
assembles as an expression of her own inventiveness.

Decorative Arts: **Bjorn Wiinblads Hus** (Ny Ostergade 11)
intrigues us. There is no single slot into which this incredible
artist fits. Is he a ceramicist? A tapestry designer? A poster painter?
A candlestick maker? An architect? An interior decorator? A
theater set designer? An opera illustrator? A cartoonist? A costume couturier? A charmer of man's limitless imagination?
Wiinblad is all of these—and before the ink dries on this page,
he will undoubtedly be into a dozen more media. If this restless
talent can have any headquarters, it is probably located in the
quaint, 18th-century half-timbered house which bears his name
in the Pistolstraede district. Though scores of polychromatic creations are visible in this living museum which is also a retail
outlet for his whimsical creations, he is just as likely to be found

in Dallas checking on the decor of the Hotel Anatole, or in Japan, Melbourne, Chicago, Sydney, Karlsruhe, or a hundred other cities where he has exhibited, decorated buildings, or otherwise enchanted the public. There is no fun like the merriment that comes from living in Wiinblad's world, whether you're buying a simple pot, a wall plate, a poster, or simply wandering through the inspired forest of one of the 20th-century's most delightful geniuses. His marvelous tables, his celebrated graphics, his deftly drafted greeting cards are all here to be purchased and to bring happiness to their new owners. Almost anything that Wiinblad touches magically becomes a collector's item. His gleefully rotund airborne ladies, his blithe harlequins, his lovable villains, all of his pasticcioed childlike critters have become the everlasting pets of modern society . . . and at such reasonable prices that you will hardly believe the stickers. Wiinblad said of himself, "When I was about 10 or 11 I painted my first porcelain, but the important thing for me always was that the things should be presents for somebody." Lucky for us Wiinblad never stepped off that path.

Department Store: **Magasin du Nord** (13 Kgs. Nytorv) is a colossal emporium that truly lives up to its name. It is the largest in all Scandinavia and gathers under its roof most of the finest products of the Nordic cultures.

English Lifestyle: **Mulberry** (Ostergade 13) A splendid store here. See "London" for details of the stock.

Fabrics: **Per Reumert** (Amagertorv 33) and **Gera Stoffer** (Ostergade 36-38, adjoining Birger Christensen) are locally the undisputed leaders of this field. If it's for either sex—if it's woven, braided, knitted, or pleated—or if it runs anywhere from 50¢ to $50 per meter—they probably have it.

Flowers: **The House of Flowers** (Kobmagergade 7) nurtured by Erik Bering is of star quality.

Foodies' Funhouse: **Kokkenes Torvehal** is in the Pistol Street district near Ostergade, the heart of the capital's finest shopping tenderloin. The name means ''Cook's Market'' and it's a fresh concept for today's busy midtowners who don't have time to pause at outlying stalls. If you are looking for a gourmet gift item, wine, fine chocolate or even a restaurant for relaxing in the middle of a purchasing spree, here they are—handy, handsome and headed for success.

Furs: More high-grade mink is raised in Denmark than in any other foreign land—and the quality and savings are unbeatable. By far the most eye-gleaming assortment can be found at the 121-year-old house of **Birger Christensen** (Ostergade 38 on the Pedestrian Mall). Purveyors By Appointment to no less than 3 Royal Courts and to most of the important foreign embassies, it offers a reservoir of the largest stocks and widest fur choices in Europe. They are so understated and so *different* that many customers now walk in to ask without specifying for ''a fur coat''— simply because they want a Birger Christensen styling and label. The specialty here is their world-famous Danish mink in a color galaxy of 20 mutations. For the unique brilliance of design and the superb quality of every pelt on the premises, the traveler gets a great market value in comparison with fine furriers anywhere. The inventory is deliberately umbrellaed to cover all age and economic groups from the cost-is-no-object models at the top, to the lovely new contemporary line, labeled Bee Cee, which includes inexpensive minks, shearlings, fur-lined raincoats, and more. Globally known Birger Christensen has now set up outlets at the Hotel Scandinavia, and the new shopping area in Copenhagen Airport as well as his own departments in New

York's Bergdorf Goodman, Texas' Neiman-Marcus, Tokyo's Seibu Department Stores and Pisa plus special Birger Christensen Fur Salons in Holt Renfrew stores in Montreal, Toronto, Vancouver and Ottawa. He has his own fur shops in London and Paris (see separate sections) where the same designer styles exist, but, naturally, at the home base the range is more extensive. As the only major house in the world to create new collections twice yearly, its fashion shows have been smash successes from coast to coast in the U.S.A., as well as in Paris and London, Gstaad, Saudi Arabia, Zurich, Montreal, Tokyo, and Kuwait. In addition, they distribute internationally the furs they make to the designs of such luminaries as Hanae Mori, Claude Montana, Donna Karan, and Ralph Lauren—a pretty discerning quartet themselves—who found the quality and expertise they were looking for. Ask for Mr. Christensen in person, the dynamic and ever-so-friendly spark behind so much of this nation's commerce. (With all of his projects he still has time for any visitor.)

Glassware: **Skandinavisk Glas** (#3 Ny Ostergade) is located on a charming spur (which is banned to traffic now too) just off the Stroget, Copenhagen's central pedestrian mall. It provides amazing versatility.

Handicrafts: **Haandarbejdets Fremme** (Vimmelskaftet 38) is the fascinating headquarters of the Danish Handcraft Guild, under the patronage of Queen Ingrid; it houses many of the patterns which another royal needlewoman—her daughter Queen Margarethe—has fashioned. The building itself is an invitation to fantasia, with tall banks of cottage windows revealing the two segments of the guildhouse. One is devoted to the imaginative apparel created by Denmark's most talented designers. The other contains a world of artistry that is manifest in knitting, embroidery, carving, pottery, jewelry, weaving, and other textiles. Not only are these treasures available for purchase in their finished form—items such as cushions by Bjorn Wiinblad, mats, doilies, eyeglass cases, handbags, tea cozies, and more—but there are scores of do-it-yourself packages which could keep any hobbyist busy for the next six centuries. The startlingly low prices and facile portability of such gorgeous flat-packing inventories make this a trove for gift items which can be carried away on impulse. In the clothing sector, here again the Danish artisans have outdone their zesty best and brought new form, hue, and texture to the flattering, lively wearables. Many of the dyes reflect only the colors which nature provides, manifest richly in capacious cloaks, heavy woven capes, scarves, vests, knitted blouses, and snugglesome woolens. Haandarbejdets Fremme operates 7 branches in the major cities of Denmark. For only about $40 per year you can become an associate member of the organization and receive the Guild's (English) quarterly magazine which includes articles, photos, as well as practical instruction in the arts and crafts which you will find represented at the "eye" of Danish needlework.

Hobby Shops: In the **Panduro** chain the most convenient link for the avid-do-it-yourselfer is at N. Voldgade 21. Far greater fun can be found in arranging and pasting up your own table mats, tea cozies, Christmas ornamentations, animals, and a galaxy of other things in the colorful felt designs of **Filt og Garnkaelderen Birgitte Norgaard** (G1. Strand 52), which are so gay, so merry, and so enchanting. Each figure is a lovable pixie.

Home Furnishings: **Illums Bolighus, Center of Modern Design** (Amagertorv 10), is the closest we've ever found to being *the* dream shop of any North American host or hostess. The level of artistry, quality, and technical soundness throughout its 4 sweepingly dramatic, air-conditioned floors is electrifying. True-life displays replace counters. You'll find a bonanza in this one-

and-only "Home House." There is a "Mini-Illums" branch which is a honey in Tivoli, open until late on Saturdays and all of Sundays.

Jewelry (Museum Reproductions): **Museums Smykker** (Gronnegade 6 and Copenhagen Airport Shopping Center) is the brainchild of Elisabeth and Finn Gotthelf. Sifting through a rich harvest of archaeological finds they've copied pieces from the Bronze Age, Viking period and the Crusades in gold, silver or bronze. Over 200 pieces are available. A catalog with black and white photos and price list can be obtained for 7 Dkr. In all the objects there is a feeling of great power and strength yet infinite delicacy as well. Owning one of these is a mystical experience that spans the millennia.

Model Theaters: These are the specialties of **Priors** (Kobmagergade 10–13), where you'll also find puppets, marionettes, and the like.

Pewter: **Tin Centret,** also known as **The Pewter Centre** (Ny Ostergade 2), built its fame on handmade pewter from Scandinavia which it still features as the focal point of all its products. Within the inventory today, however, the taste and variety have expanded to include some of the most exciting designers of 15 different nations.

Pipes: **W. O. Larsen** (Amagertorv 9) is not only one of the outstanding establishments in Europe for pipes and blended tobaccos, it also is one of the world's most fascinating centers for viewing the history of smoking. As purveyor to the Danish Court, here is Scandinavia's monarch in this particular field. Even if you don't smoke you can pass an hour of riveting interest admiring the assemblage of rare briars, bone, porcelain, and clay pipes which have been collected from all over the globe, including a unique American Indian peace pipe. Each one of the Larsen masterpieces is handcrafted with its own meticulously fashioned stem. The 126-year-old firm has been in the same family from father to son through 4 generations and the fifth is already extremely active in the business. The pipes, which started as a hobby, are now the dedicated vocation of Mr. and Mrs. Larsen. The family travels throughout the world to display the distinctive Larsen design. Grand!

Porcelain: **Royal Copenhagen** (Amagertorv 6) and neighboring **Bing & Grondahl** (Amagertorv 4) are, of course, the historic titans of this powerful industry and important craft. This pair has now merged with Georg Jensen, Holmegaard glass and Illums Bolighus.

Silver: While world-famous **Georg Jensen** (Ostergade 40) has gorgeous displays and the biggest name, you may wish to own pieces that are not so familiar but which reveal all of the distinctive Danish trademarks of finesse, line and quality finish. That should lead you to the prestigious doors of **Hans Hansen Silver** (Amagertorv 16, on the Pedestrian Mall), which we regard as the most intimately tasteful silver store in all of Denmark. Since its founding in the small town of Kolding, Hans Hansen Silver has combined honest, gifted craftsmanship with the dynamic, pure forms of the sculptor's art. Gold, silver, and rosewood are the mediums; glory is the result. Sterling-silver rings (from $35), brooches (from $35), bracelets (from $85), necklaces (from $50), and cufflinks (from $65) are among the enticements waiting to cast their charms over you. Other specialties include lyrically wrought hollow ware, elegant rosewood table accessories (inlaid with sterling silver), and strikingly creative flatware. Of the latter, Statesiders are especially fond of the "Amalie" pattern (about

$315 per 5-piece setting) and the "Kristine" pattern (about $345 per 5-piece setting). Ib Moller-Larsen will help you in this garden of temptations. The greatest, say we!

Sound & Music: **Bang & Olufsen Center** (*pa Stroget,* Ostergade 3–5) has made its own bang in the world of ultra–high fidelity as well as creating sonic booms in the realm of design. (The Museum of Modern Art has chosen its creations for their permanent collection.) Aesthetically, there is nothing that can touch the thin-line finesse of these sleekly sedate masterpieces of hi-tech engineering. Moreover, this Center is the perfect studio showcase for experiencing the multitude of concepts and applications the Danish maestros have come up with—from the unique button-touch "round-the-house" music system to Beogram and Beovox audio components which are a joy to command. Proprietor Svend Erik Hansen is on hand with his staff to demonstrate and explain the secrets of such superlative sound. Since so many tastemakers in the field are American, much of the stock is built to U.S. voltage and wattage standards. You'll get a satisfying jolt from the tax-free purchase program which brings prices far below back-home levels for the same equipment.

Sweaters: **Sweater Market** (15 Frederiksberggade) is situated on Copenhagen's Pedestrian Street. There is a splendid collection of hand-knitted Danish sweaters for every taste: classic, chic, and sporty, mostly knitted in the original Scandinavian patterns. Another specialty is the supersoft wool of the Icelandic jackets, coats, scarves, mittens, and hats, all of which are in the natural undyed colors. If your suitcases are full, don't fret, as they will ship the goods home for you and the prices quoted will be exclusive of Danish taxes. Moreover, the tab will include handling, postage by surface mail and insurance. You can also take the goods with you minus the Danish tax, as long as the amount purchased is 600 DKR or over.

Watches: **Ole Mathiesen** (Ostergade 8) is a startling discovery; Swiss watches can be found in Denmark for the same or even lower prices than those in Geneva, Lucerne, or Zurich. And what better place to go shopping for one than in the ingratiating company of Ole Mathiesen himself, the proprietor of this distinguished shop and the designer of the superb wristwatch series which bears his own name and is represented at the Museum of Modern Art? While almost any major brand is obtainable here, the house specializes in Patek Philippe, Audemars Piguet, International Watch Company, Cartier, Paris, Ebel, and some of the most exquisite antique clocks visible in a commercial shop in Europe—all part of the outstanding "Mathiesen Collection." Here is a boutique where the timepiece is preeminent and the time allotted to each client doesn't matter a tick. A splendid and superfriendly address where time and money are both well spent.

Toys: **Kay Bojesens** (Bredgade 47) offers a droll collection beloved from Singapore to Sintra to Seattle. **BR-Legetoj** (Bremerholm 4, opposite Magasin du Nord) is a child's paradise too.

Airport Shopping: The word is getting around that **Copenhagen Taxfree** is a smash hit in the international battle for super-low prices and infinite variety. Furthermore, it offers an atmosphere that challenges Tivoli in freshness, vitality and *joie de vivre*. Indeed, the same people who maintain the famous downtown wonderland also keep this airport facility pulsing with excitement and flair. The basic design focuses on an interior mall containing twenty-two shops. Perfume and cosmetics are offered with discounts of up to 65% on downtown prices. (Concessionaires vowed that their charges will not be higher than those in Copenhagen.) You'll see furs from Birger Christensen, silver from Georg Jensen, renowned porcelain from the great names of Denmark, a Good Night Shop specializing in down comforters, notions galore, Viking jewelry, men's haberdashery, smart clothing and accessories for women, Scandinavian art, handmade pipes (look for the world's largest, according to the *Guinness Book of Records*). Merlin provides a sonic boom in stereo and other sound equipment; there's a toy shop with hours of trouble for little people; fine chocolate is purveyed in a 19th-century-style boutique filled with tempters to take home or to attack impatiently while on the plane. There's also a bewildering choice of gourmet items from a supermarket carrying Danish meats, Norwegian salmon and other dainties of the North. You can drink, dine or dawdle in any of several restaurants, cafes or bars—even an American-style drugstore. If your purchases within a particular store add up to 600 DKK or more then by the simple act of showing your passport and boarding card the V.A.T. is subtracted directly from the sales price. You thus avoid the need to visit the tax refund bureau. Saves time and offers more chance for further shopping. Very, very clever. Shops within the taxfree area function from the first flight of each day to the last one at night; otherwise, boutiques outside this zone but within the airport generally operate from 7 a.m. to 10 p.m. If there is anything you have missed on your shopping spree in Copenhagen proper, don't despair because all you must provide is a little extra time and a surprisingly little amount of money to satisfy that yen before boarding your flight.

ENGLAND

SHOPPING HOURS

London: In general, 9 a.m.–5:30 p.m. with some Sat. closings at 1 p.m. and others at 5:30 p.m. Large department stores, as well as other shops, open one specific weeknight (Thurs. on Oxford St., Regent St., Bond St., Kensington High St.; Wed. at Harrods in Knightsbridge and on King's Road and Sloane Sq.); smaller shops in Chelsea, Soho, and similar districts close at 1 p.m. on Thurs., but are usually open all day Sat.; shops at Covent Garden open 10 a.m.–8 p.m. Mon. through Sat.; although everything used to be shuttered on Sun. except a few delicatessens, a scattering of food shops (mornings only), and a handful of all-night drugstores (''chemists''), an increasing number of small merchants are keeping their doors open then. If in doubt, it is advisable to check before setting out.

SALES

A bonanza twice a year: After Christmas and late June, extending into July. Planeloads of bargain hunters fly into London for these 3-ring circuses, and through their purchases save enough to pay their plane fare. At Harrods you'll even find eager shoppers camping on the doorstep overnight waiting for the morning stampede.

PUBLIC HOLIDAYS

Jan. 1, Good Fri. (April 13), Easter Mon. (April 16), May Day (May 7), Spring Holiday (May 28), Late Summer Holiday (Aug. 27), Dec. 25–26.

DIFFERENCES IN SIZES

Important! British women's clothes are 1 size larger than North American. Women's shoes: 1½ sizes smaller. Men's trousers: 1 size larger. Men's shoes: 1½ sizes smaller. Hats: ⅛ smaller. The following items are equal in size: Men's suits, shirts, pajamas, collars, and any measurements given in inches such as bust sizes. Now that Britain has partially gone over to the metric system, clothing size tags show centimeters as well as inches.

MONEY-SAVING PERSONAL EXPORT SCHEME

Upon presenting their passports, overseas visitors may buy clothes and most other goods free of the 15% Purchase Tax. Retailers make over-the-counter sales on this basis, provided that the buyers carry all of these items and the accompanying documents in their hand luggage, produce them for inspection by the Departure Customs (whose officials will sign the forms, which then must be mailed back to the stores, which will later send a refund of the tax), and export them within a 3-month period. V.A.T. is also returned on purchases shipped overseas but often, in this case, the price quoted is the export price on which the tax is already deducted—saving on the paperwork. Merchants are under no obligation whatsoever to offer this service. If they do, legally they may deduct a modest sum from the refund to cover their costs. Since a large number of the leading establishments do subscribe, however, please be sure to inquire when your purchases are substantial. (The minimum amount you must buy to be eligible for these rebates has been see-sawing, so please check locally at the time of your visit.)

NOTE · · · Now, an alternative V.A.T. refund system is operational. Tourist Tax Free Shopping (with its red, white and blue stickers) is one service. Participating stores will display the emblem to show they are associated with it.

Vouchers have been simplified and can be issued for as little as £40. Once stamped by Customs all the forms can be returned in *one* envelope to the company and the refund is made quickly by *one* check to the purchaser's home address in his own currency or to a credit card account. The rebate is minus a small administrative handling charge.

MAIL ORDERS

Large-scale mail-order traffic was in full bloom here at least a century before it became big business in North America. Over the long span when The Sun Never Set On The Empire, it provided a vital lifeline to English, Scottish, and Welsh purveyors for colonists from Borneo to Honduras to Hudson Bay to Somaliland to hundreds of other far-flung outposts. Hence, however odd the request, a proper English merchant will wrap it and send it to you.

Chinacraft's nearly 100-page color catalog shows off their merchandise to perfection. Write to them at Parke House, 130 Barlby Road, London W10 6BW to obtain them, or for even speedier attention you can phone in England (01) 9601100, Telex: 923550 or Fax: (01) 9609232. This firm provides outstanding service to the customer and we think you could not do better.

The 260-year-old **House of Floris,** Perfumers to Her Majesty and Manufacturers of Toilet Preparations to His Royal Highness the Prince of Wales, would be pleased to post to you a fully illustrated catalog of their extensive range of glorious English flower perfumes, toilet waters, bath essences, soaps, and much more. **Halcyon Days** issues free color catalogs displaying their antiques and enamel collectors' items and they take great care to expedite orders efficiently. **The Irish Shop** has brochures available that they'll send at no cost to you upon request. The famous **House of Burberry** and the charming-to-its-roots **General Trading Company (Mayfair) Ltd.** both guarantee safe arrival at your doorstep of everything processed through their seasoned Export Departments. The latter will mail you their tempting general and Christmas catalog for the equivalent of £1 plus handling charges. **Dunhill** for smokes and **Foyle's** for books both have active mail departments. **Gidden** can outfit both horse and rider with their hand crafted tack by (what else?) posting. **Frank Smythson Ltd.** is one of the world's prestige names in stationery, pads, and fine leather desk equipment; ask for the documentation. **Eximious** offers a galaxy of giftware—and, even better than ordering through the UK, it features a Stateside facility for greater convenience (with dollar quotations, too!). Write P.O. Box 8455, Winnetka, IL 60093 or Tel: (312) 446–8171. And if that's not enough—there's snuff—from **M. Landaw.**

LONDON

SHOPPING AREAS

London can be divided roughly into seven main precincts: (1) **Oxford St.** (big department stores, chain operations and boutiques), (2) **Regent St.** (more department stores and specialty shops), (3) **Bond St.** (high fashion, jewelry, and exclusive luxury items), (4) **Kensington High St.** (boutiques, chain stores, antiques), (5) **King's Road, Sloane Sq.,** and **Fulham Rd.** (youthful fashions, oddments, and "in" articles), (6) **Knightsbridge** (Harrods and Harvey Nichols the two most exclusive department stores, other top name shops and fashionable boutiques), and (7) **Covent Garden** (a potpourri).

NOTE · · · When the Conran interests rehabilitated the Michelin Building, an architectural landmark of an earlier era, **Brompton Cross** was born. It's where **Brompton Road** meets **Fulham Road**; suddenly this junction has taken on star quality. A rather different restoration program is underway in the **Docklands** district as part of an entire urban renewal scheme. Merchants both large and small have set up at **St. Katharine Docks** near Tower Hill and most recently at **Tobacco Dock** close to Tower Bridge and the **Hays Galleria,** a complex in the shadow of London Bridge. All are realities, but there is more to come. Riverbus service, the Docklands Light Railway and extensions to the London Underground system will create easy access to these rather out-of-the-way zones. Right at the center of things, a far cry from Thames River activity, is the newly unveiled **London Pavilion** building at Piccadilly Circus. This rejuvenated old edifice now contains three floors of shopping possibilities.

THINGS TO BUY

Cashmeres, tartans, Burberrys, food delicacies, silver, china, enamels, sports equipment, leather goods, rare books, stationery, antiques, Dunhill pipes and supplies, English flower perfumes, shotguns, fishing gear, saddlery, toys, snuff, Birger Christensen Danish furs, Irish crafts, boutique items, and selected men's furnishings such as Lock's famous hats.

NOTE · · · Early during their visits, travelers may wish to make a reconnaissance to either or all of the exhibits at the **Design Center** (28 Haymarket), **Contemporary Applied Arts** (43 Earlham St., Covent Garden) and the **Crafts Council Gallery** (12 Waterloo Place, Regent St.). Each dispenses information on where you can obtain their products. The first is a showcase especially assembled for goods intended to interest the import-export trades. It is run by the Design Council, which in turn receives much of its support from the Department of Trade and Industry. Admission is free; there are three floors of items all of which are for sale plus a register of thousands of British goods— many samples, too. The second shows textiles, pottery, furniture, glass, lighting, and pieces of jewelry by artists and designers who usually work for themselves. Slides are on file and the information center augments their new Commissioning Service. The last offers another index of craftsmen, a slide library, research facilities, and an education department. It sells cards, posters, brochures, craft books, magazines, and catalogs.

Antique Fairs: These form another aspect of the art market scene. Four of the most widely known and well respected include: (1) **Arms Fair** (Royal Lancaster Hotel, Bayswater Rd., W.1; May and Sept.; an armory of military paraphernalia), (2) **Chelsea Antiques Fair** (Chelsea Old Town Hall, King's Rd., S.W.3; Mar. and Sept.; all categories of goods), (3) **Fine Art and Antique Fair of Great Britain** (National Hall, Olympia, Hammersmith Rd., W.6; June; merchandise of varying calibre and wide ranging prices), (4) **Grosvenor House Antiques Fair** (Grosvenor House Hotel, Park Lane; from second Wednesday in June; top grade specimens with equivalent prices).

Antique Markets: The greatest variety at decent prices is found in the permanent indoor installations. Here the dealers know their business and the competition is keen. The 2 oldest are the **Chelsea Antique Market** (253 King's Rd.) and the **Antique Supermarket** (3 Barrett St.)—neither of which, in our view, is nearly as good as **Alfie's** on Church St., Marylebone. Each contains at least 100 stalls. Many articles cost less than $100. **Gray's Antique Market** (58 Davies St. and the adjoining 1–7 Davies Mews) is a maze of stalls with a stream running through the hall. Anything from jewelry to lace to books to oogah horns will be on display. Great fun for browsers. **Antiquarius** (135 King's Rd.) is more trendy and generally more expensive.

The open-air street markets are greater fun. **The Portobello Road Market** with its famous Collectors' Corner, **Islington's Angel Market** *(both Saturdays only),* and **Islington's Camden Passage** *(Wednesday and Saturday mornings)* are currently the hottest bets among hunters In The Know; the last, founded when 12 friends got together, has blossomed into importance. Historic **Petticoat Lane** around Middlesex St. *(Sunday mornings only)* is often characterized as the old clothes exchange of London. Finally, the **Bermondsey Market** (Bermondsey Sq., just south of

Tower Bridge, *Friday mornings*) is a lodestone for dealers rather than for visitors, and often dazzling fresh shipments from the country are put up for sale here at ridiculously low tariffs. The catch is that to be successful you must be on the scene before 6:30 a.m. At **Camden Lock** *(Saturdays and Sundays)* crafts, clothes and antiques appear.

At **The London Architectural Salvage and Supply Company Ltd.** (Lassco Mark St., off Paul St.) is for home*builders* as well as home*makers*. Need old doors, banisters, grills, knockers, knobs, hinges or moldings? Hire a container and fill 'er up.

For items related to the performing arts—books, pictures, and paraphernalia—the stage is **Cecil Court,** an alley behind St. Martin's Lane and fringing the theater district. The boutiques are minuscule.

Fulham Road and **King's Road,** Chelsea, are for those who can afford sentimentality in the more costly bracket; **Beauchamp Place** (pronounced "Beecham"), just off Knightsbridge, is another choice. **Westbourne Grove, Kensington Church St.,** and **Notting Hill Gate** remain popular-priced playgrounds. At 19 Marylebone Lane, the **Button Queen** (antique buttons) is amusing.

Where should you bargain? In all Markets and in all holes-in-the-wall that carry second-line merchandise—but never in the topnotch places, so haggle your hardest and stand your ground most resolutely there.

NOTE · · · The London and Provincial Antique Dealers' Association, Ltd., known as LAPADA, has produced an invaluable paper-back called *Buying Antiques in Britain.* Aside from listing its members both in London and around the country, it deals with matters such as export control, hallmarks, dates of important fairs and exhibitions, museums and galleries. There are clearly rendered maps of buying areas outside of London, too. Write to Heather Collingwood at 535 Kings Road, London SW 10 to order a copy. The cost is £7 (air mail) or £2 (surface post)—foreign currency checks aren't accepted, but you may send cash.

Antiques and Modern Furniture, China, Glass, Cutlery, Linens, Kitchenware and Gifts: **The General Trading Company** (144 Sloane St., Sloane Sq. and 10 Argyle St., *Bath*) lives up to its name perfectly. And it's a joy. Occupying four elegant Edwardian terraced houses, GTC evokes a unique and urbane atmosphere. Established in 1920 and owned by the Part family, this shop has a deserved reputation for well-chosen and carefully selected merchandise to suit the eclectic. Its English period pieces, prints, pewter, accessories, china and *objets d'art* are displayed in softspoken traditional surroundings while the modern furnishings are shown in a more contemporary setting. There is a comprehensive collection of bone china and porcelain tableware from Royal Worcester, Spode, Wedgwood, Herend and many others as well as fine glassware both collectable and functional. For the keen gardener there's a Burbank of choices as well as the Garden Cafe, run by Justin de Blank. As a quintessentially English Establishment, GTC proudly displays its four Royal Warrants. Export packing and shipping can be arranged to anywhere in the world; mail order catalog available.

If General Trading shouldn't have what you're hunting for, try famous, two-century-old **Asprey** (165-169 New Bond St.) for anything from an Adam fireplace to a gold swizzle stick to Ringo-Starr-designed chess and backgammon sets to historical figures in porcelain. **Algernon** (27 Bruton Place) comes up with an interesting span from antiquities to contemporary pieces. In the very top leagues **Bernheimer Fine Arts Ltd.** (32 St. George St.) of Munich fame arrived on the scene recently. Here is a treasure house of antique furniture, sculpture, Chinese art, carpets, tapestries and textiles. **Nina Campbell** (9 Walton St.), **Colefax and Fowler** (39 Brook St.) and **Parrotts** (56 Fulham Rd.) are rightfully well regarded. **Eldridge of London** (99–101

Farringdon Rd.) has been a well-kept secret for years—as specialists in *original* 18th- and 19th-century furniture. Schedule time at **Thomas Goode & Co.** (19 S. Audley St.) for traditional china, or **Peter Jones** (Sloane Sq.), **John Lewis** (Oxford St.), or **Heal's** (Tottenham Court Rd.) for modern china or glass. The area around Kensington Church St. is an especially good hunting ground for antique porcelain and pottery. **Wedgwood** and **Worcester** have showrooms, respectively at 34 Wigmore St. and 30 Curzon St.; arrangements may be made in both to visit their factories.

Art Prints and Paintings: **Stephanie Hoppen** (17 Walton St.) is both the person (charming, too) and the legend behind this name. The works (collected usually from great private estates) can be seen in a homelike, salon setting, framed and often hung with a motif in mind. Many subjects are available and you may even order a theme which Stephanie can possibly find for you somewhere across the face of Europe. Locales also at Suite 1000, 305 E. 61st, NYC and at 9 Sultan St. in Toronto.

Auctions and Art Galleries: **Sotheby's** (34-35 New Bond St.) and **Christie's** (8 King St., St. James's) are the world's greatest auction rooms, as everybody knows. The latter is more than 200 years old. Consult their listings in the London newspapers for what is being sold during your visit. As a rule, the most important sales occur in July and December. **Phillips** (7 Blenheim St., off Bond St.) reliable and good, vends less expensive things than those of the Big Two; they specialize in antique furniture; its sales days are Mondays and Fridays. **Bonham & Sons, Montpelier Galleries** (Montpelier St.) is also crowding the pacemakers. For more than 75 years, **Glendining & Co.** (7 Blenheim St.) has specialized in placing on the block small objects such as military medals, decorations, coins, commemorative medals, and the like. Although the bylaws of these houses prohibit them from issuing certificates of authenticity, their staffs are totally honest in their advice to their clients. Please never hesitate to seek this; it is entirely expected of bidders, regardless of the sum involved. Then set your limit, and stick by it. Look directly at the auctioneer and use every reasonable means to attract his attention. Above all, don't be frightened or shy—because your fears will prove to be groundless.

As for straight galleries, try **Arthur Tooth & Co.** (Bruton St.) and **Leger Galleries** (13 Old Bond St.) as two of the choicest for paintings only; **Ackerman** (3 Bond St.) for fine equine paintings, prints, and sculptures; **Harra Gallery** (next to the Hotel Connaught) for Impressionists onward; **Colnaghi** (14 Bond St.) for Old Masters to the present; and **Michael Parkin** (Motcomb St.) for English works from 1850–1950.

Books: **Foyle** (113-119 Charing Cross Rd.) is probably the world's biggest bookstore with an inventory of 4-million volumes, but **Hatchards** is coming up fast. **Waterstones** (121–125 Charing Cross Rd.) is part of an excellent chain. At the other end of the scale, **Bondy** (16 Little Russell St., W.C.1), with an apt address, sells miniature books chiefly as well as tomes for antiquarians. **Bloomsbury Rare Books** (29 Museum St., W.C.1) does what it says, but upstairs **Arthur Page** (another appropriate monicker) proffers parchments from medieval manuscripts. **J. A. Allen** (1 Lower Grosvenor), a trot from the Royal Mews, is devoted singularly to horses while **The Book Dump** (19 Great Ormond St., W.C.1) purveys its bargains in bulk and by weight. For the bibliophile, London is ecstasy under the cover.

Boutiques and Young Designers: A wave of fresh, provocative new talent has rapidly and totally changed London's fashion lookscape. The punk-rock music cult has found expression in threads as well as chords. Designers such as Dexter Wong, Helen Robinson, Wendy Dagworthy, Joseph Ettedgui, Katharine

Hamnett, Vivienne Westwood, John Galliano, Alistair Blair, Betty Jackson, Rifat Ozbek, Janice Wainright, Sheridan Barnett, Anthony Kwok, and Stevie Stewart and David Holah of Body Map are influential. Look, too, for evocations by groups such as English Eccentrics, Artwork, Arkitekt, and Design Studio. For Sloane Rangers more into the Establishment mode, names such as Caroline Charles, David and Elizabeth Emanuel, Jasper Conran, and Anthony Price are staples of the moment. Jean Muir and Zandra Rhodes are living legends who continue to excite the fashion world and the late Laura Ashley created an empire in home furnishings as well as clothing which continues. Literally hundreds of small, chic shops have sprung up, particularly on Bond St., in Knightsbridge, and in Chelsea. Now the capital is a-brim with talent which produces everything from classic to elegantly casual to fun-filled or horridly kooky models. We like the new and decoratively zesty **Bee Cee** (169 Sloane St.) which is a dashing fresh evocation from Birger Christensen and Maxwell Croft, the distinguished furrier team on New Bond St. There's a spry young look here—full of innovation. Incidentally, the same architect did up **The Way In Boutique** at Harrods to the tune of $4.2 million. The decor is high-tech to match the clothes. **Miss Selfridge** (Selfridges Department Store as well as Regent St. and Knightsbridge), in our opinions, has merchandise that is simultaneously inexpensive, sometimes junky but fashionable. **Next** is all over town (for women: 9 South Molton St., 160 Regent St., 728 King's Rd.; for men: 53 Brompton Rd., 62 South Molton St., 137 Kensington High St.). Their formula for success: classic styles at reasonable prices. **Brown's** (27 S. Molton St.) mixes the lines of Armani, Missoni, Chloe, Norma Kamali, and Sonja Rykiel with its own design label. **Lindka Cierach** (54 Hartismere Rd.) made headlines as the designer of Fergie's wedding gown. **Bruce Oldfield** (27 Beauchamp Pl.) dresses her, too, as does boy wonder **Jasper Conran** (37 Beauchamp Place). **Monsoon** (67 South Molton St. and 35 Beauchamp Pl.) takes its inspiration from the East. **Franka** (11 Dover St.) cut her first swath in couture but now has added her own boutique. A smart flair in basic conservatism. **Anouska Hempl,** owner of ultra-chic Blakes Hotel, carries her talents to yet another dimension. At 2 Pond Place (this area is really ''in'' right now) she has a design studio where she'll dress you from tip to toe. To make an appointment phone Blakes Hotel (370.6701) and they'll put you through. The name **Hartnell** (26 Bruton St. and 3 Stanhope Mews West) is back in the news. The house has been revived; Sheridan Barnett and Alan MacRae are whipping up ready-to-wear collections that are show-stoppers. **Ian Thomas** (14 Motcomb St.) stitches for the Queen herself. **Karl Lagerfeld** (173 New Bond St.) features the maestro's beautiful handmade creations as well as perfumes, shoes, and accessories. **Lucienne Phillips** (89 Knightsbridge) is a treasure trove of the high-styles of Britain's best. **James Drew** (3 Burlington Arcade) draws legions of sophisticated ladies for his dashingly created shirts in ombre- and moire-look jacquard silks, satin, crepe de chine, and fine cotton woven specially for the house; separates are also accented, as are Outlander knits. **Margaret Havell** (29 Beauchamp Place) caters to a similar clientele who like her skillful tailoring of country fabrics. **Caroline Charles** (11 Beauchamp Pl.) is another name to be reckoned with for sophisticated elegance. **Kenzo** (17 Sloane St.) serves both sexes; all ready-to-wear garments for Her originate on the drawing board of the illustrious designer himself. **Katharine Hamnett** (Sloane St., next to the Chelsea Hotel) still sticks to the basics. Remember her T-shirts some seasons ago? **Joseph** (13 South Molton St., Brompton Rd., across from the newly restored Michelin Building and 6 Sloane St.) has sharp, bright styles. The shop at the latter address is now called **Esprit. Piero de Monzi** (68 Fulham Rd.) is also currently popular among the bigger spenders; his specialties are cunningly conceived day and evening garb, casuals from France and Italy, chunky belts and bags, plus footwear.

Another current standout is **Kanga** (8 Beauchamp Pl.). The pure silk dresses are knockouts. **Palmer** (4 Motcomb St.) is a serene oasis which features up-to-the-minute selections by top-drawer English and Continental designers. Since style is the watchword here, the range of tariffs is broad. **Letetia** (18-20 Grosvenor St.) is a cheerful entry where you will find entrancingly classic Italian and French models by Corutti, Michael Goma, and other glamorous fabricators. **Wallis** (96 Kings Rd., 9 Brompton Rd., 215 and 272 Oxford St.) is worth a peek. Now for two specializing in "street fashion"; **Kensington Market** and **Hyper Hyper** vis-a-vis on Kensington High St. More up-market but also young is **Whistles** (St. Christopher St.). For the young and innocent there's the previously mentioned **Laura Ashley** (9 Harriet St., 256–258 Regent St. and Fulham Rd.).

Brass: **J. D. Beardmore and Co.** (3 Percy St.) has larger pieces as well as a mighty array of doorknobs, letter slots, locks, drawer pulls, hooks, latches, door numerals, lighting fixtures, fireplace hardware, and the like in this versatile metal. In the Notting Hill Gate area, **Jack Casimir** (23 Pembridge Rd.) is the brassiest gent for miles around; he has a whole floor of it.

Burberrys Rainwear and Apparel: Since Thomas Burberry invented his celebrated weatherproof cloth around 1856, **Burberry** has become a familiar name to literally millions of shoppers from Tampa to Tokyo. (You'll even find the name in *Webster's*.) Now its twin homes at 18 Haymarket (near American Express) and at 165 Regent St. house what is probably the world's finest collection of weatherproofs and other wearables under the sun (*and* clouds!). Because the Burberry Look has developed from a practical necessity into high fashion, the stores are shrewdly designed to cater for this ever-increasing demand. There's an extensive collection of ladies' topcoats as well as a

distinguished choice of casuals and knitwear including a Burberry logo lambswool series in a dozen flattering colors. You'll
find forests of tweeds, indescribably soft cashmeres and camel-
hairs, superbly chic Burberrys luggage, a wide range of golfing
gear, as well as a splendid Burberry fragrance for men. But the
crowning glories are those definitive trenchcoats (and overcoats)
lined either in the instantly identifiable traditional Burberry check,
or in a subtle alternative based on this pattern. (Personalized
monogrammed labels together with six months' free insurance
on rainwear are standard if your purchase is made from one of
Burberry's own stores.) These evoke a sporting mood which can
be augmented by additional matching Burberry accessories—from
a jaunty peaked cap to a smart-looking scarf to a neatly rolled
'brolly—a full ensemble that is both uplifting and timeless. And
timeless they are, a durability as prevailing as the British Empire
itself. Burberrys has recently added sunglasses, wristwatches, food
and toweling to their collection. All major credit cards (including American Express and MasterCard) are accepted. At both
Haymarket and Regent St. they understand North American tastes
and will go all out to be helpful. If you're heading for Scotland
there are branches in Glasgow, Aberdeen, and Edinburgh.

Cashmeres, Tartans and Materials: The Scotch House
(flagship store at corner of Knightsbridge and Brompton Rd., 2
others at 84/86 and 191 Regent St.) has been a titan in this field
for more than a century-and-a-half. Go to the circular Tartan
Room at the Knightsbridge home and see more than 300 patterns, plus the guides to the clans. Fabulous Highland accessories, sweaters, tweeds, cashmeres, Shetlands, lambswool and
exciting wardrobes and combinations of ready-to-wear items for
men, women and children. Also for cashmeres, you might like
a peek in the Burlington Arcade where **N. Peal** and **Berk** are
reputable purveyors.

Children's Clothes: No VAT is applied on items for kids under 14. **Anthea Moore Ede** (16 Victoria Grove) is where the Establishment goes to dress its progeny. **Anastasia** (28 James St.) is traditional as well: **Please Mum** (69 New Bond St.) is a mecca for half-pint nabobs; it's *very* expensive, as is **La Cicogna** (6A Sloane St.) an Italian connection. **Tigermoth** (166 Portobello Rd.) and **Benetton-012** (S. Molton St.) are both sprightly and colorful. **NBG** (S. Molton St.), part of the Next chain, caters for kids in an easy-going, moderately priced way. **Buckle My Shoe** (19 St. Christopher's Place) has as many eye-catching models for youngsters as its amusing name implies.

Cheese: **Paxton & Whitfield** (93 Jermyn St.) founded in 1797 sells over 100 different types and will mail anywhere in the world.

China: **Chinacraft** is the unquestioned leader in this complex field. All the prestige names are available in bewildering if not stunning diversity, thanks to Chinacraft's forty years of close cooperation with the peers of the industry. But luxury does not necessarily mean high prices. Because of Chinacraft's impressive buying power, it maintains a keenly competitive edge. Moreover, at sale times (January and July), it offers additional bargains. Shipping and insurance services are totally reliable; tax-free opportunities further enhance the shopping picture. Brides, of course, are grateful for the flexible and comprehensive Wedding List Service detailed in a special brochure. Furthermore, companies can order Christmas gifts or conference novelty items under the promotional gift plan. Whether it's china, crystal, silver or even some of the most endearing figurines imaginable, Chinacraft can keep you browsing with relentless avidity. Just a few addresses: Inn On The Park and Grosvenor House hotels, 198 Regent St., 556 Oxford St., 7/11 Burlington Arcade, 130 New Bond St., 50 Brompton Road; many others listed in their tantalizing publication.

Chocolates: **Bendicks** (195 Sloane St., 55 Wigmore St., 107 Long Acre, and 20 Royal Exchange) is world-renowned for its Bittermints. **Prestat** (24 South Molton) defies diets with hand-made truffles and brandy cherries. **Charbonnel & Walker** (28 Old Bond St.) offers number-charts indicating fillings, tongs to pick up the soft-hearted masterpieces, and lettered chocolates to spell out a message as a sweet treat. You'll be pleasantly surprised how sparkling fresh the after-dinner mints from **Marks and Spencer's** food departments can be.

Cigar Humidors: **Robin Gage** (50 Pimlico Rd., Tel. 730–2878) turns antique Victorian or Regency boxes into elegant accessories for smokers, puffing up for around $600. A man of many talents, he also creates brass and hide club fenders on order for your fireside; prices from $1,000. It's best to phone him.

Coins: **Spink** (5–7 King St.), **B.A. Seaby** (11 Margaret St.), and **Coins and Antiquities** (20–22 Maddox St.) offer the most interesting coinage in this realm.

Covent Garden "Village": Don't miss the general-purpose Jubilee Market surrounding the central area, restaurants, wine bars, a constellation of engaging stores, trendy boutiques, and other facilities. Among the unique merchants who have settled here are **Suttons Seeds** (Catherine St.) which offers 13,000 different species, **The Kite Shop** (69 Neal St.) which claims to stock the biggest range of kites and flying disks on earth, and **Glasshouse** (65 Long Acre) which is a cooperative of artisans who produce their wares on the premises and sell them in their front showroom. This is the capital's first permanent latenight shopping center, open until 8 p.m. 6 nights a week—and it is booming.

Cuff Links: **Paul Longmire** (12 Bury St., St. James's) is top drawer. Aside from the enormous variety on hand, personalized orders are welcomed.

Decoys: **Robert Coyle** (10 Holland St. W. 8) is the ducky choice for collectors of such carved decorator items.

Department Stores: **Harrods, Harvey Nichols, Selfridges, Marks & Spencer** (goodness, how ''Marks & Sparks'' is climbing!) and **Peter Jones** are the pacesetters; **John Lewis Partnership, Peter Robinson,** a pair called **House of Fraser** (Oxford St. and Kensington) and **Dickens & Jones** are also worthy.

Liberty (Regent St.), with outstanding antiques, furniture, luggage, notions, and a number of other categories, regards itself as an upper-bracket department store. Notwithstanding, we believe that the main emphasis here is on its internationally famous printed fabrics, silks, and sublime carpets. It has opened an Oriental Bazaar to bring back the flavor of an old-time trading company. A British monument.

Dollhouses: **The Singing Tree** (69 New King's Rd.) is the world in miniature—both modern and antique. All the little items that go into this microculture are here, too; write for the catalog (about $6).

Duty-Free Airport Shops: Our suggestion is to skip these marts in the Final Departure Lounges of Terminal 2 at Heathrow (''London's airport'') and at Gatwick. Reasons? First, except for perfumes, cigarettes, and spirits, the prices are no cheaper than they are in the city. Second, in these 3 discounted categories they are among the costliest airport installations in all of Western Europe. Third, the variety is downright poor, the stylings of clothing are often passe, and the camera, optics, and electronic counters do not compete with the best products on the shelves elsewhere. When you buy in town for export, your purchases will *truly* be duty-free—and their quality should be higher.

Enamels and Antique Accessories: **Halcyon Days** (14 Brook St. Mayfair, W.1 and 4 Royal Exchange, Cornhill, E.C.3) is just about as fetching as any one of its splendid little enamel boxes—a specialty that this house recovered as a lost art from 18th-century England. Enamel fired on a copper base, the luster and finish are exquisite creations in a tradition of perfect Georgian refinement. The artistic themes cover a multitude of subjects, family pets, stately homes and stately people, flowers, genre scenes, heraldry, topical statements for coronations and famous events—even special commissions for notables such as yourself or those loved ones in your family. The antiques selection is vast: 18th-century English enamels, rare shagreen, Staffordshire pottery, porcelain, papier mache, tole, Japanned ware—the techniques seem endless. In addition to snuff boxes, etuis, bonbonnieres, and other bibelots and keepsake pieces, the variety (which spans from under $50 to many thousands of dollars) includes marvelous clocks and watches, picture frames, sewing items, music boxes, decorative eggs, thimbles, and much more. Susan Benjamin is the genius responsible for these beautiful collections. Speak to her or any of her expert assistants and ask for the tantalizing catalog for back-home orders.

English Lifestyle: **Mulberry,** The Mulberry House (11/12 Gees Court, St. Christopher's Place plus boutiques in Harrods, Harvey Nichols and Liberty's). There is a lovable eccentricity that pertains to British tradition and many of its trademarks are reflected in the clothing and accessories that become cherished classics. Founder and designer Roger Saul is able to translate his awareness of these subtleties into wardrobe and study, pocket and purse, hatwear and footwear and many items betwixt and between. Whether it's a waxed jacket, a "watersilk" Swagger trenchcoat or hunting togs, the feeling and mood are quintessentially English. Run your hand over the burl of Scotchgrain luggage, feel the firm and lasting strength of a golf bag, open the printed leather agenda which would serve as a lifetime gift or browse across the mellow richness of heather hues in the woolens, cashmeres and handsomely woven textiles which are so invitingly displayed on polished wood cases. There's a haunting nostalgia of oak and cavalry twill, a dignified yet casual collection for both town and country. Women and men equally garner the comfort and inbred reliability of the Mulberry touch. The collection is meant to be almost timeless—in the way that Chestnut Sedgemoor Brogues are the creation not of passing fashion but of lasting quality that is identified with good and confident taste. Cotton trousers and skirts are staples of any age and era, but add to these bowling whites, a duster, or boaters and you have the idiom that has defined England and her people for uncounted generations. From a small beginning in 1971 this trademark has spread to other nations in Europe (see "Denmark," "France," "Germany," "Netherlands" and "Sweden") as well as to Asia. In every shop or boutique within other emporia, the interior design is a continuum of the ambience that was first created at St. Christopher's Place. There's no doubting that "Mulberry Look"—whether you're standing in a trout stream, a theater queue, a croquet lawn or a downpour. The message is clear. You can avail yourself of the tax-free shopping opportunities for overseas visitors. Open Monday to Saturday from 10 a.m. to 6 p.m. with Thursdays extended to 7 p.m. Be sure to ask for the free customer catalog—also a classic of its inimitable type.

Exotic Handicrafts: **Inca** (45 Elizabeth St.) recalls the moods and fashions of Peru.

Fishing Gear: **House of Hardy** (61 Pall Mall) and **Farlow's** (5 Pall Mall) are the hooks to any angler's hearts. Clothing, equipment, and solace are offered in taste and abundance.

Flowers: **Moyses Stevens** (Berkeley Square), **Constance Spry** (64 S. Audley St.), or **Pullbrook & Gould** (181 Sloane St.) will possibly make the biggest impression on Her or on your hostess. **Kenneth Turner** (8 Avery Row) decorates London's most illustrious tables and he's in demand worldwide, too. His dried flowers are goregous and now he's added scented candles and potpourris. He has boutiques at Bergdorf Goodman in New York and Marshall Field in Chicago, but there is nothing like seeing the original.

Footwear for Gentlemen: **Alan McAfee** (5 Cork St.) has had smartly shod feet beating a path to its various doors since this century turned its corner. While its world-wide reputation was made in custom (bespoke) footwear, modern methods now allow the same expertise to apply also to an extensive range of all-fitting stock shoes. **Church & Co.** (58 Burlington Arcade) has represented a stout foundation in this field, too, for a century. As quality goes, there's none finer. Several outlets in town, but this is the matrix. **John Lobb** (9 St. James's St.) fit boots for royalty since Queen Victoria's day. The cobblers only work from your own personal last, so expect to wait six months before you make a Lobb footprint anywhere.

Furs: **Birger Christensen** (170 New Bond St.) the Great Dane of fur fashion, is also located in London (see ''Copenhagen''). The store, managed by Jens Birger Christensen, is adjacent to famous Asprey, a diamond's toss from Cartier, and a neighbor of some of the grandest names in merchandising. No longer must travelers wing up to Denmark in order to buy these superluxurious Danish furs. London, being the most important gateway to Europe, affords almost any serious shopper the opportunity to fondle, try on, and enjoy their own mirrored reflection in these sumptuous wrappers. Furthermore, the very same lines and exciting variety that appear in the Copenhagen boutique are available here. The identical price structure, the recognizable quality and the exacting stylings are extended to Birger Christensen's world-class clientele. For North American customers there is a 15% reduction effected by the tax rebate. Moreover, any customer can acquire these prizes at a sum that is *fixed in dollars*. If you don't wish to carry your new fur, it can be delivered to your doorstep for the guaranteed price *in dollars* so that you need not fear any complication with international currency fluctuations. (On a high priced item that can be a crucial factor.) In his new 2-story redoubt, you will find exactly the same open-style decor and the open-hearted spirit that has made womankind beat a path to the Copenhagen boutique of Birger Christensen. He is the first fashion innovator to bring ready-to-wear fur to London—a unique cache which provides the buyer enormous selectivity along with certified distinction. In addition to the "classics," B-C enjoys international renown for his sporting moods composed of fur-lined coats, parkas, fun furs, and stunning models trimmed in leather. Some of these gems are marketed for as little as £1,000 to £1,500. Naturally, because of the "Danish connection," the predominant fur is mink. And what could be better when you swoon over this apparel than to be revived by a few whiffs of Cheetah, the magnificent essence created by Birger Christensen's custom perfumers?

Gift Boutiques: **Rally** (11 Grosvenor St.) rallies an interesting collection of glossy imports in belts, costume jewelry, gold-plated goodies for the bathroom, and other specialized items; although worthy, t'aint cheap. **Eximious** (10 West Halkin St.,

Belgravia) devises highly personalized surprises such as custom monogrammed playing cards, soaps, trays, tablemats, paperweights, or even ice buckets reproduced from your color photographs. Travel items are a big thing, too. **Zarach Ltd.** (48 South Audley St.), also costly, is even more unusual. **Presents of Sloane St.** (No. 129), for The Man Who Has Everything, stocks just about every conceivably amusing gadget which moves, jumps, crawls, shines, creeps, glistens, hobbles, squeaks, or bubbles. **Saville-Edells** (25 Walton St.) has those embroidered cushions you've seen in other people's houses with cutsie messages such as "Age Does Not Matter Unless You Are Wine." Their mail order catalog (available by writing to 41 Queen Victoria St.) is loaded with ideas for the home and fashion accessories. **The Upstairs Shop** (22 Pimlico Rd.) fairly bursts with beautiful closet accessories, quilt covers, hangers with matching sachet hearts, pillows, and the like; ask for Lady Young. **Habitat** (206 Kings Rd. and 156 Tottenham Court Rd.) has a large patronage of young marrieds who are decorating their homes in the modern mood. The atmosphere of Chelsea Green is like a country village. Around its perimeter are two delightful finds. **Christine Schell** (15 Cale St.) deals in antique silver frames and objects of tortoise shell. Brian King can advise you as to the do's and don't's of importing the latter into the States. **Felicity Wigan** (8 Elystan) has a wee house with a burgundy painted door. It's chockablock with delights obviously chosen by someone with a discerning eye and eminent good taste.

Genealogy and Heraldry: The **College of Arms** (Queen Victoria St.) is a venerable institution where all the official records of all the coats of arms granted are housed. They will pursue your lineage for you as will the **Society of Genealogists** (37 Harrington Gdns.). The latter contains a library open for self-service of your very own self.

Glass: **W. G. T. Burne** (11 Elystan St.) is a specialist in antique English and Irish crystal. **Delmosne & Son** (4 Campden Hill Rd.) is highly esteemed, too.

Gourmet Provisions, De Luxe Generalia: **Fortnum & Mason** (Piccadilly) used to be one of the greatest centers for gourmet delicacies in existence. The food products may be in a temporary slump of sorts but there is still nothing like it as a period piece of a genteel era that's otherwise bygone. The famous haughty attendants in striped trousers and cutaway coat still flit among the rows of canned goods and will discourse with you for hours on the virtues of a certain brand of lychee nuts or what to look for in your cock-a-leekie soup. Its ground-floor restaurant is still good for light lunches. Wearables and another restaurant are upstairs. The splendid **Food Halls** in Harrods and in Selfridge's win our local Blue ribbon for versatility.

Hairbrushes: The Mason & Pearson brand is one of the best. Widely stocked in London stores.

Hallmarks: For the novice silver collector, a reliable and concise booklet entitled "British and Irish Silver Assay Office Marks 1544-1963" has been compiled by Fredrick Bradbury, FSA, and published by J. W. Northend Ltd., Sheffield 1, U.K. From its illustrations and detailed descriptions, the reader can instantly identify all registered marks on silver, gold, imported plate, and Old Sheffield Plate; assay offices and relevant dates are also listed. It costs a trifle.

Handknits: **Beatrice Bellini** (74 and 85 Pimlico Rd., Belgravia) specializes in handsome handknitted coats, suits, day dresses, evening dresses, and other feminine fancies which are crafted by highly qualified women who operate on a piecework basis. Because the ready-made inventory is limited, be prepared to allow from 8 to 10 weeks for your order to be completed. Although the price tags are high, the workmanship is so fine that both the investment and the wait were well worth it to us. At the latter address, just across the street, the homely art of tapestry and other thread magic come into their own.

Handpainted Children's Furniture: **Dragons** (23 Walton St.) is masterful; it even has a lock on Winnie the Pooh and other A. A. Milne characters for decorative purposes. Your own child's name can be applied as well; ask for a catalog.

Hats (Ladies'): Most English women wouldn't be caught bareheaded at most social occasions. This is really big business and the Royals lead the fashion parade. **John Boyd's** (91 Walton St.) creations can always be seen in the best places—society weddings, Ascot, garden parties, luncheons, and charity affairs.

Hats (Men's): Continuously since 1759, there has existed only one top-ranking center in the western world—**James Lock & Co., Ltd.** (6 St. James's St.). The lid on this prize package is the hat—every conceivable male headgear for formal or leisure wear.

Health Food Products: **Cranks** (8 Marshall St.) is perhaps the most highly regarded practitioner in this field. If you're an apostle of this fast-growing culinary way of life, here is an excellent place to enjoy lunch as well.

Irish Specialties: **The Irish Shop** (11 Duke St., Tel: 935.1366) is the answer if you want to avoid the humdrum atmosphere of department store shopping. Go to this intimate London establishment for its out-of-the-ordinary selection of tweeds, traditional Irish linens, Belleek china, Claddagh rings—symbols of friendship and love, Celtic jewelry, handicrafts, and that classic of classics, Waterford crystal. There are rich Aran hand-knitted sweaters, ladies' jackets and capes by Avoca plus that stunning Royal Tara china from Galway. You can even find books and Irish music.

Jewelry (Antique): **Cameo Corner** (in Liberty, Regent St.) stocks a particularly lovely collection.

Jewelry (Costume) **Butter & Wilson** (S. Molton St.) has fakes galore. Their knock-off of the highly-publicized flamingo pin of the Duchess of Windsor caused a furor. **Arabesk** (156 Walton St.) uses beads for its one-off sophisticated necklaces, bracelets and belts. Wrapped in one of their thirty-six strand jobs where the colors melt into each other you'll feel like an African princess, at least. Magically, these can be worn in three different startling ways. Special orders for their dazzling accessories are always welcome.

Jewelry: **Garrard** (112 Regnet St.) has been a synonym for the finest British jewelry almost since the day it opened in 1735. Queen Victoria recognized such excellence by issuing Garrard appointment as Crown Jewelers, a royal warrant which continues in the current monarchy. The United States has long held tenure to one of Garrard's more noteworthy creations, the *Auld Mug,* also known in yachting circles as *The America's Cup.* The famous silver ewer is only one of many important trophies created for the world of sport. Garrard also has responsibility for the most noble assemblage of gems in the British (or any) realm: the Crown Jewels both at the Tower of London and in the Royal Collection. Still, one doesn't have to be a sovereign to be favored with such splendid attentions. There are gifts for every occasion, many at very reasonable prices—crystal, leather, desk sets in wood, aluminium or semi-precious stone, suede-lined jewel boxes, ebony and ivory condiments, the renowned English antique silver collection and many items of French and English porcelain including Garrard's exclusive designs. As an addendum, look for Garrard's new houseline in jewelry and watches, to be followed soon by their own branded silver, china, gifts, ties and scarves. With a heritage of more than two-and-a-half centuries to preserve, you can well expect the legendary service for which Garrard is known.

Alex (41A Burlington Arcade; Tel.: 493–2453) is a talented designer of masterful fresh creations. He is more than willing to refashion pieces you own, producing startling results for you from old stones. A bit difficult to sniff out the correct doorway, but once you've got it, ring the bell and go upstairs. These digs are temporary so phone (the number remains constant) just to be sure. His prices are quite reasonable in today's market. **Annabel Jones** (52 Beauchamp Place) is a treasure trove of antique and contemporary pieces and they have carefully selected silverware plus Old Sheffield Plate.

Lace: **Lunn Antiques** (86 New King's Rd., Parsons Green) will pamper you with bed linen and table linen edged in gorgeous lace. Everything is white, fresh and romantic in a 19th-century mood.

Leather Clothing: **Ci Bi** (49 Beauchamp Place) puts pizzazz into all its outfits. Head-turning styles in pastel hues as well as gold and bronze; classic black often augmented with unexpected materials and finishes that are almost painterly. Evening wear that is innovative. They are certainly not hidebound here in their creative endeavors.

Left-Handed Travelers: Bill Gruby's **Anything Left-Handed Limited** (65 Beak St.) comes as a salvation to the worldwide fraternity and sorority of benighted southpaws. Pens, saucepans, scissors (33 models), irons, can openers, corkscrews, playing cards, garden tools, artists' palettes—even special kitchen sinks have been designed to mitigate the constant irritations encountered by these souls in our 88% right-handed civilization. More than 40 utensils or gadgets have been tailor-made for easier and more comfortable manual dexterity. It's about time Mr. Gruby came along!

Linen Specialists: **The White House** (51/52 New Bond St.) goes beyond its linen genre to glamorous silken nightwear to Victorian organdy cradles to quilted coverlets to table sets and personal attire for ladies, gentlemen and youngsters. Accessories, too, with quite a lot of the merchandise chosen from the finest of France and Italy. The store itself is one of London's handsomest keepsakes. At the **Monogrammed Linen Shop** (168 Walton St.) you'll be able to fill your cupboards with luxurious sheets and towels. Loads of bed and bath extras and present ideas galore. Specialist embroiderers who'll stitch a coronet as easily as an initial. The **Irish Linen Company** (35 Burlington Arcade) is tucked away at the Burlington Gardens end of this elegant covered walk. Have a look at the handkerchiefs and panoply of household chic.

Maps: **Edward Stanford** (12–14 Long Acre, W.C.2) is one of the oldest in the business, having begun in 1852. The collection is vast and global. **The Map House** (54 Beauchamp Pl.), encompassing five galleries, concentrates on old England. **Jonathan Potter** (1 Grafton St.) is a well-regarded expert. His catalog may be obtained for a fee. **Weinreb & Douwma** (93 Great Russel St.) stretch round the globe.

Mediterranean Moods: **Casa Pupo** (56 Pimlico Rd.) has caught the temperament of Europe's sunniest climes and translated it into a new dimension in gracious living. Well, not exactly new—since it has just celebrated its Silver Jubilee as an extraordinarily successful mover and shaker in the realm of home living. *Cachepots* with ceramic grapes and other harvests of vibrantly colored fruits cascading in decorative festivals, lemon pyramids, pineapple shaped lamps, Spanish woolen rugs in rich colorations and the lighter touches of beech and cane furniture marry the merry moods of the modern home. Additionally, there are wicker accessories for boudoir or bath, dining salons or conservatories or just the piece to brighten the sullen effects of ordinary corridors. As specialists in European ceramics there will be many items of giftware, table decorations, jardinieres and associated crafts which you will want to carry home with you. But also for developing larger spaces you will surely want to study the variety of furniture of vast color choices, finishes and textures for remodeling areas or entire rooms in your house. Deliveries of headboards, sofas and the full range of interior design can be effected handily.

Model Trains and Boats: **Steam Age** (19 Abingdon Rd.) chuffs for buffs of famous engines, vessels, or all sorts of steam-powered machinery. The reproductions are painstakingly perfect; the high prices match the dedicated artistry. Kits for hobbyists, a vast library of technical manuals and coffee-table books; well-informed salespeople who get up quite an enthusiastic head of steam themselves for their products.

Nautical Gear: **Capt. Watts** (45 Albermarle St.) offers just about everything imaginable for anyone who ever puts out to sea—clothing, safety items, chandlery products, books, charts, much, much more.

Naval Prints, Marine Paintings, Marine Maps: **Parker Gallery** (2 Albemarle St.) has some gems. If you are looking for salty antiques, dock at **Trevor Philip & Sons** (75a Jermyn St., S.W.1).

Needlework: For unusual designs try **Needle Needs** (20 Beauchamp Place). You'll find a fascinating variety. **Luxury Needlepoint** (same street) is another eyeful. **Woman's Home Industries** (85 Pimlico Rd.) is an institution in the same passionate pastime. If you're *really* into this craft, you'll want to visit **Ehrman** (21–22 Vicarage Gate) which has a loyal following. Incidentally, **The Royal School of Needlework** (5 King St.-Covent Garden) will give lessons in any needlework technique, depending on ability. The actual workshop, where restoration and the like is done, is to be found in Apartment 38 of Hampton Court Palace. The **Contemporary Textile Gallery** (10 Golden Square, off Regent St. behind Garrard) has continually changing exhibits of yarn and textiles turned into art objects. They are all for sale and very desirable.

Paper: **Falkiner Fine Papers** (4 Mart St.) is England's leading center. It continuously scouts the globe to supply bookbinders, calligraphers, picture framers, printers, artists, and others. Among its clients are the restoration departments of a number of museums.

Pens (Antique): **Mansfield** (158 Walton St., 30–35 Drury Lane) is into nostalgia in a big way. These collector's items run from a modest $75 to $1400 for a 1920's model and on up into the thousands for gold writing instruments. So, ransack your attic before you get here; bring them an oldie and they might buy it. The traveling cases and luggage evoke reveries of the Orient Express—some have original interiors, others have been relined. All sorts of pocket and purse oddments, too.

Perfumes and Toiletries: **J. Floris** (89 Jermyn St.) Founded in 1730 by Juan Famenias Floris, quickly established itself as the leading perfumer in London and remains so today. In its eighth generation of family management and in the same charming but extended premises in which it was begun, Floris offers an exquisite range of unique flower perfumes, toilet waters, bath essences, soaps, and talcum powders. Among the 18 classics, Florissa, Lily of the Valley, Jasmine, Stephanotis and Red Rose remain firm favorites, joined recently by the newest Floris perfume, Edwardian Bouquet—a floral elixir based on sandalwood and blended with the fresh white flowers of hyacinth and jasmine. The well-established "Traditional" range of Lavender, Moss Rose and Wild Hyacinth in soaps, talcs, bath oils and toilet waters remains enormously popular, as do the luxury toiletries for men in two fragrances—No. 89 (a subtle blend of sandalwood and citrus oils) and Elite (pamplemousse and bergamot leaf oil, tempered with exotic notes of sandalwood, vetiver and tuberose). For the home: room sprays, pot-pourris, drawer sachets, and vaporisers. To complete the picture there is an extensive choice of bathroom and other luxury accessories from natural sponges and swansdown puffs to a new range of handmade ivory-effect shaving and hair brushes. You'll receive a 10% discount on all mail orders and a free comprehensive catalog on application.

And now, right next door at #88, you'll find **James Bodenham & Company,** a Floris off-shoot. They are specialists in skin care products whose milks, creams and oils (perfumed or unscented) will pamper you from tip to toenail. In addition there is a small line of luxury food items (without preservatives and artificial colorings) plus other gifts.

Pewter: **The Pewter Shop** (16 Burlington Arcade), has mugs that range from $70 to $100 and napkin rings go from $20 up. On our most recent visit the premises were being shared with a souvenir stall. It's possible they've given up entirely now, but please check this out if you are especially interested.

Pipes and Tobacco: **Dunhill** (30 Duke St., St. James's, S.W. 1) should need no introduction to anyone, because no other establishment anywhere has ever offered more consistently fine quality in its smoking products; it also stocks gifts, clothing, ladies' accessories and mens' toiletries.

Postcards: Post Card Gallery (32 Neal St.) combines nostalgia and contemporary messages.

Prints and Maps: **Roger Baynton Williams** (14 Sheen Common Dr., Richmond) charts your way to the finest. Months could be spent prowling through the 100,000+ prints—so many types that they boggle the mind. His interest in—and selection of—maps is enormous and he has written a definitive tome called ''Investing in Maps.''

Reject China, Crystal and Affordable Gifts: **The Reject China Shops** (Beauchamp Place, S.W.3, 134 Regent St., W.1, and in Windsor at 1 Castle Hill) began life with the sale of seconds and odd-lots, but quickly found in the heady days of early success that it had the buying power to obtain first-grade merchandise at competitive rates. The sales volume is so potent that these bargains are passed along to you. You are not paying for glossy advertising or fancy theatrical effects. Since so many of the top brands are already known to you, you can probably find exactly the styles and pieces you desire for surprisingly low sums. Moreover, the stocks on hand are vast and greater inventories are readily (and swiftly) available from the manufacturers. Personally, we have shopped here for years and seldom have found a marketplace that provides more elastic for our dollars. The shopping is tax free, packing and shipping services are reliable, and you can pay for your purchases by credit card if you wish.

Rental Clothing: Its advertising slogan, ''Practically Every Well-Known Man in the Country Has Used the **Moss Bros. Hire Service** at One Time or Another!'' is the flat truth. This remarkable British institution, with headquarters at Covent Garden, 38 branches throughout the country, and 2 branches in Paris, would be pleased to doll you up in a jiffy, in a well-fitting, absolutely correct garment for *any* required occasion.

One Night Stand (44 Pimlico Rd., S.W. 1 and 148 Regent's Park Rd., N.W. 1) hits the nail on the resident headliner as well as the unsung visiting female who vitally needs some glad rags but who doesn't feel like spending £600 for a one-use ballgown, a slinky cocktail dress or any mode for any mood that pops up. Inventory of 400 stylish lovelies plus accessories; £50 to £75 rentals for 3 or 4 days. (If you MUST have it, you can also buy it; and there are especially good bargains at their clearance sales in Aug. and Feb.) Dressmaker on hand for minor hitches and stitches. Phone Joanna Doniger for an appointment (Tel: 730 8708). Recommended for taste, hygiene and strategic planning.

Sam Walker (41 Neal St., W.C.2) deals in second-hand clothing: laundered, pressed and usually in good shape. Gents can even find a suit of cricketing whites, Edwardian buttons or fine old English brogues.

Saddler: **W. & H. Gidden Limited** (15d Clifford St., New Bond St.) established in 1806, is Seventh Heaven for the equestrian, with a seemingly limitless galaxy of beautifully made saddles, bridles, bits, harnesses, horse clothing, horse boots, other accessories, and chic riding outfits for both genders. Ask for Michael Gidden.

Shirtmakers: **Hilditch & Key** (with 3 addresses on Jermyn St.: #'s 73, 87 and 37, plus at Harrods and 42 Beauchamp Place) represents a partnership that was cemented just before this century was born. Their world-renowned talents now extend to women as well as to men. **James Drew** (3 Burlington Arcade) does his numbers in silks and cottons just for ladies. Stocks, ruffles, bows, full-cuts and built-in elegance.

Shoes: **T. Elliott & Sons** (76 New Bond St.), the **Chelsea Cobbler** (165 Draycott Ave. and 33 Sackville St.), **Rayne** (15 Old Bond St. and 57 Brompton Rd.), and **Manolo Blahnik** (49/ 51 Old Church St.) cater to a variety of happy feet for ladies.

Shotguns: **Purdey** (57–58 S. Audley St.) goes back to the early days of fine hunting guns. **Holland & Holland** (13 Bruton St.), also remarkable, is almost as expensive. Both are side-by-side in quality. Both can personalize your gun or sell one off the rack.

Silver: **Mappin & Webb** (170 Regent St.) has long been one of the pillars of an industry which has made English silver so respected throughout the world for the past two centuries. The sterling, of course, is the measure by which most other silver is compared. But simultaneously, many of these prestigious designs also have become available in Mappin & Webb's silver plate (officially designated as *Mappin Plate* and considered the best in the world); it carries a lifetime guarantee and costs approximately one-fifth of the sterling price. All the well-loved classical patterns such as Fiddle, Lotus, Athenian, Rat Tail, Kings and many more are stocked in profusion for you to study and evaluate side-by-side. The voluminous catalogs and price lists are supplied as an added customer service. Details—even to the edging on serving platters—are clearly delineated. One could almost retain these publications as a constant home companion for ordering gift items for any occasion. But then, if you wish to fly to London on the Concorde, the savings you would realize simply in the purchase of certain Swiss watches carried by Mappin & Webb would approximately pay for your flight.

The **Silver Vaults** in Chancery House (53/63 Chancery Lane) offers new and second-hand collections and a vast underground shopping area comprising about two dozen shops.

Snuff: **M. Landaw** (4 Eagle Place, Piccadilly, Tel.: 734–1477) is among the very few suppliers of this unusual form of tobacco in all of London. (In the 18th century there were 400 snuff emporiums.) They carry the Fribourg & Treyer blends and have a booming mail order business. Two-ounce tins cost anywhere from $4.50–$7. **G. Smith and Sons—The Snuff Centre** (74 Charing Cross Rd.) boasts 22 of their own blends. Their brightly colored handkerchiefs are a novel expression of the lore.

Souvenir Items: **The Old Curiosity Shop** (13/14 Portsmouth St.) couldn't be more touristy. Loaded to the scuppers with ''antique'' china, pottery, silver, glass, pewter, plaques, playing cards, silhouettes—you ask for it and they'll find it, because the gent who owns the place isn't about to lose a single customer. Open 7 days a week (!). You might try some of the wacky holes-in-the-wall around Trafalgar Square for canned London fog, tins of country air, pieces of the White Cliffs of Dover, and similar tomfooleries.

Sporting Equipment and Sportswear: The glittering 6-floor jungle of **Lillywhites** (Piccadilly Circus) is a paradise for outdoor types.

Stationer: **Frank Smythson Limited** (54 New Bond St.), which holds the Royal Warrant of Stationers to Her Majesty the Queen, is a delight in its atmosphere, its tastes and its friendly welcome. Courtly General Manager Thomas Neate would help you. For ourselves we've discovered more than a dozen of enchanting exclusives here. Suddenly, you'll become a prolific correspondent because **Stokes** (Elizabeth St.) and **The Walton Street Stationery Co.** (13 Walton St.) have such desirable writing materials—beautiful papers, unusual pens, unforgettable ink colors and desk accessories.

Sweaters: **Edina Ronay** (141 King's Rd. and Burlington Arcade) is not merely to keep warm. Here is the leading edge in smart sweater fashion—from cashmere, cotton, silk, ribbon, Fair Isle (with lace) to ensembles that produce a "total look." Tweeds, too, and even styles for men. Don't miss this one. She is now stocked by Harvey Nichols if you don't make it to her own shop. **Moussie** (109 Walton St. and 28 St. Christopher's Place) has hand knitted sweaters that you'll warm up to immediately. A calendar, the alphabet, naif images, a ski motif, flowers and animals—these are all highly amusing. There are dressy, beaded cashmeres for evening and bobbly stitch casuals. Co-ordinating skirts, culottes, waistcoats and embroidered blouses complete the picture. Both shops charming enclaves with painted wood floors. It's just right for the country-club set.

Tea: **The Tea Centre** (Regent St., near Lillywhite's) is an aromatic delight to tempt any tea lover. **The Tea House** (15a Neal St.) is another cuppa. It also sells all of the items that should suit you to a tea: pots, caddies, strainers, infusers and other tack for teatiming.

Toys: **Hamleys** (188–196 Regent St.) will gladden your young or old heart. Infinite variety; prices refreshingly lower than many in the States. **Pollock's** (1 Scala St.), resembling a 3-story Victorian museum of playthings, carries a large line and specializes in miniature theaters.

Toy Soldiers: **Under Two Flags** (4 St. Christopher's Place) is the leader, with the highest standards and finest quality. The owner turned his lifelong hobby into this business more than a decade ago. New, unpainted types are also stocked. Its quotations are commensurate with its superiority. At **Tradition, Ltd.** (Shepherd's Market) and **Stall 410** in the Antique Supermarket, the conditions of their ample offerings vary from excellent to poor, with the prices adjusted accordingly. The best source for information on this commodity is Mr. John Ruddle, Secretary, The British Soldier Society, 22 Priory Gardens, Hampton, Middlesex, whose phone is 01–979–7137.

Walking Sticks: **Swaine Adeney Brigg & Sons Ltd.** (185 Piccadilly) has stomped down the gales of all its competition since 1836. All types of canes, seat sticks, hunting-and-shooting paraphernalia, umbrellas, dog collars, whips, picnic baskets, small gifts—and everything in high quality. A landmark.

WINDSOR

SHOPPING AREAS

Any of the streets radiating from the Castle.

Clothing: **Knitwear of the Islands** (Church St.) is your sweater center, especially for fully fashioned, hand-finished Guernseys. These have the flavor of the sea about them, but are also useful for the field. Aran knits and Scottish tartans fill the shelves as well. **House of Tweed** (same lane, next to Nell Gwynn's house) offers similar merchandise in somewhat more dressy moods. The superb quality is immediately apparent.

China and Gifts: **The Token House** (26 High St.) is just the niche if you have a knack for knickknacks. Porcelain and glassware dominate the intimate scene.

Perfumery: **Woods of Windsor** (Queen Charlotte St.) is a delight to the nostrils, whether in soaps, sachets, colognes, bath cubes, shampoos, powders, drawer liners or whatever is made better through fragrance. The inventory will always bring back a whiff of Windsor and the scent of English woodlands.

ELSEWHERE IN ENGLAND

While visiting the British Isles you may wish to see craftsmen at work and make some factory tours. The British Tourist Authority has published a handy little booklet entitled *Made in Britain*. There are about 30 addresses in England, Scotland and Wales where you can buy candles, carpets, cheese, china, crystal, fishing gear, pencils, ropes, sheepskin products, wood work, pottery, whisky, hand-knitwear and woven items. In addition the calendar of craft events is very useful when planning your itinerary.

FINLAND

SHOPPING HOURS

Weekdays, 9 a.m.–5 p.m., except 8 p.m. for department stores
on Mon. and Fri.; Sat., 9 a.m.–2 p.m. Holiday eves have Sat.
closing times. On some summer Sundays shops along the Esplanade are open from noon–4 p.m. Please check locally for details.

NOTE · · · The **Senaatti Center,** located between the marketplace and the Lutheran Cathedral, is one of the most charming shopping complexes in the north. Its atmosphere is completely
different from what you will find in pedestrian malls, department
stores or shopping areas anywhere in the world. It comprises
about 40 boutiques offering Finland's finest in handmade, hand-
painted and handwoven articles plus silver, leather, fur, silk,
wood, linen, wool; it even has a bakery, a confectionery shop
and a tantalizing game restaurant. Built at the beginning of the
last century, the origins have its roots in 1812 when a merchant
named Kieseleff first began trading locally. The farsighted progeny of Helsinki's commercial scene have wisely rescued it and
restored these precincts in order to preserve the nostalgia and
maintain an area of serenity. Entrances on Unioninkatu, Alex-
anterinkatu, and Sofiankatu. Open 10 a.m. to 6 p.m. weekdays,
3 p.m. closing on Saturdays; noon to 4 p.m. Sundays in summer.

PUBLIC HOLIDAYS

Jan. 1, Epiphany (always a Sat.), Easter (April 15–16), Ascension, Pentecost or Whit Monday, April 30 (May Day Eve or Vappu Night), May 1, Midsummer's Day and Finnish Flag Day (Sat. nearest June 24), All Saint's Day (Nov. 4), Dec. 6 (Independence Day), and Christmas (Dec. 24–26).

MAIL ORDERS

Sorry, but we've never ordered by mail from Finland. One impeccable source is the 70-plus-department **Stockmann,** the greatest merchandising institution in this nation. In one recent year it shipped more than $2 million worth of goods to foreign embassies, business firms, news bureaus, and individuals in the Soviet Union alone, prompting one U.S. diplomat to affirm, "Without Stockmann's there wouldn't be any Americans living in Moscow!" Hence, if you want information about *any* Finnish specialty, here is your linchpin. Since organized mail-order commerce in this land is almost totally nonexistent, however, our only suggestion concerning our other listings would be to communicate directly in the hope that this type of service would be understood and expedited by them.

HELSINKI

SHOPPING AREAS

Esplanade Boulevard is lined with many fashionable addresses. The harbor offers open-air market browsing.

THINGS TO BUY

Weaving, glass, textiles, rya rugs (ready-made or in do-it-yourself kits), raanu wall hangings, birch and pine furniture, Arctic gems, crystal, porcelain, ceramics, sauna accessories, bath and beachwear, jewelry, women's and children's countrywear, lighting fixtures, and myriads of individualized handicrafts, some made of scented juniper wood *(kataja)* or reindeer fur and horn, plus sheath knives *(puuko)* and chip baskets *(pave kori)*.

TAX REFUND FOR PURCHASES

The 11% sales tax (included in the original price of each article) on purchases over FIM 150 is automatically deducted if the item is mailed to the U.S. Stores that are part of the Finland Tax-free system issue checks for the duty imposed which can be cashed upon departure from the country if the goods are hand-carried. This applies even if payment was made by credit card.

NOTE · · · The visitor might find it expedient to go to the **Finnish Design Center** (Kasarmikatu 19, Door B) before proceeding to its shops. In its 3 small rooms, some of the nation's greatest artists and artisans—in weaving, ceramics, glass, textiles, furniture, silver, and more—display their masterpieces. You cannot purchase anything here—but this nonprofit organization will direct you, upon request, to the appropriate atelier, workshop, or retailer to which you have taken a fancy.

Art Galleries: **Backsbacka, Strindberg, Pinx,** and **Bulevardilla** set the pace.

Bathwear and Sauna Items: Within the small and charming premises at Aleksanterinkatu 28, the **Sauna-Soppi-Shop** collection of sauna-related articles is the most comprehensive you can find north of Hades.

Crystal, Porcelain, and Ceramics: In its handsome showroom at Pohjoisesplanadi 255, Arabia has combined with Nuutajarvi to form the **Arabia Nuutajarvi Center.** The former contributes the porcelain and ceramics, the latter the glass. In flair and elegance, it is in the Very First Rank. For its stoneware and earthenware seconds at 25% below retail levels, call (Tel: 790211) and ask for the Head Guide at Arabia and make an appointment to visit the factory out at Hameentie 135 from Monday through Friday. Major disadvantage: Since no shipments are made to individuals from this factory, you'd be forced to tote your purchases to an outside agent. **Emma** (Fredrikinkatu 41) comes up with a fairly unusual collection of kitchen gadgets of her own fashionings—ceramics, aprons, potholders, and fabrics in cotton and linen.

Department Store: World-famous **Stockmann** (Aleksanter-inkatu 52B) is Finland's largest retail operation—a northern Saks-Magnin's-Macy's-Gimbel's rolled into one. This century-old landmark is a national institution, with branches at Tampere and Turku. Its Finnish arts and crafts are especially fine—as are its lighting fixtures by Orno. The merchandise runs the gamut from distinguished to routine, depending on the price tags. Warning: Its branch in the airport is not a duty-free shop. **Sokos, Elanto,** and **Pukeva** are solid but far less prodigious and versatile alternatives. **Aleksi 13** (corner Aleksanterinkatu and Mikonkatu) is a 5-storey wonder. Once again, our advice is to brouse through the **Senaattii-Center** complex.

Fashion: Widely heralded **Marimekko** can be found at **Vintti** (Keskuskatu 3) and **Marimekko** (Pohjoisesplanadi 31). **Pentik** (Pohjoisesplanadi 27) is sensational for suedes and leathers. Its prices are the same for both genders. In addition there are slippers, mittens, trousers, and bags. Everything is made up in Lapland. Wool and knits are cunningly combined with softest skins in striking styles.

Florist: **Dan Ward** (Etelaesplanado 22) blooms brightest.

Fur Hats for Men: Try **E. R. Wahlman** (35 North Esplanade). He'll charge you from $20 to $200.

Furniture: In **Artek** (Keskuskatu 3) look for the late Alvar Aalto's globally revered designs for grownups and children; the rest here didn't impress us much. **Asko** (Mannerheimintie 18-20), while less expensive, seemed very commercial and dull.

Handicrafts: **Kalevala Koru** (Unioninkatu 25) contains a sizable handicrafts section among which you'll find whimsical sheep made of curly birch, door chimes, rugs, sweaters, and additional lures such as woven pictures and unique custom-made (4–6 weeks) copies of ancient dress from Viking times. These will cost about $1600. In **Sokeain Myymala** (Annankatu 16) absolutely everything—baskets, furniture, souvenirs, a little jewelry, other items—is made by the blind. It's so worthy that we profoundly wish it could be more fascinating.

Jewelry: You'll flip when you see the gloriously conceived and crafted works at **Galerie Bjorn Weckstrom** (Unioninkatu 30–Agora). The distinctive style of his contribution to the Lapponia Collection—rings, bracelets, pins, necklaces, and others—combines thousand of years of jewelers' art with the stunningly original, world-famous designs of this genius whose sculpture is displayed as well. We rate this house as the very finest of its industry in the North. When Arctic gems are added **Kaunis Koru Oy** (Senaatti-Center) has unusual and distinguished stocks of spectrolites and other semiprecious stones mined above the Arctic Circle. There's a wide range from inexpensive to fairly costly silver brooches, bracelets, men's cuff links, necklaces, and rings. **Kalevala Koru** (Unioninkatu 25), mentioned above, also specializes in reproductions of ancient Finnish designs in silver and bronze. **Tillander** (Aleksanterinkatu 8) is the oldest jeweler and goldsmith in the nation. We particularly like their enameled items as exemplified in the Rainbow Range of spoons in 30 colors based on sterling silver. Their miniature egg jewelry carries on the Russian traditions of the firm which has its origin in St. Petersburg of 1860. Handsome and individual tableware, too.

Open-Air Market: From 7 a.m.–2 p.m. (plus evening hours), the w-o-n-d-e-r-f-u-l **Kauppatori Market Square** at the harbor bristles and bustles with stalls and throngs. You'll find flowers, vegetables, fish, wearing apparel, small articles of furniture, paintings—just name it or spot it, and it's yours. Go *early* to savor the best of its delightful color.

Weaving: **Neovius** is our purl among pearls. It is replete with lovely, lovely rugs for wall-hanging ($125 up), interesting cushions, topflight wools for knitting, and similar products. Its various branches have differing stocks. Check in at Olavinkatu 1 and Keskuskatu 7 to find out just where they store their rugs, yarns, clothing and woven articles. **Metsovaara** (Pohjoisesplanadi 23) displays beautiful Finnish prints, weavings, and other treats. **Vuokko** (Pohjoiseplanadi 25) offers textiles in natural fibers designed by Eskolin-Nurmesniemi for dresses, skirts, and decorating usage.

Wooden Articles: **Aarikka** (Pohjoisesplanadi 27) is the showroom for Kaija Aarikka's clever designs in all types of wood: Household and tableware (plates, candlesticks, salts and peppers, bowls, cups, napkin rings), curtains, toys, chunky necklaces and bracelets, and gift ideas. Different and interesting.

ELSEWHERE IN FINLAND

If you go as far as *Rovaniemi*, just below the Arctic Circle, there are a number of outstanding handicraft shops that are well worth visiting. **Lauri-Tuotteet Oy** (Pohjolankatu 25) is a log chalet in the center of town. From its workshops emerge puukko knives, jewelry, curly birch whimsies, wood and leather articles. Visitors are welcome to watch the manufacturing processes which start with such raw materials as reindeer antlers and pussywillow roots. Its farmhouse cafe is also the sales center.

Throughout the country, local handicraft associations abound. There are more than 150 educational centers nationwide teaching and exhibiting the wares. There's a commercial side, too. In *Rovaniemi* **Miessi** (Korkalonkatu 12), **Koru ja Kivipaja Inarin Hopea** (Joulupukin Pajakyla) and **Polarpiste** (Napapiiri Arctic Circle) are loaded with exceptional regional specialties here at the gateway to Lapland.

Further north at *Inari* (that's beyond *Ivalo*) is the silver workshop **Inarin Hopea,** run by Tapio Tammisto. He and his dedicated band are experts in the traditions of Lappish jewelry— rings, pendants with animal motifs, chest brooches known as "Inarin risku," and lovely polished spheres with suspended rings (ask for an explanation of their heritage). For the fisherman who has *everything* this studio has created a silver lure for salmon trout which if it doesn't get a record winning strike will at least be the envy of every other angler on the beat. You get hooked for about $50. It is unique! **Tapsan Tapuli** is a roadside souvenir stand right on the main drag. Reindeer products, Lapp felt jackets and hats, boots, you name it—they've got it.

THINGS NOT TO BUY

Imported items (silks, mechanical gadgets, and the like) are saddled with colossal import duties. Nearly all antiques have either been snapped up or used for firewood. Many paper products, to our astonishment (we still do not understand the economics of this), carry exorbitant price tags. Even though almost all brands of cigarettes are now manufactured under Finnish license, you'll be rocked by the startling prices as a result of the vigorous official antitobacco crusade that bans its advertising and prohibits smoking in the public rooms of all airports, railway stations, theaters, airports, and elsewhere. Finally, due to such high-quality standards versus such low production quotas, an increasing supply of cheap, junky "handicrafts" are imported from Japan or Germany—so make sure their source is Finnish before you shell out your beans.

FRANCE

SHOPPING HOURS

Most of the deluxe establishments stay open on Sat., but are closed Sun. and Mon. mornings. Hairdressers, however, function on Mon. Food stores operate all day Sat. and some of them do business on Sun. mornings, too, but many are closed Mon. Department stores are busy every day except Sun., with store hours from 9:30 a.m.–6:30 p.m. Boutiques and specialty shops generally open at 10:00 a.m. and lockup around 7–7:30 p.m. Many stores no longer shutter during the lunch hours, particularly those in areas heavily traveled by tourists (Champs Elysees, Faubourg Saint-Honore, Saint-Germain-des-Pres, Place des Victoires). If you find a very small shop darkened during normal business hours usually there will be a sign taped on the door that reads ''Be back in ten minutes'' which means the owner is also the salesperson. Summer holidays are taken very seriously in France. From mid-July through Aug. it is not unusual to find curtains drawn at varying periods for some establishments. There is no general rule.

PUBLIC HOLIDAYS

Jan. 1, Easter Mon., Ascension Day, May 1, Whitmonday, July 14, Aug. 15, Nov. 1, Nov. 11, Dec. 25.

TVA TAX CUSTOMS REFUND

Many tourists and quite a few business travelers visiting France still do not know that a tax refund is theirs for the asking provided *a minimum purchase* is made in stores and boutiques. This refund—from 13% to 23%—represents the TVA (*Taxe de Valeur Ajoutee*) which is included in the price of every item of merchandise you buy, with the exception of food. (Some department stores such as Galeries Lafayette and Au Printemps give an across-the-board 10% discount.) It is refundable to non-resident travelers who will leave France within a 90-day period, taking their purchases with them.

How to claim your refund? Simple. And well worth the effort. Once you have reached the minimum purchase required (see below) just ask the salesperson for a *Fiche de Douane*, letting it be known that you are a non-resident tourist and would like to recoup the TVA when you leave France. He or she will ask to see your passport (proof of non-residence) and then fill in the necessary forms allowing you to claim the tax refund. Do not lose the form you are given and also DO NOT FORGET to have it validated by French Customs officers at your point of departure from France.

Ways in which the TVA can be refunded: (1) You can have the tax refund mailed to your home. It is usually a check in francs and in the process of converting it to dollars your U.S. bank will probably charge you a fee that can diminish your original saving slightly. (2) You can have the tax refund credited to your credit card account directly. This might be the best method. (3) You can receive the tax refund in cash at the following airports: Charles de Gaulle, Orly, Le Bourget in the Paris area and at Nice/Cote d'Azure in the south of France. Again, you'll receive francs, which, if you're leaving the country, you'll have to change.

TVA tax refund mailed to your home or credited to your

credit card account: When completing the forms, the salesperson will ask you where you'd like the refund to be sent—either your home or to your credit card account. Sometimes it is best if you fill in your address or account information yourself—that way, no mistake can be made. The tax form will be enclosed in the store's self-addressed envelope. AND REMEMBER! Be sure to present this envelope (or envelopes if you have made multiple purchases) to French Customs at your point of departure; they will validate the forms, send them back to the stores where your purchases were made, and the stores will mail your refund to you or to your credit card account. It may sound complicated, but it's not. All it takes is a bit of extra time.

TVA tax refund in cash at major international airports in France: A number of larger stores and important boutiques now can supply a form which allows you to receive your tax refund in cash if you exit France via one of the major international airports designated by French Customs. You must ask the salesperson if the store can supply the cash refund form, because not all shops have made such arrangements. Upon arrival at the airport go to the appropriate French Customs desk to have your forms validated; the officer will then direct you to a bank on the premises where you will receive the refund. A word of *caution:* Allow yourself up to an hour and a half extra when claiming the refund in cash—lines can be long and slow moving.

Minimum purchase requirements: If you hold an American passport then you must buy a minimum of 1200 French franc's worth of merchandise in any one establishment in order to qualify for the TVA tax refund. If you're buying a variety of small items shopping in a department store might be a benefit since you can total up *all* the purchases to reach the minimum.

NOTE · · · When packing your French purchases put them all in your carry-on luggage because French Customs officers may request to see them. If you have purchased bulky clothing items and are forced to pack them in your suitcases then visit the French Customs desk *before* you undergo the normal check-in formalities. Articles that cannot be verified against the purchase forms could jeopardize your refund.

What should you do in case you failed to have the TVA tax refund forms validated? Should you have forgotten this all-important step in the process then your only hope is to mail them back to the stores where you made your purchases. If management is dependable they will process the refund through Customs themselves and then arrange to have the money sent to you. However, bear in mind that this takes a fair amount of paperwork and a great deal of time. It could be a year before you see your refund—if ever. The best thing is NOT TO FORGET to have those forms validated and to allow enough additional time to have it done.

MAIL ORDERS

Almost universally, this type of purchase holds very little appeal to the French. Perhaps it is because as an element of the national character its citizenry prefer to *see* and to *hold* the merchandise as a cautionary measure before acquiring it. However, there are several conspicuous exceptions that we know which have surmounted this psychological stance and built their mail-order commerce into important subdivisions of their daily and weekly turnovers. **Baccarat,** that household name among discerning collectors and lovers of crystal, for more than 2 centuries has dispatched its exquisite creations to every major country on the global compass. **Denise Francelle's** fashionable French gloves and scarves remain outstanding favorites among stay-at-home shoppers either as up-to-the-minute additions to their own accessories or as sophisticatedly chic, reasonably priced Christmas or special-occasion gifts; another plus is that they can be airmailed for a trifling extra sum. **Quimper Faience** of Brittany, Paris (see

"Faience") and Storington, Conn. offers a US catalog ($2) which may assist you in reordering to expand your collections. **Charles and Philippe Boucaud,** the antique pewter specialists, publish a catalog in French. If you should be interested in anything offered by these illustrious firms, please follow our earlier suggestions in "Mail Orders: At Your Service Today and Tomorrow."

SHOPPING AREAS

Right Bank: **Faubourg Saint-Honore** (boutiques, haute couture, galleries), **avenue Matignon** (galleries), **rue de Rivoli, Place des Victoires** (boutiques), **avenue Montaigne, avenue George V,** and **rue Francois 1ᵉʳ** (haute couture), **Place Vendome** (jewelry), **Champs Elysees** (the full gamut—including automobile showrooms), **Opera** district (department stores), **rue de Paradis** (crystal and china). *Left Bank:* **rue de Seine, rue Bonaparte,** and **rue de Bac** (galleries), **Saint-Germain-des-Pres, rue des Saints-Peres,** and **rue de Grenelle** (boutiques), **rue d'Alesia** (bargain-priced designer clothing).

THINGS TO BUY

Perfumes, gloves, lingerie, scarves, handbags, fine jewelry, shoes, boutique items, glassware, china, high fashion clothes, leather goods, hats, tapestries, potpourri and home fragrances, luxury foods, fine wines, spirits, books, antiques, fashion sunglasses, active sportswear (ski, tennis, etc.).

Antiques Centers: **Le Louvre des Antiquaires** (2 Place du Palais-Royal), a huge commercial complex dedicated to the purchase and sale of antiques, is in the former Magasins du Louvre just opposite the Louvre Museum. The multi-storied, 12,000-square-yard site houses 250 different shops representing many kinds of specialties, plus cafes, restaurants, and exhibition halls. This project, open from 11 a.m.–7 p.m. on Tues.–Sun., impresses us as strictly routine. Far better is the **Village Suisse** (78 av. Suffren). A bit different and infinitely more charming; lovely people in lovely precincts with beautiful merchandise; open daily except Tues. and Wed. from 10 a.m.–7 p.m. Yes, it's expensive. One of our most delightful discoveries is a cluster of 18 individually owned centers of this category in a picturesque setting—**Cour aux Antiquaires** (54 rue du Faubourg-St.-Honore). Vast variety at your command; generally costly but generally reputable; open from 10:30 a.m. but closed Sun. and Mon. mornings; pleasant for browsing as well as for buying. After the above, loaf along any of these famous streets and make your own selection according to what's on hand that day. **Carre Rive Gauche** is a geographical designation that will assist you in finding at least 120 dealers within a square surrounded by rue de Bac, rue de l'Universite, rue des Saints-Peres and the Quai Voltaire.

Art Galleries: Literally hundreds. Among the most tried-and-true landmarks are **Galerie de France** (3 rue du Faubourg-St.-Honore), **Artcurial** (9 av. Matignon, 14 rue Jean-Mermoz), **Galerie Claude Bernard** (3 rue des Beaux Arts), **Karl Flinker** (25 rue de Tournon), **Drouand-David** (52 rue du Faubourg-St.-Honore), **Katia Granof** (place Beauveau), **Alex Maguy-Galerie**

de L'Elysee (69 rue du Faubourg-St.-Honore), **Lucie Weil** (6 rue Bonaparte), **Maeght** (13 rue de Teheran), and **Galerie Bellier** (32 avenue Pierre-1er-de-Serbie). Serious devotees should first pick up a current copy of *l'Officiel de Galeries* (15 rue de Temple), the definitive source of what painters and sculptors are being shown where in the whole nation.

Auctions: Auctioneers in France are unable to compete with their peers around the world because the government has imposed so many taxes on them. They have not been the prime movers in the art world in at least two decades. It is hoped that in 1992 when the Common Market is completely regularized fiscal reform will make for equality. In the meantime they struggle on losing the great sales to London, Geneva, and Monte Carlo. The historic **Hotel Drouot** today resides at 9 rue Drouot. In both architecture and operational facilities we belong to the great throng who regard it as a disaster. So do a number of its members who either have moved or plan to move out. Nonetheless it continues to be the largest national center of this traditionally regulated industry. One of the most valid objections is that sales are conducted on 3 different floors—7 in the basement, 2 at ground level, and 7 up 1 flight. Expert Souren Melikian of the *International Herald Tribune* put it exactly right when he stated "Walking into (it) any day, one sees a mixed assortment of furniture and furnishings that would not be out of place in a flea market. The bustle and squalor further justify the parallel. . . . Even the specialized sales are poorly organized. . . . One weakness is the breathtaking high-handedness, particularly among lower echelon employees." Open daily except Sun.; mixed sales held Mon., Wed., Fri., 2 p.m.–6 p.m. with viewing on the previous day from 11 a.m.–6 p.m. or on auction day from 11 a.m.–noon. **R. G. Laurin** (7^e rue des Sts.-Peres on the Left Bank) and **Guy Loudmer** (73 rue du Faubourg-St.-Honore) are respected independents who have their own exhibition rooms. Both are defi-

nitely worth examining. Highly regarded art auction houses are
Versailles (5 rue Rameau in Versailles) and **Gallera** (Espace
Cardin); the latter often operates in the evening. Most days at
10:30 a.m. there are sales at the **Credit Municipal de Paris** (55
rue des Francs-Bourgeois) of pawned articles (unredeemed). Call
42712543 to find out what's on the calendar. To have a work of
art appraised, take it to the **Chambre Syndicale des Experts**
(52 rue Taitbout), open Tues. and Thurs. from 2:30 p.m.

NOTE · · · Two indispensable publications for antiques en-
thusiasts are *La Gazette de Drouot* (a weekly) which gives the
dates of fairs and auctions both in Paris and the provinces and
the *Guide Emer,* a directory of dealers throughout the nation
plus another schedule of important fairs.

Bakery Products: **Poilane** (8 rue Cherche-Midi) If you arrive shortly after 4 p.m. you might join a line 50 yards long of
patient clients waiting for Papa Poilane's and Lionel's (son)
products to emerge hot from the ovens.

Books: **Galignani** (224 rue de Rivoli) is regarded as the oldest foreign bookstore on the Continent. It has been a Parisian
landmark for nearly 2 centuries, always stocked with the finest
reading material on the world literary market. Go in and browse.
The storekeepers even encourage it, knowing this is how customer loyalty is developed. The choices invite leisurely study
and when it comes to asking questions, the staff is so well read
that a sage opinion is usually available on almost any volume.
Many are in English. **Brentano's** (37 avenue de l'Opera) is also
an old standby; paperbacks are best found at **Nouveau Quartier
Latin** at 78 Blvd. St. Michel. If you are hunting for thrillers or
English-language magazines, then **W. H. Smith** (248 rue de Rivoli)—a neighbor to Galignani—should be your target zone. Paris
wouldn't be Paris if it didn't have those little stalls lining the

Left Bank of the Seine. Aside from secondhand volumes the *bouquinistes* have antique maps, prints, and engravings. Who knows what little treasure you may unearth—and even if you don't, you'll be *a la mode*.

Boutiques: As has been intimated, Paris abounds with so many hundreds of interesting and different ones that your happiest fun would be to search out your own favorites. However, as a guideline you should know that three areas have become very important along with the traditional rue du Faubourg Saint-Honore. They are (1) place des Victoires in the 2^e, (2) the Saint-Germaindes Pres quarter in the 6^e and (3) the historic Marais in the 4^e. (The latter zone contains, among other things, the Bastille, the new Picasso Museum, the Pompidou Center and some of the best Jewish delis in town. Take the metro to St.-Paul/Le Marais and start roaming.)

Here's a thumbnail sketch of what you'll find along the Faubourg Saint-Honore: Starting at the Hotel Bristol end near the avenue Matignon, **Angelo Tarlazzi** (#67) for beautiful ready-to-wear and accessories from one of the leading designers in Paris today, (#73) **Christian Lacroix,** the man-of-the-moment, with his ready-to-wear line, **Sonia Rykiel** (#70) who put French knitwear on the map, **Chloe** (#60), **YSL** (#40) for ladies, **Ungaro** (#25) and his fabulous prints, **Gucci** (#25) for gift items, **Leonard** (#28), **Les Must de Cartier** (#23), **Lanvin** (#20) for women and across the street **Lanvin** (#15) for men, **Gianni Versace** (#4) the famous Italian designer, and **Daniel Hechter** (#12) for men. In addition, the French Institution of **Lubin** (#64), makers of *Idole* and other regal perfumes, features small to *haute elegance* gift items that excite the feminine soul. *Formidable!* **Roger & Gallet** (63 rue du Faubourg-St.-Honore), recently doubled in size and in stocks, offers outstandingly attractive accessories for Her or Him. **Rety** (a step down the street at #54) has justifiable appeal to the affluent. **Chanel** (31 rue Cambon) revised its boutique downstairs by soft-pedaling its line of bags, belts and similar articles to concentrate on its famous "little suits." (This inspired the company to inaugurate more than two dozen similar ventures in other countries including the United States.) A suit and blouse could run about $1,900 here against perhaps $8,000 upstairs. Rue de Passy in the 16th arrondissement is virtually lined with a parade of boutiques too. **L'Eclaireur** (26-84 Champs Elysees) is the brain-child of Marithe and Francois Girbaud. It offers high class rough wear, far out leather clothing with great panache and wonderful sweaters under the label Maillaparty. Lots of belts worked in silver and leather, oil-linen fabrics cut for jackets and pants that are sensational.

Not stopping in the newer, more fashionable and updated area, Place des Victoires, would be an oversight. Stroll around and be sure to view the following: **Victoire, Thierry Mugler, Mercadal et Fils** (see under "Footwear"), **Stephane Kelian** (women's shoes), **France Andrevie** (with-it women's ready-to-wear), **Kenzo,** and **Cacharel** (for men). Just off the *place* is **Tokio Kumagai** (for trendy shoes and accessories), **Structure** (beautiful, classic menswear) and **Mulberry Company** (45 rue Croix des Petits Champs plus additional Left Bank location at 14 rue du Cherche-Midi—English accessories—see "London" and "Stockholm"). Nearby is the newly restored **Galerie Vivienne** (4 place des Petits-Champs) a Belle Opoque building where, among other things, you'll find silk flowers by **Emilio Robba** and a welcome pick-me-up brew at **A Priori-The,** if your energy is flagging. The price tags at **Gaultier Junior** (7 rue de Jour, close to Les Halles) aren't astronomical. This is a new venture for the renowned designer.

A proper shopping spree would require a trip to the Left Bank arriving at Saint-Germain-des-Pres, again, one of the most with-it boutique areas in town. Make your first stop at **Yves Saint Laurent** (6 Place St. Sulpice), the king of all French ready-to-wear. Here you'll find women's and men's clothing, accessories, shoes, and even his perfumes and men's colognes. Move over to the rue de Grenelle where you'll find **Sonia Rykiel's** flagship store. Next door is **Emmanuelle Khanh, Claude Montana**'s on tap, too, and also **Michel Klein** (noted for a distinctive, sporty approach to dressing). Rue des Saints-Peres offers a galaxy of big names: **Maud Frizon** (shoes), **Angelo Tarlazzi, Tokio Kumagai, Pat-Lang** (shoes), **Sabbia Rosa** (gorgeous lingerie), **Catogan** (great knits), **Stephane Kelian** (more footwear), and **Enrico Coveri** (youthful styles, marvelous colors).

Boxes and Decanters: **Coffrets et Flacons** (7 rue de Castiglione) is the pride of Nicole Brissonneau who specializes to an exquisite degree in these two areas of antiques. Pick a period or a style and she will have it or search every corner of Europe—and even Asia—to obtain it for you. We are especially fond of her select collection of portable writing desks.

Brassieres and Foundation Garments: Historic, world renowned **Cadolle** (14 rue Cambon) is *the* French corsetier. Fittings in only a few days. Terrific!

Brushes: **Franquet** (rue Saint Honore 209) has one of the most complete assortments—from shaving to shoe, from backscrub to beauty.

Buttons and Trimmings: **Fil d'Ariane** (40 rue de Ponthieu) seems to have sufficient on hand to supply every clothing manufacturer in all of Gaul within minutes.

Canes and Antique Umbrella Handles: **Madeleine Gely** (218 blvd. St.-Germain) is a marvelous little center with beautiful examples of these specialties. It offers a highly unusual collection of canes with hidden compartments which conceal swords, flasks, and even miniature violins. These range from $120 to about $350, while the handles are priced from $150. No aficio-nado of these articles should miss it.

Canine Frivolities: "Coddle" is the wrong word here; "spoil to a ludicrous degree" better describes the facilities of **Aux Etats-Unis** (229 rue St.-Honore) and **E. Goyard Aine** (233 rue St. Honore). Among the too, too with-it set, the former is regarded as even more chic than the latter. Among their more useful wardrobe items are vinyl raincoats, their hand-knitted pullovers, and their specially designed carriers. But when we saw the fancy collars fashioned to match the clothes of the master or mistress (even a black-tie formal outfit, for God's sake!), the plates and bowls on which Fido's likeness is hand painted (you supply the photo), and the special line of cosmetics that includes a canine toilet water, we burst out laughing at their absurdity. What Fools We Mortals Be!

Cheese: **La Ferme Saint Hubert** (21 rue Vignon) nurtures a permanent collection of 180 different varieties from every region of France composed, of course, of the best cheese-makers of these districts.

China and Accessories: **Villeroy & Boch Creation** (21 rue Royale) has been a preeminent name in porcelain ever since its founding in Luxembourg in the middle of the 18th century. The dignified and beloved patterns are now exported to 83 countries throughout the world with annual production running close to fifteen-million! Here is a beautiful showcase for those wonderful trademark designs which have captured the imagination of homemakers all over the globe. How often we see the noble marbleized finish in pale russets of *Sienna,* the very essence of autumn in Tuscany. Or the rich golden hue of *Indian Summer;* though delicate to the eye it's still tough enough to resist the rigors of the automatic dishwasher. Or *Naif,* the joyful picturization of rural life. *Basket* (the darling of so many *nouvelle cuisine* chefs) casts a friendly glow over any table. *Manoir, Petite Fleur, Riviera* and *Amapola* are also enduring favorites which blend so well into any household, conservatory or garden setting. If you are traveling to other European destinations the Villeroy & Boch dinnerware as well as gift items of exquisite taste are available in the following **Creation** outlets: London, 155 Regent St.; Berlin, Kurfurstendamm 20; Dusseldorf, Koeningsallee 92; Strasbourg, 8 rue Merciere; Zurich, Seidengasse 13 and Gerbergasse 4, and Copenhagen, Illum A/S, Ostergade 52. Virtually every important retail shop of taste and every major department store in Europe carry Villeroy & Boch's products. Be sure to pick up a free catalog.

Lalique (11 rue Royale) is majestic. For retail sales try **Paradis Porcelaine** (54 rue de Paradis). *Sevres?* At the **Musee National de la Ceramique** (near the Pont de Sevres metro station) you'll find examples of this exquisite porcelain from its several periods along with those of other great French manufacturers. However, hidden away, almost unknown, is a salesroom where one can purchase Sevres factory production. Because the government monopolizes most of its output, the company doesn't encourage individual buyers. While today's designs might not attract you, it is possible to find reproductions of their most famous patterns created by using the original techniques. To give you an idea of prices, a dinner plate might cost over $100, but if you asked for a special pattern it could be 4 times as much. They estimate that it takes from 3 to 5 years to execute a complete service. Come prepared to do all your business in French and come prepared to meet resistance, but if you are serious they will honor your requests. Museum hours are daily (except Tues.) from 10 a.m.–12:30 p.m. and 1:30–5 p.m., entrance fee is about $1.

Chocolate: Look under ''Teas'' for **Christian Constant.**

Commercial Centers: **The Tour-Maine-Montparnasse** complex of about 80 establishments was much touted before its completion but proved a dreary disappointment. Almost all of the merchandise we saw was so tacky and so junky that our long trek was a waste of time. The **Palais des Congres de Paris Boutiques** (Porte Maillot) contains over 100 shops and includes a Japanese department store.

Costume Jewelry and Trinkets: **Paris Chic** (198 rue de Rivoli) The name says it all—the latest baubles in the world's most fashionable and up-to-date city. This house, a smash-hit success since it opened in 1976, carries exclusive lines and the latest creations in French costume jewelry. The prices are so reasonable that you may think you are visiting on that opening day more than a decade ago. Only $2 to $100 for some of the smartest selections of the house; immaculate representations of Cartier, Dior, Chanel, and Gucci lines, plus those intriguing sportswear ornaments in elephant hair and ivory. (Be careful of the latter two while passing customs.) You'll find a sparkling mine of zirlonium stones, rainbows of French silk ties, original belts which are noteworthy for their uniqueness, and a dazzling array of scarves. Ask Michele, who is the last word in kindness, to help you with the tax rebate program (returning to you immediately 20%) as well as the ultra-swift mail order facility.

Other targets might be the previously mentioned **Lubin** and **Roger & Gallet** (special items only)—then **Line Vautrin** (3 rue de l'Universite) or **Burma** (16 rue de la Paix and 2 branches). For updated fashion-right pieces head for **Anemone** (rue Saint-Honore 235) and **Ancolie** (nearby at #231 and 8 rue de Sevres).

Creative Jewelry: **Jean Dinh Van** (7 rue de la Paix) gave birth to the ''Square Jewel'' design; half-circle bracelet; rectangular link chain; interlocking rings; the angular hand-cuff clasp and octagonal watch face replicas of Paris city clocks. He has reinvented the engagement ring and added a new line for men with rings and cuff links in the shape of thumbtacks or fourholed buttons.

Crystal: In 1764 **Baccarat** (30 bis, rue de Paradis) obtained royal authorization from Louis XV to create a glassworks in Lorraine and became a household name among discerning collectors and its exquisite creations continue to appeal to all lovers of crystal. Factory with retail shop at Baccarat, Meurthe & Moselle; branch in N.Y.C. A breath-taking fairyland.

Custom Clothier (Men and Women): **Charvet** (28 Place Vendome) first rolled up its cuffs back in 1836 and ever since has taken the measure of kings, emperors, princesses and everyday *beaus* and *belles* who revel in tasteful apparel.

Cutlery and Silver: **Peter** (191 rue du Faubourg-St.-Honore) is one of the leaders. Tea services, hand-forged carving sets, scissors, caviar knives, the works; antique cutlery collection; a gracious shop. See Mr. Peter. **Christofle** (12 rue Royale) has been at it, hammer and mold, for more than a century and a half. Its silver now blankets the world—perhaps the blanketing being more democratic than when it answered a commission to make a maharaja's bed (and did so out of 640 pounds of sterling). At **Puiforcat** (131 blvd. Haussmann) everything is of the highest order.

Department Stores: Our favorite now is **Au Printemps** (64 blvd. Hausmann), followed by (1) **Aux Trois-Quartiers** (17 blvd. de la Madeleine), (2) **Au Bon Marche** (138 rue de Sevres), and (3) **Galeries Lafayette** (40 blvd. Hausmann). All are good—and all are close together. **"Au Printemps-Nation,"** opened a 5-story branch on Paris' eastern edge, for suburban shoppers.

Exceptional Gifts: **La Boutique** is the aptly named luxury redoubt which resides just inside the main entrance of the distinguished **Hotel de Crillon,** overlooking the Place de la Concorde and a few steps from the U.S. Embassy. In concert with some of France's finest craftsmen and most renowned manufacturers French stylist Sonia Rykiel brought to life the stunning black-and-gold line: items discreetly signed ''Le Crillon'' or bearing the Crillon crest. Next to the prestigious gifts, any budget-conscious customer can find classy, yet affordable presents. Open Mon.–Sun. 9 a.m.–6 p.m.

Faience: **Quimper Faience** (84 rue Saint-Martin, near the Centre Pompidou), is the capital's representative of the most famous earthenware factory in the lovely Brittany town of *Quimper.* It is also a blood relative of **Quimper Faience** in Stonington, Connecticut.

Feline Frivolities: **Au Chat Dormant** (15 rue Cherche Midi) is definitely for people zonked on cats. Their images are portrayed in statues, crafted into puppets, embroidered on pillows, drawn, painted and burnished onto boxes, ceramics, jewelry and all sorts of kit-schy decoration and ornamentation. Open: Mon. 2:30–7 p.m., Tues. and Wed. 11 a.m.–noon and 1–7 p.m., closed Thurs. and Sat., Fri. 11 a.m.–7 p.m.

Forum de Halles: The most significant architectural development to hit France since the Centre Pompidou opened on the site of the legendary wholesale food market which was abandoned in 1969. This $153,000,000 commercial center is built on 4 levels which create an unusual cascade effect. On its 14-acre spread there are fashion boutiques, restaurants, shoemakers, interior decorators, beauty parlors, theaters, and garage parking for 1,650 cars. The architecture of this massive, way-way-out complex, while certainly eye-popping, still stirs up white-hot controversy—especially that of its underground commercial "forum." Many of the original stalls on the streets in this district have been taken over by hippie-type artisans who peddle old furniture, clothing, shoes, costume trinkets, and the like at prices which are often absurdly high due to this colony's current vogue. Unfortunately, the Forum has not worked out the way its planners and promoters had hoped—many of the better shops have already relocated. It has become very seedy, full of questionable types and no great shopping treat.

Footwear (Ladies): Top French manufacturers now build sizes to please the American foot, since the export business is today such an important aspect of their sales. (Some while back there was only one width which pinched profits—and the ladies—mercilessly.) **Carel** (22 rue Royale), **Celine** (58 rue de Rennes and 24 rue Francois ler) and **Dior** (26 av. Montaigne) are classics. **Francois Villon** (27 Faubourg Saint-Honore) is for high steppers looking for *the* boot or evening shoe—madly expensive. **Mercadal et Fils** (3 Place des Victoires) is one of France's leading lights in enlightened, full-fashion boots and shoes. **Andrea Pfister** (4 rue Cambon) features way-out models which can be fun if you are in that bizarre mood. A bit less expensive is the **Cedric** line (11 rue du Faubourg Saint-Honore plus many branches). **Charles Jourdan** is getting to be a pretty costly linkage; it's a chain that was very much a la mode but is now inclined toward more classic themes. The rue de Sevres is loaded with shops and worth a stroll.

Fun Wear: **Mod'Shop** (210 rue de Rivoli) is up-to-the-instant in its lighthearted approach to travel notions and international souvenirs. Here is *the* place to pick up that sweatshirt or T-shirt that will tell the back-home throngs that you have just returned from abroad. Their lettered or patterned legends declaring "Paris

University'' or somesuch illustrate the monuments of the City of Light and include a full range for adults and children. This portable humor starts at around $10 per giggle. There is also an engaging, if not disarming, selection of costume jewelry with crystal rings resembling diamonds, sapphires, rubies or onyxes for as little as $7. Not only that, they have bracelets to match which are similarly low in cost for the impression they provoke. You may also be tempted by the umbrellas, the silk ties or the items from the souvenir counter which Miss Christine will be happy to show you. Open from 9:30 a.m. to 7:30 p.m. every day including Sun. A bonanza for the last-minute shopper.

Furniture Reproductions: **Mailfert-Amos** (26 rue de Notre Dame de Recouvrance, Orleans, Tel.: (33) 38627061) If you are planning a visit to the Chateaux country or want an unusual excursion from Paris then please turn to the section ''Elsewhere in France'' at the end of this chapter for a very special recommendation.

Furs: **Birger Christensen-RAD** (412 rue Saint-Honore) is an on-going news blitz in the fashion whirl—the furs of Denmark's Birger Christensen have come to the City of Light! And, very importantly, prices in Paris are precisely those you'll find at the Scandinavian home base. They are also featuring fur designs by Christian Lacroix and Claude Montana made by Birger Christensen for worldwide distribution.

Gifts: **Delrieu** (89 rue de Rivoli) began offering its fine collections of crystal, china, silver and gift wares to the public as early as 1907 and still retains the aura of that gracious period when the century was young—beveled windows, rich moldings and original furniture. The discernment with which they have assembled their finery is legendary.

Chez Perrette (15 bis rue de Marignan) is a nonprofit organization to which mentally handicapped people, many of them elderly, contribute their artistry. You will be shown a parade of beautiful creations which these talented unfortunates have made in their homes. While finest quality hand-embroidered pillow-cases, handkerchief cases, shoe bags, quilted bed covers, suede-lined leather boxes, and other merchandise are more for adults, the things for children steal the greatest thunder here. Typical illustrations within the very own province of the latter are the smocked dresses up to size 6, the wee sheets and pillowcases, and the marvelous little cloth dolls cut in circles and threaded on elastic. Great for your Small Fry, with every purchase an Act of Grace. **Strich** (5 rue d'Arcole) is a small, amiable haven with small, amiable decorative *cadeaux*. Jewelry, match boxes, odds-and-ends for the person, table, or home; reasonable price tags. For higher quality and costs, **Michel P. Pigneres** (3 avenue Vic-tor-Hugo) may prove rewarding; large ceramics, silver bibelots, jades, and similar objects are here. **Jansen** (9 rue Royale) is where you'll find a fascinating choice of *objets d'art,* decor items for the home, unusual presents—not cheap, but in beautiful taste. There's a boutique to the rear.

Gloves and Scarves: **Denise Francelle** (244 rue de Rivoli) has been a favorite since 1946—and she gets better every year. There is room inside this dollhouse shop for exactly 5½ custom-ers—and it's always crowded!—but her selection is so smart and her prices are so sensible that her vast international clientele couldn't care less. They come from every point of the compass to this Lilliputian magnet for 2 principal reasons. The first is that her a la mode stocks are always one jump ahead of her compe-tition. The 2nd is that she and her small staff are all so sweet, so dedicated, and so *caring* that to them each of their customers becomes a valued individual rather than a face across the counter. Somewhere on the premises, though, she must have a storage room which either climbs half the height of the Eiffel Tower or dives 20 thousand leagues under the sea—because in gloves alone (not to mention her other specialties) she carries all sizes of about 400 different models in each of the popular colors. You'll find styles for every mood. One popular gimmick is her beaded or Beauvais gloves. Full assortment of scarves—square or long, printed or brocaded; handmade beaded bags in all colors. The latest (and oh-so-successful!) addition to her line is her lovely umbrellas, both decorative unlined types and luxury lined types. Problem-solving dividend, even when you're back in the States: For a normal postage fee, the staff will AIRMAIL a pair of gloves per box to your Christmas or Special Occasion designee. And what a sensation they cause—direct from Denise Francelle, Paris! Ask for lovely Mlle. Edith. Reliable and excellent.

Gourmet Foods, Liquors, Gifts: **Hediard** (21 place de la Madeleine) is Paris's answer to boutique foodies as opposed to the glitzy supermarket atmosphere evoked by giant Fauchon. Shopping here is more tranquil and some might avow even a bit more select.

Another deluxe gastronomic establishment, **Maxim's de Paris** (Galerie Charpentier on rue du Faubourg-St.-Honore), was launched with equal sponsorship by the venerable restaurant of this name and Pierre Cardin. Now the latter has fully taken over both. In addition to delicacies and wines it sells linen, glasses, dishes, ashtrays, and champagne buckets that are copies of Maxim's wares.

Haberdashery (Men's): **John** (250 rue de Rivoli) has had itself around the necks of such early luminaries as Maurice Chevalier, Picasso, Cocteau and a Milky Way of American and international stars of recent times. Begun in 1944 as a specialist in ties and cravats—more than 2000 in stock always in silk, wool, cashmere and other noble materials—it has spread to incorporate shirts, accessories, and a rich harvest of distinctive pamperings for gentlemen. You'll find world-class names such as Paco Rabanne, Balmain, Scherrer, Nina Ricci, Guy Laroche, Clarence and others for the neckwear—and be sure to ask for the choice of two ties for a set charge of 180 FF. Apart from a vibrant and luxurious private collection of shirts, there are also smart tailorings from Yves Dorsey, Yves St. Laurent and Otto Hoffman. Even fanciers of bow ties can find those *rara avises* here plus well-chosen pocket handkerchiefs and cashmere mufflers. Miss Douchka will explain how you can obtain the tax rebate (a whopping 20%) immediately in the shop for charges totalling $200 or more. Mail order requests (over $400) can be satisfied within 2 days, a service standard which is almost unheard of in these lackadaisical times.

Hats (Million Dollar Variety): **Paulette** (63 avenue Franklin D.-Roosevelt) is both the most chic and most astronomical. Madame died in Sept. 1984 but we believe her salon remains open. **Jean Barthet** (13 rue Tronchet) probably is now the unchallenged successor in this realm. You'll pay less in the high-fashion boutiques—but only a cool three-quarter-million or so.

Hats (Practical Variety): **Willoughby** (7 rue de Castiglione) for the fold-up-to-nothing model: $65 in felt for men or women, or $70 to $90 for the women's silk version.

Hats (Fashionable Variety): **Jean-Charles Brosseau** (rue des Saints-Peres) creates models for many of today's top designers. His styles are fresh and fun. **Philippe Model** (Place du Marche Saint-Honore) works wonders in felt. **Anthony Villareal** has turned the simple beret into a work of art. **Marie Mercie,** a relative newcomer, continues to receive rave reviews. She sells through select boutiques, so be on the lookout for her label.

Haute Couture: Freely translated *haute couture* means high-fashion clothing made expressly for *you*—made to order. Furthermore, the best names in France are at your disposal. All you need is a wallet fat with francs of high denomination. (Business-wise fashion, in all its guises, ranks as the country's 10th biggest money maker.) Yes, prices are VERY HIGH, but if your pocketbook permits, you can treat yourself to a rare and exciting experience.

Here's how it works: Twice each year the top haute couture designers in France show their collections to a select audience of international journalists, celebrities, and well-heeled individuals. These shows take place in Jan. and July. After the shows, the clothes go to the designers' salons where they are put on display for customers. These clothes are the prototypes against which you make your selection and have things made to order. To help you choose what's best for you there is usually a videotape of the collection running continuously in the salon giving you an idea of how to put yourself together complete with the right accessories. Additionally, most of the top houses conduct shows in their salons for small groups of clients.

As of this writing there are 21 world-famous names to contend with when speaking of Parisian haute couture: Balmain, Cardin, Chanel, Dior, Givenchy, Gres, Lacroix Lanvin, Laroche, Patou, Ricci, Saint Laurent, Scherrer, and Ungaro—to list just a few. Officially, they are known as *grand couturier*. They must employ a minimum of 23 seamstresses, have two collections a year showing no less than 75 models each time, everything must be custom-tailored and, in addition, have 45 private fashion shows. It's an expensive business. Courreges had to bow out of this elite group when he couldn't meet all these requirements. It is interesting to note that the Chambre Syndicale de Haute Couture has suggested that there are only about 3,000 people world-wide who could frequent these realms. Another amazing figure is the one that estimates that about 70% of French couture is purchased by Americans.

The press viewings held in July and Jan. are "closed showings" and invitations and admittance are strictly limited. However, during Aug. and Feb. the haute couture houses are very accommodating to interested prospective clients. The best way to visit one of the *couturier* salons is to ask your hotel concierge to arrange it. Or, upon your arrival in Paris, you can call directly and request an invitation. The individual houses will tell you the times they will be holding the shows and send a welcome to your hotel.

Should you choose to buy something be prepared to spend in the vicinity of $6,500–$8,500 for a little daytime number and from $10,000–$13,000 for evening wear. Prices are also dependent on fabrics and the complexity of the garment chosen—beading and embroidery become truly astronomical. Furthermore, do not expect to have something made for you in a day or two. After selecting what you want you will have at least several fittings to undergo while the clothes are being made and it might take a month until delivery.

Haute Couture Ready-to-Wear: All of the major houses have established boutiques where you can buy their clothes ready-made at about half the price of things made to order. Perhaps the most famous of these are the Saint Laurent "Rive Gauche" shops (for men and women), which you will find located in the best shopping areas of Paris. The majority of such types of boutiques can be found along avenue Montaigne, avenue George V, and the rue Faubourg Saint-Honore. The salespeople speak fluent English and are happy to serve you. These boutiques also sell wonderful accessories such as belts, scarves, shawls, costume jewelry, handbags, and leather goods.

NOTE · · · When you buy haute couture ready-to-wear in Paris you're automatically saving between 35%-50% of the price you'd pay for those same clothes in the U.S.—and that goes for accessories, too.

Haute Couture at 50% Discounts: There are dozens upon dozens of outlets in the capital where you can buy original creations of France's most exalted fashion shrines for half-price. But remember—it's a hit or miss proposition because the stock situation is sometimes very low, picked over, or non-existent. These break into 3 categories: ''Trocs,'' wholesalers, and *degriffe* stores. ''Troc,'' which means ''exchange,'' is the least practical form for most North American visitors. It requires that your bring in your dry-cleaned Givenchy or similar of *this* years model to trade it for another authentic raiment of your choice, the cash difference subject to settlement with the management. (You may also sell it outright.) Wholesalers, which have the best bargains, vary in their operations. Their stocks can be current or from the next-to-latest showings. In some you must have an introduction. In others, which are also retail, all you do is ask if they accept private customers. Many will admit you with the provision that you make a minimum purchase of about $50. Last year's designs, all unworn, are the most frequent. Of special note are **l'Entrepot de la Mode** (103 rue Reaumur) and **Cacharel** (171 rue de Belleville). **Didier Ludot** (24 rue de Montpensier) carries Chanel suits, Hermes purses, and other fillips. **Kenzo** (Place des Victoires) simply slices the costs on this period of merchandise in his basement. *Degriffe* means that the labels have been removed—while in actuality some are not. **Le Mouton a Cinq Pattes** (8 and 10 rue de St. Placide, Tel.: 45.48.86.26), which claims that it was the originator of this genus, is the most popular—so successful, in fact, that it has opened a second establishment named L'Annexe some steps away. **Toutes**

Griffes Dehors (76 rue St. Dominique on the Left Bank, Tel.: 45.51.68.14) specializes in the Guy Laroche and Ted Lapidus lines. **Dorothee Bis Stock** (76 rue d'Alesia Tel.: 45.42.40.68) open 10:15 a.m.–7 p.m., closed in Aug., has jogging and tennis clothes at 50% off. If you can't find what you want in these, there are many other good ones along the rue St. Placide.

NOTE · · · One of the best outlets for secondhand clothing is **Reciproque** (95 rue de la Pompe, Metro: Pompe) open Tues.–Sat. 10 a.m.–6 p.m. Its racks are crammed with low-priced designer labels; the bargains are incredible. Each article is in excellent condition and not more than a season old. Children's clothes are next door and a men's shop is nearby. Traveler's checks but not credit cards are now accepted.

Following is a very special list that should really bring you great bonuses in discounts. **Andre Courreges** (7 rue de Turbigo, Tel.: 4233.03.57) open daily 10 a.m.–6:30 p.m. and on Sat. 10 a.m.–1 p.m. and 2–5 p.m.; generally a 30% to 40% discount; clearance sales in Jan. and June an extra 50%. **Emmanuelle Khanh** (6 rue Pierre Lescot, Tel.: 4233.51.62), open 10 a.m.–6:30 p.m.; 50% discount; silk blouses approximately $43; big choice for men, too. **Pierre Cardin** (11 blvd. Sebastopol, Tel.: 4261.74.73) open 9:15 a.m.–1 p.m. and 2–6:30 p.m.; 30% to 50% discounts; for men also. **Mendes** (65 rue Montmartre, Tel.: 4236.83.32) carries Saint Laurent, Chanel, and Ted Lapidus. It's sister shop (rue Montmartre 140, Tel.: 4236.02.39) specializes in fabric remnants—especially silks—from the Saint Laurent and Chanel collections. Those are treasures from the cutting room floor. **Paco Rabanne** (7 rue du Cherche Midi, Tel.: 4222.87.80) open 9 a.m.–noon and 2–6:30 p.m., closed Sat.; 50% discount. **Jean-Louis Scherrer** (29 rue Ledru-Rollin, Tel.: 4343.58.34) open May–July on Mon., Tues., Thurs., and Fri. from 10 a.m.–6:30 p.m. and Sept.–April on Mon., Thurs., and Sat.; 50% to 60% discounts. For men, **Bidermann** (114 rue de Turenne, Tel.:

4277.15.20), open 8:30 a.m.–noon and 2 p.m.–6 p.m. Mon.–
Fri. with no midday closing Sat., a manufacturer for Yves Saint
Laurent and others, offers at wholesale levels suits which were
made the previous season.

NOTE · · · In January 1986 a new museum opened in Paris—
the Musee des Arts de la Mode. Contained in five floors of the
Louvre's Pavillon de Marsan, on the rue de Rivoli next to the
Musee des Arts Decoratifs, this should be of keen interest to
anyone fascinated by fashion. Curators have an inventory of
10,000 costumes and more than 32,000 accessories to work with.
Exhibitions will change three times a year.

Health Foods: Nutrition centers here are small shops that follow the French marketing style. One of the most elegant is **La
Petite Marquise** (also known as La Maison Des Produits Natu-
rels) at 3 place Victor Hugo and 93 rue Convention. In addition
to its specialized stocks of comestibles and wines (a rarity in this
type of establishment), there is a takeout counter for organic
grilled chickens, sandwiches, and salads. **La Vie Claire** (25 rue
Annonciation) is part of a chain of 15 outlets in the city (some
with restaurants) and about 135 more in the nation. **Clairevie**
(51 rue de Miromesnil) is not related to the complex directly
above. Its typical customers are young, and it is said to carry
the most avant-garde products available. **La Samaritaine** (rue
de Rivoli) has set aside a segment of its basement which emphasizes salt- and sugar-free packaged goods. Honey pound cakes,
oils, dried fruits, nuts, brown rice, and herb vinegars are also on
hand.

House Beautiful: **Atelier Melisande** (175 Ave. de Versailles) is the brain-*enfant* of talented Marie-Francoise Gruere.
Decorators and home-living editors are lining up to order and

see the marvelous lamps and shades she makes (using all manner of bases) and the beautiful screens she designs and has executed for her. The latter can take any shape or dimensions you want; they can be painted or covered with fabulous antique or modern fabrics (which she is a wizard at finding), or paper and parchment just as the lamp shades are done. The versatility is endless. For chic candlelit dinners, see the unique hand-painted hurricane lamps. She is wowing Paris (where most people are pretty blasé) with her unusual tables, her cloths to cover them, and with her flower arrangements combining both silk and natural blossoms. Just the silk flowers may be purchased for those not living in the capital. She's an expert at shipping anywhere! Open Tues.–Sat. 10 a.m.–7 p.m.; Tel.: 42.88.67.38; closed July 15–Aug. 15.

Un jardin . . . en plus (224 blvd. Saint-Germain, 64 rue St. Denis and 66 ave. Victor Hugo) blooms with paper, fabrics, china, pottery, lamps and shades in an atmosphere of eternal spring.

Kitchen Equipment: **Dehillerin** (18 rue Coquilliere, near Les Halles) wins by 6 skillets and a wok, in our opinion.

Leather Accessories: **Morabito** (1 Place Vendome) There could be no more central address than this craftsman's showcase. Since 1905 this has been the ancestral pride of a great family who are masters in their trade. Evening bags form an impressive part of the inventory; luggage in leather, vinyl, rigid-or-soft-sided is another major aspect of the treasury. But, naturally, there are the classics such as desk sets for the office, handsome finely finished attache cases, handmade belts with gold-plated buckles, plus a tempting gift array of lighter cases, wallets, pads, key rings, scarves and even jewelry and watches. Indeed, they are trend-setters *par excellence* who merit their primary position in European craftsmanship.

Leather Goods and Travel Specialties: Beautiful **Hermes** (24 rue du Faubourg-St.-Honore) personifies all of the legendary flair, tradition, sophistication, and elegance of the best of French craftsmanship. What isn't Gallic is also exquisite. Now upstairs they've added tempters for home, garden, and yacht. **Louis Vuitton** (78 bis avenue Marceau and avenue Montaigne) is as much a Paris landmark as the Eiffel Tower and the bags and luggage you'll find there are about as enduring. **La Bagagerie** (41 rue du Four, 13 rue Tronchet plus other branches) stocks a very successful breed of distinctive nylon and leather suitcases made by Cassegrain-Longchamp. **Lancel** (8 Place de l'Opera) is of general interest and **La Peau de Porc** (240 bis blvd. Saint-Germain) specializes in—pigskin, what else?

Linens: **D. Porthault,** the unchallenged national leader (and purveyor to Mrs. Jacqueline Kennedy Onassis, the U.S. Ambassadors to France and St. James's, plus every French Embassy in the world), has a plush 2-floor retail shop at 18 avenue Montagne, opposite the Hotel Plaza-Athenee. Their designs are GORGEOUS. You'll find everything from the most costly pair of sheets on earth ($4400), to towels in all ranges, to terry-cloth robes, to humble bathmats and hot-water-bottle covers—so many, many exquisite gifts that you can spend very little or very much, depending upon your whim. A treat to visit, even merely to browse.

Lingerie: **Cordelia** (21 rue Cambon) features many items from the Dior line. The female member of this writing team thinks of them as "yummy." The male member of this writing team thinks of them—often. Exceptionally fine. **Sabbia Rosa** (73 rue des Saints-Peres) is a real find for sexy underwear—especially the fabulous lace and satin teddies. To add to a glamour girl's wardrobe are scented satin hangers, lingerie cases, garters, bath robes, and peignoirs.

Markets: Most famous is the **Flea Market** ("Marche aux Puces," Porte de Clignancourt), part of which has already been condemned to make way for new construction. The 3000 merchants here turn over an estimated $80 million in francs per year. Its teeming, trash-filled streets are overrun by tourists and nationals whose quest for "bargains" is too often illusionary. Although it operates on Sat., Sun., and Mon. only, the best time to buy is Sat. morning. Foreign youths have set up their own informal (and technically illegal) Flea Market in front of American Express; everything from cars to camping equipment to guitars to other personal possessions is traded.

Marche Serpette (110 rue des Rosiers, St. Ouen—about 5 miles from Paris) is an up-grade grabbag. We understand there's ample space to show the wares in well-lit, carpeted surroundings *and* it's indoors, too. Also open Sat., Sun., and Mon.

Marche Biron a collection of 250 stands housing an extremely interesting antique collection is actually a part of the aforementioned Flea Market. **Marche St. Pierre,** the textiles-and-remnants market (rue Charles Nodier, foot of Sacred Heart Church), is a maze of stalls which work during the ordinary business hours. **The Dog Market** (15e at 106 rue Brancion) parades canines once per week, from 2 p.m.–4 p.m. on Sun. **The Bird Market** (place Louis-Lepine) cheeps along on Sun.; the **Flower Market** (place Louis-Lepine and Quai de la Corse) blooms Mon.–Sat. 8 a.m.–7:30 p.m.; the metro stop for this is Cite. **The Stamp Market** is perforated with philatelic bugs on Thurs., Sat. and Sun. along avenue Gabriel (between avenues Matignon and Marigny). Dicker your head off in all of these. Other, lesser-known grab-bag markets are located near the **Porte de Vanves** (southern outskirt), the **Porte Montreuil** (on the eastern edge of Paris) where there is said to be some silver and secondhand books on view Sun. a.m., and at **Place d'Aligre** (12e), where of a Sun. morn, among the comestibles, you might find a bit of

clothing, china, and silver, too, and the **Hospice du Kremlin.**
All 4 are raw but fun.

Miniature Soldiers and Ancient Arms: Aux Soldats
d'Antan (12 rue de l'Universite).

Mini Potpourri: **Changrila** (14 rue de Beaune) has a collection of unusual-shaped pillboxes with mother-of-pearl tops, wood
or painted enamel jewel caskets, small, lidded, jasper jewel caskets originally made for pomades and unguents, and miniature
Oriental porcelain dishes, as well as other tiny tempters. **Pulcinella** (10 rue Vignon) offers a galaxy of similar articles.

Museum Gift Shops: The **Association of National Museums** (Reunion des Musees Nationaux, 10 rue de l'Abbaye)
orchestrates the reproduction of pieces from the collections of a
bevy of important museums. This organization has two shops of
its own: Forum des Halles, Porte Berger, second level (10 a.m.–
7 p.m. daily except Sun.) and 89 ave. Victor Hugo (same hours
plus Mon. closing). There is also a department within **Galeries
Lafayette** dedicated to this as well. The **Louvre's** gift shop (9:45
a.m.–5 p.m. daily except Tues.) has a wide-ranging assortment
of copies of ancient jewelry and textiles from its own treasure
troves as well as those of other institutions. The **Paris Opera**
has a shop (11 a.m.–5 p.m. daily and until intermission on per-
formance evenings) dedicated to musical themes. The **Musee de
la Mode et du Costume** (10 a.m.–5:45 p.m. daily; closed Mon.)
is all fashion. The **Musee des Arts Decoratifs** (107 rue de Rivoli—closed Mon. and Tues.) was established at the end of the
19th century in an effort to preserve some of the finest examples
of French craftsmanship—and this is a continuing preoccupation
of its curators. The glassware and china collections are particularly extensive and important with special emphasis upon the art-

nouveau and art-deco styles. Don't think, however, that the glorious 18th century has been forgotten—far from it. Recently, the museum embarked upon a program of allowing replicas of some of its wide-ranging inventory to be made and here, on the premises, these are sold. You will be buying history with every piece you purchase and aiding a very worthy cause, too.

Oriental Potpourri: **Compagnie Francaise de l'Orient et de la Chine** is a melange of Eastern clothing, baskets, pottery, and a number of other categories. It was sold sometime back and no longer deserves top billing as there are hundreds of imitators now. Go to its branch on blvd. St.-Germain, if you must—not to its headquarters in the Tour-Maine-Montparnasse Commercial Center, which is too far. For Indian handicrafts try **SONA** on the Faubourg Saint-Honore.

PERFUMES

This remains the number one bargain in France, which as a nation is fighting to retain its firm grip as *parfumeur* to the world since America, Germany and Italy have entered the competition in a very lively way. Certainly by a wide margin more famous scents are still produced in France than in any other land, a fact which puts this industry among the top seven export items of the country. As a non-resident you're entitled up to a 40% saving on perfume purchases—obviously a great way to save money.

When buying perfumes it's a good idea to first do some homework. You should be aware of the regular retail prices of those you want to buy in France. This way you can calculate how much you are actually saving. Posted retail prices can vary a bit from shop to shop and in some of the ritzier places be as much as 50 francs higher.

Perfume manufacturers keep adding fragrances and deleting

them from their lines. It's a fast-moving industry. Listed alpha-
betically the leaders today include the following: Balmain, Ca-
charel, Capucci, Caron, Cartier, Carven, Chanel, Chloe, Jean
Desprez, Dior, Givenchy, Gres, Hermes, Lagerfeld, Lanvin, Guy
Laroche, Missoni, Montana, Morabito, Paloma Picasso, Patou,
Paco Rabanne, Oscar de la Renta, Nina Ricci, Sonia Rykiel,
Jean-Louis Scherrer, Valentino, Van Cleef & Arpels, and Yves
Saint Laurent. Brand leaders for men are: Azzaro, Bogart, Giv-
enchy, Gucci, Halston, and Lanvin.

Perfumes and fragrances bearing the names of certain famous American designers are made in France and the discount
still works in your favor. The same applies for certain Italian
ones as well. A quick glance at the bottle will tell you the country of origin. Statistics suggest that 95% of all of these have
been concocted by Gallic maestros anyhow. Now, no designer
is worth his buttons unless he's launched a scent.

Some perfumes like *Chanel No. 5* and Guerlain's *L'Heure
Bleu* remain classic best-sellers, to name only a few. However,
some newer fragrances have made a success. The biggest for
American customer's include both classics and newcomers like:
Opium by Yves Saint Laurent, *Bal a Versailles, Chloe, Yendi*
by Capucci, *Or Noir,* in its fabulous package by Morabito, *Missoni, Oscar de la Renta* and *Valentino.*

Others that are sought after are Leonard's *Balabe,* Rochas'
Lumiere, Coco by Chanel, *Diva* by Ungaro, Alain Delon's *Le
Temps d'Aimer, Parfum d'Hermes, Paloma, Ombre Rose* by Jean
Charles Brosseau, *Ombre Bleu* and *Paris* by Saint Laurent, *First*
by Van Cleef & Arpels, and *Phileas* (for men) by Nina Ricci.

Within the last several years the shelves have expanded with
Scherrer 2, K L Homme, Guy Laroche's *Clandestine, Montana,*
Herme's *Bel Ami* and Givenchy's *Xeryus* (both for men). Per
Spook, Benetton and Cacharel have been busy in the labs, too.

Here are some interesting statistics: Cacharel's *Anais Anais* sold the most by volume in 1987, of all French perfumes, while *Opium* rang up highest dollar sales.

Guerlain is the only producer who insists on selling direct to the Paris public (4 shops in the city). Chanel has branch factories in New York, London, Brazil, and Italy; experts opine that the French original is far superior because elsewhere it is alleged to be made with denatured alcohol.

The French perfume industry is beset by the problem of imitation. It is thought that almost $80 million a year is lost in sales because bottles not unlike those used for a genuine scent are labeled with a name that sounds not unlike the original and buyers are bilked. Sometimes salespeople try to hard-sell a house abomination or another shoddy unknown brand as ''outstanding,'' and to offer a huge ''discount'' on a 10th-class product which yields an enormous profit. Therefore, it's worth the time, before leaving home, to comparison shop in the perfume department of a local department store and come prepared not to be taken in.

Don't let purveyors in *Grasse,* the tourist-choked perfume-flower center on the Riviera, gull you about Grasse products, either. More about this in the next section.

Remember, also, that *most* (not all) of the above leaders are ''restricted brands'' by U.S. Customs. Your import into the U.S. is limited, in these cases, to 1 or 2 bottles of each scent *per person* (in a few cases, a bottle not exceeding 3 oz.). Likewise, direct mail shipment to America is often prohibited. *Be sure to check these restrictions before you buy,* because excess amounts are confiscated by our Men in Blue. While it sometimes looks as if savings are greatest on inflight sales offers, selection is often so limited that you don't really get what you wanted and waited for; hence it's recommended you do your buying on the ground. That way you won't be disappointed. And don't wait to do your buying at the Paris airport tax free stores because savings in town are definitely greater.

Assorted Fragrances: **Sagil** (242 rue de Rivoli, Tel: 42607181) attracts its discerning clientele from every corner of the scented world. Located in the same fashionable area of Paris since 1932 Sagil has an undisputed reputation for chic. The most important service that is offered to shoppers is the highest export discount available, *higher than at any airport!* Here you will find a selection of such famous designers and labels as Chanel, Patou, Yves St. Laurent, Paco Rabanne, Dior and Lavin. Also featuring Nina Ricci, Chloe, Bal a Versailles, Givenchy, Molinard, Armani, Paloma Picasso, Oscar de la Renta and many others. New perfumes such as Panthere by Cartier, Gem by Van Cleef, Ungaro, Montana and Gianfranco Ferre are represented too. This boutique offers cosmetics (Dior, YSL, Orlane, Lancome and French beauty products) as well as a choice of splendid leather goods, silk scarves, hair ornaments, Lacoste sportswear, cashmere sweaters and watches from such collections as Van Cleef, Cartier, Yves St. Laurent and Ebel. And ladies, if your conscience is bothering you, you will find prestigious ties by Cerruti and Christian Dior; also sunglasses by Porsche and Vuarnet for the man in your life. You will be given the best discount possible—no matter what the amount of your purchase. Items can also be mailed to your home at the same tremendous discount rates! And the English-speaking team is there to assist you in choosing all the latest fashions in this fast-paced field of haute-couture. You will also be provided with a beauty service a few doors away; hairstyling, makeup applications and consulting, waxing, manicures and pedicures. Call the talented Veronique who will make an appointment for you (Tel: 42607054).

Home Fragrances: These have become extremely popular in France and the selection of particular scents—ranging from the pleasantly familiar to the downright exotic—has expanded enormously over the past decade. **Jean Laporte L'Artisan Parfumeur** (84 bis rue de Grenelle, plus branches) is in tasteful

Directoire style. One of their best-sellers is *Le Parfum a Bruler* (perfume to burn). Actually, it evaporates at a leisurely rate when heated by the aid of a lamp bulb. The scent is contained in an oil which is put drop by drop on a porous ring—a few drops lasting several hours on the ring which rests on the illuminated bulb.

Personalized Silk Scarves: **Alice Landais** (5 Faubourg Saint-Honore, one flight up in the courtyard) is wrapped into high-fashion's silkiest shopping district. And well it should be, as you will agree when you spy these elegant wares. Ask this artist to show you her distinctive chiffon personalized creations, the squares, the stoles, and limited but highly select masterpiece collection which springs from her own special genius. The lace and linen handkerchiefs are unbeatable gems, too. When you witness and touch these glories for yourself, you'll then want to ask about the tantalizing export discounts which are available and their excellent mail service. Here is a true bastion of cordiality, patience and genuine concern for the customer—alas, rare properties in today's rushed commercial whirl.

Pewter: **Charles and Philippe Boucaud** (25 rue du Bac) specializes in antique pewter. You can totally rely on this establishment. A catalog in French is available.

Pipes: **Sommer** (15 Passage des Princes), founded in 1850, is regarded by many smokers as ranking almost neck-and-neck with Dunhill as the greatest pipemaker in the world. Its individually fashioned briar and meerschaum models range from $30 to $700. The prizes have 1 to 4 tiny white rectangles set into their stems, with 4 designating its ultimate in craftsmanship.

Precious Enamel Jewelry: **Michaela Frey Team** (42 rue du Dragon, Tel.: 45441220) commands one of the best locations in this city for its showcase—the very heart of Saint-Germain-des-Pres. You'll certainly be wowed by the newly renovated boutique which reflects the potent design themes carried out in the Michaela Frey Team collection. Here is a gallery as much as a store. In the beautiful sets of precious enamel creations you will find bracelets, necklaces, rings, brooches, earrings and belts in thrilling variety. As an added design bonus which is absolutely irresistible, each line features its own matching silk scarf for the perfect fashion combo. Don't panic. Prices range from a modest $15 to $250! Also see ''Vienna.''

Silk Blouses: **Cocon** (255 rue Saint-Honore) is that pot-of-gold at the end of the rainbow—a spectrum of colors, 30 of them, made up into some of the prettiest and most elegant blouses and blazers you'll find. The prices are silky, too—amazingly low considering the quality.

Silk Flowers: **Trousselier** (73 boulevard Hausmann) wears the crown as the finest creator of artificial flowers in silk anywhere in the world. When we asked how many species they could duplicate, we were told ''every one nature produces.'' Without exception, everything on the shelves—Peace and American beauty roses, anemones, tulips, water irises, lots more—has been lovingly handcrafted. A one and only.

Stationery: **Agry** (14 rue de Castiglione) and **Cassegrain** (rue St. Honore 422) are the last words for your written *mots*. Their paper, stylings and note-worthy finesse put them at the top of their craft. The former is also acclaimed for blazer buttons (personalized, *mais oui*) which begin at $2000 (that's per set, not each). *Belles lettres,* indeed.

Swimsuits: **Eres** (corner rue Tronchet and Place de la Madeleine) probably offers the best and sexiest selection. Don't forget that France is the true birthplace of the bikini and even the word *maillot,* used to denote a one-piece job, is French. Their stretch elastic beauties are world-famous and there's an enormous color range.

Table Arts: **Au Bain Marie** (12 rue Boissy d'Anglas) is a feast for householders, well situated off the Concorde. There's everything here to enhance gastronomy. The ideas for settings, utensils, decorative fillips and food accessories are simply legion. What a tasteful assemblage!

Teas: **Christian Constant** (26 rue du Bac and 37 rue d'Assas) is *the* name in Europe for tea-timing (40 varieties!). Additionally, C-C is a unique specialist in cocoa: pure beans from Trinidad, Venezuela and Indonesia.

Wine Products: **'Esprit & Le Vin** (65 boulevard Malesherbes) is one of the finest equipment shops you'll find anywhere in the beverage realm. There are the usual corkscrews as well as the unusual ones (a baffling assortment of 30!), cooling buckets, lovely thermal bottle jackets, bar tack, 80 different decanters (including their own fabulous "duck" model), cast-iron or brass wall-mounted bottle openers in antique reproduction, plus a vast collection of glasses. They also have a catalog for mail ordering.

NOTE · · · In the Airport Shops in the International Zone at Orly, almost NONE of their merchandise is tax-free.

Watch out for such special items as cheap ready-made clothing (shoddy quality), almost anything mechanical (it has a penchant for breaking down), or electronic (because even with the tax discount it will be overpriced).

THE RIVIERA

Antiques: Be extra wary about these at the large, itinerant fairs, flea markets, and individual street stalls in this entire area. There are a number of companies here which specialize in vending old wood, old glues, old dowels, and old tools which are heavily patronized by crooked "antique" merchants. Some of these counterfeiters employ expert cabinetmakers and other furniture artisans on full time for "restorations" wildly beyond the accepted 15% limit. Nine old tables, for example, might be cannibalized to make 2 or 3 which are represented as genuine pieces. Anywhere you wander along this coastal strip, please do business *only* inside legitimate shops in this field.

Boutiques: *Nice* boasts a shopping attraction which we find so far superior to all of the similar establishments on the entire Riviera that it is enthusiastically commended to your special attention.

Encompassing the prestigious **Royal Salon of the Hotel Negresco,** an edifice which has been enshrined as a National Historical Monument, is its unique cluster of glittering boutiques. Not only does this grand circle present the creations of the greatest names in French wearables and accessories in articles for ladies, gentlemen, and children, but it also offers a new line of modern beachwear, plus its own personal and exclusive gifts (initialed scarves, bags, wallets, china, silver articles, etc.).

Not only are your purchases almost completely duty free, but, in addition, there is no city tax either. This is a year-round operation that ticks over 9 a.m.–7:30 p.m.

Lace: **Dentelles de France** at 16 boulevard Victor-Hugo in *Nice* is tiny and unique. The specialty here is enameling or otherwise petrifying lace patterns in bowls, dishes, plates, lamps, lampshades, and other bric-a-brac. There's a wonderful range of subtle colors, and the variety of models is impressive. Prices start at under $15 for a covered bonbon dish. Unusual and engaging.

Perfume: This can be one of the best buys—but our enthusiasm for some of the much-touted distillations of this region, notably *Grasse,* is very much on the dim side. These products all have their virtues and advantages, which are excellent *within the limits of their categories.* But don't let anybody tell you that they're the same as the Big Name brands, because emphatically they're NOT! In fact, we now avoid purchases even of topline products in Grasse because of the howls of protest from so many readers who have been disappointed in this town.

It is true that most of the basic essences that go into the making of French perfumes come from this region. It is equally true that the formulae for the great ones are among the most closely guarded secrets in the world. Why, then, the factory-retailers in Grasse persist in hawking their wares for the real thing is beyond us. Not only are their labels strangely familiar, but the names highly suggestive. For instance, "5" (*Chanel #5?*), *Bella (Bellodgia?), Xmas (Christmas Night?), Harp (Arpege?), J.K. (Jicky?).* . . .

Rimay (52 rue d'Antibes in *Cannes*) is THE one you can trust! And that is a fundamental element to remember as you'll see along the Riviera—a jungle of scents and outlandish claims from a multitude of competing outlets. Rimay's beautiful new premises provides an amplitude of space for sampling scores of world-class brands like Armani, Balmain, Chloe, Dali, Dior, Krizia, Chanel, Guerlain, Maxim's, Ricci, Van Cleef, Bulgari, Cartier, Hermes, La Prairie, Patou, Shiseido, Valentino, Clarins, Lancome, Picasso, St Laurent and Versace. There's also a knockout Beauty Institute to add more razzle and dazzle to your day. Daniele, Daisy, Martine Audrey, Isabelle and Robert Ottobre, the friendly multi-lingual staffers have the time and the disposition to discuss the variety of products. Every article is sold tax-free and they even offer the possibility of free delivery to your hotel plus duty-free shipment to the United States. You can ask them to send you the latest hotline on perfumes when you are ordering by mail. To round out the picture there are deluxe leather goods, crystal and coiffure acccessories. Winter hours: 9:15 a.m.–7:15 p.m. with Sunday closing; summer schedule: 9:15 a.m.–8 p.m. without interruption except for Sunday. A splendid establishment—on top of the market and the best in the marketplace since 1946!

Provencal Patterns: **Souleiado** (8 rue de France) on a walking street in *Nice* offers some charming Provence-style skirts, blouses, children's dresses, scarves, and other articles for home decorating—including yard goods. This is a long-established company with branches in Paris, other French cities, Brussels and Madrid, to name a few.

Rugs and Home Furnishing Fabrics: **Tissus Lauer-Tapis de Cogolin** (Cogolin, 5 miles from St. Tropez) Here at the factory-showroom it's possible to observe how these famous hand made floor coverings and tapestries are produced. Three month minimum wait for all orders—some much, much longer since only two inches can be completed a day on the very complicated patterns! If you're lucky, there might be upholstery material in stock that suits you, but again it's chancy. Decorative cushions are on sale, however. In Paris they have an outlet at 5 avenue de l'Opera.

NOTE · · · The Riviera Airport (which has added, incidentally, a delightful open-air restaurant and rest rooms with showers) now offers a large and impressive shopping complex in its waiting room for international passengers. It's a great place to load up with spirits and tobacco at tariffs which can't be touched domestically. But are its perfumes and parade of other articles tax-free, as clerk after clerk after clerk have so blithely assured us, or are they priced the same as in Nice or Cannes? We'd bet our shoes on the latter. Payments are accepted in foreign hard currencies only (no francs).

Otherwise, we're strictly lukewarm about shopping possibilities along this coast, except for branches of a few ultrachic Paris landmarks. The average local stores seem poor and the stocks disappointingly limited, for such a supposedly glamorous resort complex.

If you happen to be at *Biot* (about 13 miles from Nice), intending to visit the magnificent Fernand Leger Museum on the outskirts, stroll down the main street of this delightful town. There you'll find **St. Sebastien,** which specializes in the reproduction of antique sundials—a rare trade, indeed.

Cannes is loaded with fashionable boutiques. It is Paris all over again. Especially attractive are those along **Gray Street**— part of the Hotel Gray d'Albion complex. For lovers of antique jewelry, you won't find better than in the velvet cases of **Sylvie Nissen's** shop in the Grand Salon of the Hotel Carlton. (Her Paris address is 116 rue Lauriston.) Here, the name of the game is browsing and watching the gilded world go by.

Heading up to *Eze Village* along the winding road (Av. du Jardin Exotique) above the parking lot, you'll come across **Anicroche.** Miniature arrangements of Provence-style hamlets decorate the shelves. These clay houses are hand-made by one particular artist in Cannes and sold here and at St. Paul de Vence. The settings can be bought already made up with from five to seven buildings. Alternatively, you can be your own town planner and buy the pieces individually. There are seven models. Using your own imagination the results can be striking. This is definitely an unusual type of souvenir of your visit along the Riviera.

ELSEWHERE IN FRANCE

Most of the nation's individual craftsmen are tucked away in rural towns and villages. If you're driving through the provinces, often it's great fun for the curious shopper to smoke them out en route. Here, in general, is what to look for:

Alsace-Lorraine: Pottery, embroidery, and sculptured wood. *Auvergne:* Decorated wooden clogs and lace. *Brittany:* Quimper faience pottery (see "Paris" for details), lace, hand-crocheted gloves, handloomed skirts and linens. *Burgundy:* Wine-tasting cups (silver and pewter) and corkscrews of vine stocks. *French Alps:* Hand-turned walnut and olivewood articles, wrought iron, wooden butter molds, and cowbells. *Jura:* Wooden toys, chess sets, and handcarved briarwood pipes. *Normandy:* Pottery, copper pots, and lace. *Northeast:* Lace, velvet, and embroidery. *Provence:* Santons (Christmas creche figurines). At *Villeneuve-les-Avignon,* a suburb of Avignon, **La Maison Provencale** (10 place Saint Marc) carries the superior Valdrome label of provencal material made up into clothing and items for the home. You won't go out empty handed because owner Andre Zavejski has filled the tiny premises with so many other tempting regional products. *Pyrenees:* Basque linens and wooden articles. *Rhone Valley:* Marionettes, silks, and enamel jewelry.

Loire Valley: Furniture reproductions: **Mailfert-Amos** (26 rue Notre-Dame de Recouvrance, Orleans, Tel.: (33) 38627061) Here is one of the prize treasures on the French shopping scene: specially skilled cabinetmakers who replicate magnificent 18th century French antiques. Probably you have seen many in museums; others are designs from pieces in private collections; all are chosen because of their inherent beauty and the aesthetics which blend with today's interiors. One cabinetmaker (or *ebeniste*) maintains supervisory control over every masterpiece. Precise fidelity to the materials and the techniques of creating the originals are brought together under his discerning vigil. These furniture virtuosi not only create the image of the antiques, but they augment this with a patina of time's passage, as if the examples of their craft had actually been used for generations in private chateaux. For example, after the centuries-old "French Polishing" method has been applied—coloring the wood with a water-base stain, rubbing this with denatured alcohol, applying Oriental shellac, rubbing and more rubbing—finally there is a depth of character which can accommodate specks, variations in color, dents and other small "accidents" which can only occur over the decades. You might even find an ink stain inside a drawer as an amusing *beau geste.* Ten to twelve coats of lacquer are required for a perfect rendition of that special finish—a technique dating back 2,500 years—which has always been appreciated by connoisseurs. The workshop and showroom are in Orleans, the city of Joan of Arc. You can see gilt-wood sconces, mirrors, barometers and the fine large pieces. Even the most critical eye will be impressed with the leather desk tops by Mailfert-Amos—beautifully tooled in gold and embossed, custom-wrought marble for table tops, intricate hand-carving and other displays of the art. Prices range from $400 for small occasional tables to $4000 for a chest of drawers in fruitwood to several thousands for their most elaborate works. Average delivery is about three months since most pieces are custom-made. Photographs are available on request. Business hours from Tues. through Sat. are 10 a.m.–12:30 p.m. and 2 p.m.–6:30 p.m. Closed in August. Don't miss this very original copy.

GERMANY

SHOPPING HOURS

A federal law now standardizes them throughout the country: 9 a.m.–6:30 p.m. on weekdays; Sat., 9 a.m.–2 p.m., except to 6 p.m. on the first Sat. of every month and each Sat. of the month-long Advent period.

PUBLIC HOLIDAYS

Jan. 1, Shrove Tues., Good Fri., Easter Mon., May 1, Ascension Day, Whitmonday, Corpus Christi, June 17 (German Unity Day), Aug. 15 (in Bavaria and Saarland), Nov. 16 (Prayer Day), Dec. 25–26.

PURCHASE TAX REFUND

VAT is 14% and it's returned, minus handling charges, if you've spent over 150 DM. All major stores have the necessary documents for you to fill out. Once customs has stamped them, mail them off and soon you'll receive your rebate. (By ordering the return directly onto your credit card account the yield will be the highest since your shopkeeper has less paper work.) There is also immediate rebating at some airports and borders. Naturally, the VAT is not charged on shipped goods.

MAIL ORDERS

Among the shops that follow, the only one which has brilliantly promoted retail business by post all over the world is Dr. Hans Zoellner **(Porzellanhaus Zoellner)** of Munich, the nation's largest dealer in Rosenthal china, crystal, and cutlery as well as one of its most prominent purveyors for other manufacturers of similar or allied lines. Should you send for his catalogs and either make your selection from them or specially request anything on his vast shelves, your guaranteed-safe shipment would be delivered for up to 50% less than you would pay for it in North America. A bonanza! Particular attention by shutterbugs is also solicited in this chapter. Immediately below they might wish to read the 9-point section on what to seek and what to avoid in purchasing photographic equipment—yes, by mail, too—in this traditional Mecca of technical expertise. Then we urge that they communicate ANY related problem, no matter how large or how small, to **Kohlroser** in Munich or **Foto Hobby** in Frankfurt.

HOW TO BUY A CAMERA

Here are some private tips from one of the world's most illustrious and respected photographic suppliers, gleaned from more than 40 years of direct experience in his famous establishment:

(1) Never buy it near the end of your visit.

(2) Tell your dealer what *kinds* of pictures you will want to take, so that he can advise you which model among the myriads of types is precisely the best one for your purposes.

(3) Give him sufficient time to explain all of its mechanisms and functions to you. Then, in front of his eyes, check all these yourself.

(4) Read every word of the instruction booklet without delay.

(5) If you're puzzled about even the smallest point, return to him on the following day so that your understanding and familiarity become 100% complete.

(6) Be certain that all of your electrical sources are fresh—both when you buy and later. Whenever the batteries in automatic cameras, in light meters, and in flashguns are run down, they give incorrect readings.

(7) BEWARE OF THE CHEAPEST OFFER—especially from the discount-houses in Germany who are pushing for a quick sale with glib promises of "servicing" which later may never materialize. Since it is almost impossible for the layman to spot most technical alterations, it is common practice for them to peddle models that are already out of production. High-grade German cameras and equipment are sold *ONLY* through legitimate, well-established shops; other types of outlets often are forced to dig up their merchandise elsewhere. Although you'll find these so-called bargains here and in various other European lands, you'd almost surely end up as the loser. Any photo apparatus that does not come directly from the factory does not carry a bona fide guarantee. Charges for repairs of unguaranteed purchases are very often shockingly high.

(8) Thus, be *sure* to patronize only a topflight expert who has a well-trained staff. Should repairs be necessary during the term of your international guarantee, he will instantly advise you how to get them done either without charge or at the lowest cost.

(9) The aim of the legitimate dealer is not to sell you the most expensive type, but the *right* type expressly for your own personal requirements. You can count upon his honesty, his candor, and his dependability throughout a lifetime of association. After all, as our friendly great specialist comments, "It has *got* to be this way. A completely satisfied client is any company's best and most profitable recommendation!"

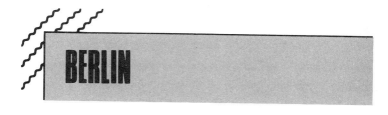

BERLIN

Antiques: Keithstrasse (a street) has a lineup of 12 or 14 shops in a row.

Books: **Marga Schoeller Bucherstube** (Knesebeckstr. 12) is outstandingly versatile; it carries many U.S. reprints.

Boutiques: There are scads upon scads, many of which feature French and Italian imports. If you are walking along the Kurfurstendamm you'll find higher quality shops beyond the Hotel Kempinski rather than in the direction of the Europa Center. **Lange** (Fasanenstr. 29) is just one example. However, their prices are so lofty that there's no sense in listing more of the names of the many we have scouted. You can do much better in other hubs.

Cutlery: **Henckels** has a fine branch (Kurfurstendamm 33). **WMF** (Kurfurstendamm 229) is also excellent.

Department Store: Historic **KaDeWe** (Tauentzienstr. 30), Berlin's largest and most famous, became a stunner when it was completely rebuilt; now we are finding it dull, dull, and duller when compared to similar rivals almost anywhere. In our opinion, its management needs a super-pep shot in the arm—but where to go, when there's none better here?

Flea Market: A most unusual one is in the deactivated underground station of **Nollendorfplatz,** on its 2 platforms and in 16 disused subway cars. It's open Wed.–Mon. from 11 a.m.–7 p.m. Otherwise, there's a small one in benign weather on Unter den Eichen at Asternplatz; this is so unimpressive that it scarcely seems worth your time.

Medals: **Berolina-Medaillen-Vertribes** (Malteserstr. 104a) has a chestful—almost every Saxon decoration you can request (antique or modern). Other choices as well.

Optical Goods: **Sohnges** (see ''Munich'') has sizable branches at Kurfurstendamm 139 and 210 and Reichsstrasse 83.

Porcelains: Go to the factory of **Staatliche Porzellan-Manufaktur Berlin** (Wegelystrasse 1) for 25% to 50% off on second or third qualities; the main store (Kurfurstendamm 26a) is very beautiful.

Stamps: **Schlegel** (Kurfurstendamm 34), or **Dieter Schmidt** (Albrechtstrasse 131).

COLOGNE

SHOPPING AREAS

Hohe Strasse starts close to the Cathedral. It, as well as **Schildergasse,** are popular pedestrian zones. Both are crowded, noisy

and crammed with many undistinguished shops. The big department stores line the latter. **Mittelstrasse** boasts the *Bazaar de
Cologne* complex. **Pfeilstrasse** has a lock on the city's chic boutiques and antique shops. Nearby, **Ehrenstrasse** and **Breite
Strasse** are worth a stroll.

THINGS TO BUY

Antiques, books, 4711 Cologne, porcelain. This is a city rich in
antiques and art. Of all the metropoli we have visited in Germany, Cologne is the most impressive in terms of variety, periods covered and price structuring. There are scores of boutiques
for these products, many of them located along St.-Apern-Str.

Antiques: **Lothar Huebel** (Breite Str. 118–120) could as well
be a museum as a commercial enterprise. The overwhelming display includes rare African, Asian and Polynesian artifacts of superb quality. It also can locate talismans, charms, sculptures,
textiles, jewelry or almost anything you might desire from any
exotic realms. Many of the staffers are multilingual walking en-
cyclopedias who will help you explore these treasures. Though
you would think prices are astronomical, they are quite reasonable. Branches in Dusseldorf, Frankfurt and Munich. **Kun-
sthaus Lempertz** (Neumarkt 3) specializes in art from the
Rhineland while **Abels** (Stadtwald Burtel 32a) focuses on silver
(A.D. 1600 to 1850), old masters, as well as modern artisry.
Dautzenberg (St.-Apern-Str. 66) is an expert on clocks, pewter
and furniture of the classic period; on the same street (No. 13)
you might also like to look into the windows of **Helmut Mohr-
holz. Faust** (Am Hof 34–36) is strong on Egyptian, Greek and
Roman artifacts. **Sterzenbach** (Lintgasse) is outstanding for furniture and silver while **Goyert** (Hahnenstr. 18) emphasizes
graphics of all periods. As for auction houses, both **Sotheby's**

(St.-Apern-Str. 17–19) and **Venator** (Cacilienstr. 48) are major names locally.

Books: **Konig** (Ehrenstr. 4) is internationally famous for its connoisseurship. The original shop on Breite Str. now is probably the world's largest postcard purveyor of old and new printings.

Cologne: Here's the town that invented it, so be sure to visit the ''4711'' headquarters at Glockengasse where you can also watch the amusing Glockenspiel performances from the courtyard. The famous title, incidentally, derives from the French occupation when all houses were given military serial numbers—*4711* is where the ''miracle water'' was conceived. The full range of products is on display.

English Lifestyle: **Mulberry** (Apostehln-Str. 5) does its wonderous British thing here (see under ''London''). A great collection.

Fashion: **Franz Sauer** (Minoriten Str. 13) is the most exclusive; it carries labels such as Escada, Hermes and Chanel. You might also like to browse at **Jansen** (Breite Str. 21 and Hahnenstr.) or at **Bleyle** (Mittelgasse). There's plenty of dash also at **Boutique Louise** (St.-Apern-Str. 21 and Kreishaus Galerie).

Gifts for the Home: **Katrin Bierther** (Pfeilstr. 36) glows with handicrafts, silk flowers, tableware, textiles and many small packageable decorative pieces.

Glass and Porcelain: **Kristall Passage** (Wallrafplatz 6) contains the great names of Europe. It is the Rolls Royce of its field. Anything you might want from Meissen to Herend to Royal Copenhagen you can find here. Mrs. Paffrath will also explain how you can receive a 14% tax rebate. Superb for gifts little and large.

Records: **Saturn** (Hansaring 97) rings in with a huge inventory of recordings in wax and tape plus many electronics items.

SHOPPING AREAS

Kaiserstrasse, Goethestrasse and **Steinweg** are the toniest shopping streets. At **Hauptwache** both aboveground and underground a galaxy of stores beckon. **Grosse Bockenheimer,** affectionately known as ''Fressgasse,'' or _Gourmand Alley,_ panders to your appetite with wine shops, cafes, delicatessens and restaurants. The larger department stores are on **Rossmarkt** and **Zeil.** Nearby is the _Kleinmarkthalle,_ a covered market with foodstuffs from all over the globe. **Schillerstr.,** a pedestrian zone, has home furnishing stores. Secondhand shops flank **Braubachstrasse** and **Fahrgasse.** The **Romer** (City Hall Square) has been revived. **Ladengalerie am Theater** in the BFG skyscraper has several floors loaded with boutiques—all you need is money.

THINGS TO BUY

Cutlery, Rosenthal porcelains, cameras, optical equipment, toys; you can trust almost any mass-produced German product.

Antiques: There's good hunting now around the Romer. Since the square has been improved, lots of interesting shops have moved in.

Books: The area in and around the Hauptwache affords satisfying browsing. By the way, Frankfurt is the home of Dr. Heinrich Hoffmann's "Struwwelpeter" (Shock-Headed Peter) a children's hero and often depicted graphically in the amplitude of literature about the wild-haired youngster.

Cameras: **Foto Hobby** (Rossmarkt 23, in the very center of the city and only a few steps from the Frankfurter Hof) has been one of the leading houses of Germany for more than three decades and a specialist in the prestige Leica brand. Since they buy, sell and exchange in this field, your opportunities for beginning a photographic hobby or trading-up to professional levels of equipment are all available under one roof. Mr. Manuel Titsch-Rivero or Jurgen Uhl can show you the comprehensive stock of cameras, lenses and accessories—new, of course, but also a wide choice of used and even splendidly antique items for the collector. While Leica is the linchpin of its international fame, you'll find Rollei, Ricoh, Canon, Nikon, Contax, Yashica, Minolta and Minox, plus Zeiss, Tokina, Vivitar and a bagful of other great names in photography. Be sure you focus on the 14% tax refund offered. They also provide worldwide export and mailing services for reorders so ask for price lists and other data while you are on the scene. If you want to inquire by phone the number is 233555.

Confection: **Bethmannchen** are globe-shaped marzipan creations decorated with 3 almond halves. Their history goes back to 1840 when they were first made in the house of the banker Bethmann. It's a Christmas specialty, but can be found all year round—great gift idea but short shelf-life.

Cosmetics: **Parfumerie Douglas** sprinkles at least 10 branches over the town. Each time you sniff you'll discover one along a major street. Very wide selection; chic beauty accessories.

Cutlery: Our first call on German soil is usually **J. A. Henckels,** now in 7 more German hubs, plus others outside the country. Almost no one disputes that the pert ''Twins,'' trademark and colophon of this giant since 1731, symbolize excellence. Look also for the silverware of **Robbe & Berking** which is of great artistic merit. **WMF** (Kaiserstr. 15, Schillerstr. 2, Zeil 107) stands for Wurttemberg Metalware Factory. This giant with about 91 outlets throughout the nation offers a great diversity of production. Their hottest new line called La Galleria began with ice buckets and champagne coolers. Everything for a *haus* beautiful.

Delicatessen: **Ploger** (Fressgasse) presents delicious looking fresh offerings at their take-away counter if you're planning a picnic, plus shelves stocked with tins and packages of exotic foodstuffs.

Department Stores: Many locals prefer **Hertie** (Zeil 90) to **Kaufhaus** (Zeil 98/104). It's a tossup.

Fashions (Women's): **La Lac** (Am Romerberg 20/22, 2 Theaterplatz Ladengalerie) is very smart. **Renate Bamberg** (Am Romerberg 26) stocks stylish sweaters. **Escada** (Goethestr. 13) is one of the brand names Americans love. **Toni Schiesser** (Kaiserstr. 19–21) was highly touted, but I didn't see much of interest on my visit. To repeat, Goethestr., Kaiserstr. and the Ladengalerie will wear you out.

Flea Market: This is located on the south side of the river near the Flosserbrucke in the *Schlachthof* (slaughterhouse) area;

operative every Sat. from 8 a.m.–3 p.m. in winter (until 4 p.m. in summer). Not special.

Fur: The center of this trade is near the railway station. **Gerson** (Dusseldorfer Str. 1–7) is highly reputable.

Jewelry and Gold Objects: **H. Stern** (see ''Paris'') has shops in town at Laden Galerie on Theaterplatz, in the Frankfurter Hof Hotel, and in the Hotel Intercontinental. Their two airport facilities are open seven days a week from 8:30 a.m.–9 p.m.; tax-free plans available. (If you're going on to Dusseldorf, you'll find a branch at Koenigsalle 21–23.)

Leather: **Gold-Pfeil** (Kaiserstr. 22) is Germany's leading manufacturer. Superb quality, handsome styling, made-to-last finishing. Their sport collection bears a classic English look. The Caracciola line evokes memories of the racy driving ace for whom it was named. Pegasus Club primarily appeals to fashion-conscious business travelers, but the inventory is variegated.

Lederhosen: Squeeze into **Leder Vater** (Kaiserstr. 6). **Trude Hahn** (Bethmannstr. across from entrance to the Frankfurter Hof Hotel) caters to children. **Pfuller** (Goethestr. 15–19) also had a few models for small fry.

Porcelain: **Behaghel** (Kaiserstr.) is *the* place in town. Several rooms of gleaming glass and china displays; large sales staff; very attentive, knowledgeable and helpful. **Lorey** (Schillerstr. 16), part of the same company, is known for its household effects.

Prints: Visit the Braubachstr. area.

Regional Dress: **Liesel Steinmetz** (Rathenauplatz, between Hauptwache and Fressgasse) is a specialist in *trachten*. Finest quality loden and the distinctive costumery of country life.

Rosenthal: **Studio-Haus Gilbert** (Friedensstrasse 10, next to Frankfurter Hof Hotel) is our local magnet for this most famous of German china.

Shoes: **Linda** and **Stivali** (both along Goethestr.) are up-market while **Salamander** (Zeil 65) is more popular in appeal and price.

Toys: **Behle** (Adam-Opelstr. 2) might be a good stop if you want a Maerklin model train, a Steiff teddy bear, a Fischertechnik building kit, a Kaethe-Kruse doll or, perhaps a complicated jigsaw puzzle. The **Kaufhof Department Store** also produces a varied assortment.

SHOPPING AREAS

Briennerstrasse, Theatinerstrasse, and **Maximilianstrasse** are the most chichi. **Kaufingerstrasse** is a pedestrian's pasture. Between the **Marienplatz** and **Karlsplatz** are most of the large department stores. **Leopoldstrasse**—in fact, Schwabing in general—is not what it used to be, in our eyes.

THINGS TO BUY

Cameras and photo supplies, sunglasses and optical aids, leather goods, Rosenthal china, Nymphenburg porcelains, cutlery, fashions, sportswear, gourmet delicacies, paintings, handicrafts.

Antiques: **Herbert M. Ritter** (Prannerstrasse 5) is excellent. **Kunsthandlung Franz Hanfstaengl** (Karlsplatz 6), is also fine.

Art Galleries: **Franz Hanfstaengl** (see above) has a lovely selection, plus flower prints, etchings, watercolors, and works in other media. **Wolfgang Ketterer** in the Museum Villa Stuck (Prinzregentenstr. 60) and **Galerie am Haus der Kunst** (Karl-Scharnagl-Ring 60 opposite the Haus de Kunst) are also worth a look.

Books: **Hugendubel** (Marienplatz, Salvatorplatz, plus other branches) can satisfy most reading needs.

Cameras and Accessories: **Kohlroser** (Maffeistrasse 14, near the Hotel Bayerischer Hof and American Express) is our favorite camera dealer and photo consultant in Germany—not only because the stock is so extensive, but also because Mr. Kohlroser and assistants Mr. Schindler and Mr. Honig are so honest, so knowledgeable, and so interested in doing the best possible job for you, for us, and for every other client who steps across its threshold into its high-tech atmosphere. Again in the past year, we've had at least 3 dozen letters from readers of both this *Shopping Guide* and our *Travel Guide* about how they went out of their way to be helpful and thoughtful—an unusual trait in the extra-cold world of German commerce. Kohlroser will refund the turnover tax (value added tax) of about 12% through the Tax Cheque Service Organization after the Customs declaration form is returned. Every camera in the shop is guaranteed for a minimum of 12 months, even if shipped. On their shelves you'll find among others, the new automatic Leicaflex R5 and R6, Leica M6, Bauer Video VHS and the new Video 8, Agfa, Kodak, Minox, Linhof, Hasselblad, Voigtlander, Fuji, Olympus, Nikon, Canon, Asahi, and Minolta, plus the new Minox AF autofocus as well as the new and light Canon and Metz video 8 cameras; there are new pocket-size Zeiss, Leitz and Voigtlander binoculars, opera glasses, zoom lenses from 28–200 mm for German and Japanese cameras, automatic slide projectors, flea-size electronic computer flash units, and goodness knows what else; furthermore, the house provides two-day service on Ektachrome. Sample prices at this writing: Automatics, $99–345; Leica R6, $2330; the freshly unveiled Minox AF, $230; new small autofocus cameras, $120–380; latest fully automatic small and light Video 8 cameras, less than ever. Superb stocks, superb values—but the most important asset around Kohlroser's is the careful personal attention of experts steeped in the technology of optics and photography. A shutterbug's heaven.

Candles: **J. & W. Furst** (Sporerstrasse 2) is first, in our judgment: Narrow in size, wider in selection, widest in charm.

Cutlery and Souvenirs: **Bestecke & Praesente** (Karlsplatz 25) commands a position on the leading edge for cutlery and, as you know, Germany has always ranked as the primary manufacturer in the world for this art.

Department Stores: **Kaufhof** (Marienplatz), **Beck's am Rathaus,** and **Karstadt** and **Hertie** (Bahnhofplatz) are all popular.

Dirndls, Regional Dress and Loden: This fashion is really in high gear for men and women all over the world. At the following five you should be able to find any ensemble or accessory to give your wardrobe a genuine alpine flavor. **Loden-Frey**

(Maffeistr. 7–9) is perhaps the biggest purveyor in the nation. The quality is exceptional and the selectivity is vast. **Dirndl Kobler** (Theatinerstr. 45) tilts decidedly in an exclusive direction for dressy occasions. **Heimatwerk** (Burgstrasse 50) belongs to the nearby Ludwig Beck department store interests. Here the emphasis is on tradition and authenticity. A great deal of historical research went into the creation of the dirndls alone. Cozy premises where you'll want to linger and try on loden capes and coats, and colorful sweaters. Lots of charming household items, too. **Frankonia Jagd** (Maximiliansplatz 10) evokes a mood of smart country attire and sport. **Resi Hammerer** (Maximilianstr. 27) puts her own swanky hallmark on her personalized collections for summer and winter.

Dog Coats: Bavarian-style loden coats in green with gray trim and sculpted silver buttons are a feature at **Alles fur den Hund** ("Everything for Dogs") at Schwanthaler 2. They cost from $20 up. They would make your 4-footed companion the best-dressed in the neighborhood.

Furniture, Furnishings, and Gifts for the Home: **Vereinigte Werkstatten** (Amiraplatz 1) is a treasure trove. This is the marketplace of many self-employed Bavarian furniture and bric-a-brac craftsmen. Branches in *Hamburg, Dusseldorf, Bremen,* and *Bremerhaven.* Gorgeous. **Pilati** (Amiraplatz) is the decorating arm of a famous architect. The feeling here is of sleek sophistication.

Handicrafts: Our pick is **Wallach** (Residenzstrasse 3), with its 2 floors packed to the rafters—and a basement bulging with antiques. Worth a browse. Also interesting is **Deutsche Werkstatten** (Briennerstrasse 54 and branch), the commercial outlet of many independent local artisans, with accent on furniture, fabrics, lamps, and wooden paintings. The contemporary surroundings of the **Bayerischen Kunstgewerbeverein** (Pacellistr. 7) set off to perfection splendid examples of bookbinding, ceramics, stone sculpture, pewterware, textiles, glass, toys and games, gold and silver jewelry and enamel work—a very superior grouping of finely designed objects.

Hats: **Joh. Zehme** (Perusastr.) is just right for Bavarian models. The Mayser brand is what local heads head for.

High Fashion: **Maendler** (Theatinerstr. 7) resides in Munich for a reason—the most fashionable city in a country which is rapidly becoming very, very important in the design field. German names which now span the world come from the innovative drawing boards of Marc Kehnen, Renzo and Uta Raasch. Here at Maendler you will find the creations of Jil Sander and Edith Sonanini to name just a few. The sweaters by Iris von Arnim have become legends in only the twinkling of an eyelash. There's the cool, casual Iceberg knitwear which has become so identifiable in smart circles. A lot of the sport as well as the town-and-country apparel and accessories are downstairs. Don't overlook the dazzling evening dresses which are always in great demand in this ever-partying city. Select items from the collections of such internationals as Krizia, Claude Montana, Genny, Patrick Kelly and Christian Lacroix fill the cupboards, too. The Maendlers (Robert and Rosi) have put together a showcase which is one of the most modish you can find anywhere in this nation of burgeoning stylists.

The **Palais Boutique** in the Bayerischer Hof Hotel arcade (Promenadeplatz) tends towards the Italians. Sanny Gehrig will show you the latest from Armani, Enrico Coveri, Valentino and Miss V.

Jil Sander (Wurzerstr., around the corner from the Vier Jahreszeiten Hotel) has her own boutique where you can see the explosive talent of this fashion leader.

Jewelry: **Hans R. Rothmuller** (Briennerstrasse 1) is the most distinguished house, with the most distinguished price tags, too.

Leather Goods and Travel Aids: **Zimmermann** (Briennerstr. 1) has fashionable stylings that are soft and supple. **Karl Thalmessinger** (Theatinerstr 1 and 15, Maximilianstr. 16, Karlsplatz 25 and more) carries the highly-renowned Gold-Pfeil marque that speaks quality and elegance.

Markets: One of Germany's best is on **Viktualienplatz.** Here everything from flowers to flounders is for sale—including some of the most scrumptious cheeses we've ever savored. It's open from 9 a.m–6 p.m. every day except Sat. afternoon and all day Sun. Three mammoth rummage sales, with stalls extending for blocks around the Gothic church in Mariahilf Square, are held annually. Custom has it that they commence on a Sat., run for nine days and are open from 9 a.m.–9 p.m. In addition, there must be 320 stalls. The Spring Fair ("Fruhjahrsdult") is normally end-April; the Summer Fair ("Jakobidult") is normally end-July; the Fall Fair ("Kirchweihdult") is normally mid-Oct. Everything is there, from cookie molds to porcelains, candlesticks, fur coats, bratwurst stands, furniture, false teeth—a huge stewpot of buyables and junk. Don't miss them if you're there. Terrific!

Optical Goods: **Sohnges** (Briennerstrasse 7 and Kaufingerstrasse 34; plus *Berlin* branches) is one of the 2 or 3 top optical complexes in the world today. You can find anything from binoculars to sunglasses to contact lenses. The service is extremely cordial and the precision is noteworthy.

Regional Furnishings: **Die Alpenwerkstatten** (Schafflerstr. 22) is the top of the Alps for giving your bedroom, salon, kitchen or den the highland flavor that you found so enchanting on your

European tour. Everything from sofas and lamps to textiles, bookshelves and typical dolls. The company will even panel your walls and put porcelain plates on your table.

Religious Items: **Karl Storr** (Kaufingerstr. 25 with entrance at Liebfrauenstr. next to the Dom) has as its specialty hand-carved religious pieces of inspired quality. Some (not all) bear reverential prices.

Shopping Center: One of Europe's largest underground shopping centers—$4.2 million in cost, 100% air-conditioned, 44 separate stores—is in action beneath the **Stachus,** Munich's main square. **The Marienplatz,** in front of the Rathaus, is now an island for strollers or buyers.

Skiwear: **Das Bogner Haus** (Residenzstr. 15) is headquarters for the world-class German leader in winter sportswear. Fashions which will make your snowtimes glisten. Skis and equipment upstairs.

Sporting Goods: **Sport-Scheck** (Sendlingerstr. 85), though an emporium, could qualify handily as a museum of modern sport. Virtually every competitive and challenging pastime is represented and every required accessory in stock and highly visible. One of the most dramatic displays you'll see is a 6-story rock interior wall created for climbers to test their gear.

Tableware: **Porzellanhaus Zoellner** (Theatinerstrasse 8). Germany's biggest Rosenthal sales tycoon—a private pilot by hobby—and porcelain expert, Dr. Hans Zoellner, is the son of the factory's original Technical Managing Director (1892 to 1935). His spacious, beautifully decorated store offers the full range of the Rosenthal ''3 C's''—china, crystal, and cutlery including their Classic Rose Collection (with shape ''2000''). There's the entire assemblage of Hutschenreuther, which has been producing china since 1814, plus the best of Hummel, Swarovski, and others. Prices? An astonishing 50% *average* saving against the same merchandise at home! This outstanding shop (near City Hall) carries all—repeat, *all*— Rosenthal Studio Lines products as well as the complete "Classic Rosenthal" traditional dinner sets ($800 to $6000). Gift items from $10 to $600 are also available. The management and staff here are warm, friendly, and helpful. Safe shipment guaranteed; huge export and mail-order business; Dr. and Mrs. Zoellner or Mr. Schrottle stand behind the great reputation of their firm. None better.

Nymphenburg (Odeonplatz 1) has been producing its exquisite *objets d'art* since 1747. Ask here about visiting the fabled Schloss Nymphenberg on the outskirts of the city.

Tree Cake and Other German Pastry Specialties: **Conditorie Kreutzkamm** (Maffeistrasse 4) has been baking *Baumkuchen* for over 150 years and mails them to any destination on the globe. They make an unusual and delicious gift—especially if the recipient lives within visiting distance of your home.

ROTHENBURG OB DER TAUBER

This beautiful walled townlet is recommended as your base for touring Germany's glorious Romantic Road. It is also the best headquarters for shopping throughout the entire route: greater variety, best presentation and extremely convenient for all needs.

Antiques: **Fritz Weiss** (Untere Schmiedgasse 5) contains some of the greatest prizes in the nation even though it is tiny in size. Liselotte Hintze knows the insides of a multitude of fine homes, castles and manors where she personally visits on her collection forays.

Art Prints and Drawings: **Ernst Geissendoerfer** (Obere Schmiedgasse), only a few steps away in mid-hamlet, offers its more popular collection on the ground floor. If you are searching for a specific print (even something as exceptional as a Durer) then ask the jovial St. Nick—the twinkle-eyed proprietor who frequently wears his white beard over a bright red smock—to show you the treasures in the cellar.

Christmas in July? **Kathe Wohlfahrt's Christkindlmarkt** (Herrngasse 2) can do a lot better than celebrating Noel in July. Here you'll discover that holiday mood twelve months of the year. Step inside to this wonderland any season and you will see a frosted Bavarian scene sparkling with over 80,000 lights and comprising approximately 50,000 hypnotizing items such as cuddly bears, dolls that blink, maybe an 18-foot Christmas pyramid, or possibly a colossal wooden "nutcracker" which inspired the Tschaikowsky suite—the full inventory of Santa's busiest North Pole factories. The famous Steiff animal collection is a classic in petable zoology. You'll wander up staircases and along aisles that glitter with the urgency of the festive season, provoking thoughts of everyone back home who must be remembered with some appropriate gift. While the carols fill the snow-buffed air you can assemble all of your year's givings in one shopping spree—and receive an impressive tax discount on purchases of 150 DM or more. (If you can put this through your credit card the handling charges will be reduced and your rebate will be yet an extra holiday gift.) Tell either of the Wohlfahrts (father or son) or any of the principal staff supervisors that you have come through Fielding and they will present you with a lovely free tree ornament for your own home. Merry Christmas—whenever it comes!

Glassware: **WEHA-Kristallglas** (Obere Schmiedgasse 23 and 20) carries numerous trademark items but also blows its own horn (and glass) in the manor of the 16th century. It is a good show whether you buy or not.

Edible Cigars: All of the local butcher shops purvey these trick items made from sausage meat. The mocks are wrapped and packaged just like the real thing. These items are said to have a shelf-life of about 3 weeks but I suspect from the several boxes which we have purchased the cigars could be smoked (literally) after a month or so.

Toy Soldiers: **Tradition H. Zorn** (Obere Schmiedgasse 6 and Ortsteil Bettenfeld 21) contains armies of these, all from various epochs, nationalities and states. There are kits for painting or molding your own combatants. The support troops include military books, prints, and fascinating antiques of this medium.

Trachten: **Der Bergtorladen** (Herrngasse 36) provides a tantalizing wardrobe of regional country-style dress. Prices are surprisingly low for such wearable costumery.

Wax Works: **Wachskunst-Ingrid Huhnlein** (Untere Schmiedgasse 18) is an endearing atelier where the craftsman does most of his artisanry in the streetfront window. His inventory includes tiny inexpensive table decorations to sculpture in human size. Many colors; all forms in heat-resistant wax which will not melt in transit; most prices in the $5 to $15 range; packaging facilities for overseas mailing (don't worry as they are sturdy little creatures); excellent for any gift occasion. This house also sells the superb Nurnberger Lebkuchen (a delicious spice cake common to this entire region) of the Gottfried Wicklein brand; these come in ornamented boxes and containers with polychromatic paintings of local landmarks.

ELSEWHERE IN GERMANY

Hamburg: Possibly Germany's richest city, the shops are often hidden away and almost become family properties for the legacies that have resided in the area for centuries. Your best bet is to search through the arcades called **Galleria** and **Hanse Viertel** for your whimsical moods. **Hamburger Hof mall** (Jungfernstieg 26–30) is another conglomerate of stores worth a look. **Milchstrasse** is a rewarding fashion venue. Both **Alsterhaus** (Jungfernstieg 16) and **Kaufrausch** (Isestrasse 74) are your best options for department store browsing. You will also find an *outdoor market* on the **Isestrasse** on Tuesday and Friday mornings.

Nurnberg: Gingerbread: **E. Otto Schmidt** (near the Hauptmarkt) is globally known for its *Lebkuchen* which is in the nature of spiced pastry with honey. The shop displays dozens of opportunities for gift selection: large presentation boxes for approximately $40, down through a multitude of packaging ideas to colorful tiny envelopes for as little as $1. The shelf-life for this distinctive bakery is adequate for shipping anywhere in the world. If you would like to reorder the address is Zollhausstrasse 30.

Regional Dress: **Frankonia Jagd** (Dr.-Kurt-Schumacher-Str. 23) is probably the greatest name in sportswear for men and women in Europe. It specializes in clothing, loden, huntwear and fashion, but also carries a fabulous range of weapons, optical equipment and accessories associated with field sport. The stylings are smashing and whatever the purchase you can feel confident that you have obtained the finest available anywhere.

GREECE

PLUS CORFU, MYKONOS AND SANTORINI ISLANDS

SHOPPING HOURS

In an experimental move, the government has switched shop-hours so that they vary on alternate days. Currently, on Mon., Wed., and Sat. they are from about 9 a.m.–2:30 p.m. only, closing down in the afternoons. On Tues., Thurs., and Fri. they operate from 9-ish to 1:30 p.m. and 5:30–8:30 p.m. Sales are rung up in the Plaka till at least 9 p.m. Because this awkward and uneconomical system might well be temporary, please check upon your arrival.

PUBLIC HOLIDAYS

Jan. 1, Jan. 6, Clean or Shrove Mon. (First day of Lent), Mar. 25 (Independence Day), Good Fri., Easter Sun., Easter Mon. (please remember that these last three refer to *Greek* Easter; those dates are calculated by the Orthodox Church and do not usually coincide with the Protestant calendar.), Aug. 15, Oct. 28 ("Ochi" Day), Dec. 25–26.

MAIL ORDERS

There are only a few establishments in this land which subscribe to the mail-order concept. One, however, is noteworthy because you will probably not want to hand carry your original purchase and almost certainly you will wish to reorder and re-reorder over the years. **Karamichos-Mazarakis,** the nation's leading creator of *flokati* (gorgeous, fluffy, inexpensive, virgin-wool floor coverings) distributes price lists and guarantees safe delivery to your threshold.

SHOPPING AREAS

Constitution (Syndagma), **Omonia,** and **Kolonaki** Squares and the streets surrounding them are the prime targets. (**Voukourestiou St.** is a particularly chic promenade where shade trees substitute for noisy traffic.) The last of this trio is in the center of an expensive, fashionable residential district. The first two are right in midtown. The **Plaka** district is stuffed with small shops and cheap wares.

THINGS TO BUY

Hand-woven ladies' apparel, regional handicrafts, exquisite jewelry, gold coin creations, unique *flokati* rugs, ceramics, *komba-*

loi ("worry beads"), icons, books, Flea Market antiques and trinkets.

Antiques: At **Mati** (Voukourestiou St. 20) gleaming silver crowns ($875 for ancient originals, $40–75 for reproductions) mingle with Byzantine coins that have been fashioned into pins, pill boxes, letter openers, money clips, cuff-links, striking 100-year-old Ipiros silver belts ($375), exquisite icons, and beautiful strings of *komboloi* (worry beads). Another popular dealer is **Antiqua** (4 blvd. Amalias) which may have just the article of yore which you are seeking. Please remember that no antiquities or authentic icons may be exported without a valid license. Contact the Archaeological Service, Section of Antique Dealers (13 Polygnotou St.) for all the necessary information. **The National Archeological Museum** (1 Tositza St.) sells copies of ancient works which have no export restrictions. So does the **Benaki Museum** shop.

Art Galleries: **Nees Morphes, Zoumboulakis, Zygos, Ora, Hellenic American Union,** and the **British Council Library** are all worth perusal. Please check with your hotel concierge about the exhibitions and the opening hours.

Baby Clothes: The word "enchanting" best describes what we saw at **Bambino** (Ermou St.), **B.B.** (Kanari St.), and **Fantastia** (15 Hermes St.)

Books: **Eleftheroudakis** (Nikis St.) and **Pandelides** (11 Amerikis St.) have mouth-watering supplies of U.S. and British originals, reprints, technical tomes, and the like. Perfect for browsers. **Les Amis du Livre** (9 Valaoritou St.) will be of interest to collectors of rare books, engravings, and maps of Greece; open Mon.–Sat., 9:30 a.m.–3 p.m.

Candy: **Aristocratiko** (Voukourestiou St. and Intercontinental Hotel) is where locals go to satisfy their sweet tooth; chocolate, Turkish delight—a dentist's dreamland!

Department Stores: **The Minion** (Patissia St.) and **Lambropoulos Bros.** (Aeolou and Stadium Sts.) are the national pacesetters. Unfortunately, in our opinion, they don't begin to compare to their counterparts in the rest of Europe.

Flea Market: **Pandrossou** St. is the start of its Athens equivalent (known as **Monastiraki**)—grand fun for the shophound. It seethes Mon.–Fri. from 8 a.m.–1:30 p.m., resuming from 5–8 p.m. and on weekends from 8 a.m.–2 p.m. You'll find bulky knits, copper and brassware, embroidery, sandals, bags, woven articles, jewelry, everything but the kitchen stove—well, maybe that, too at the Plateia Avissinias section. When you've finished exploring this bylane, cross the artery at its end and ramble up its extension named Ifestou St. Good hunting but tough bargaining.

Furs: **Dora Furs** (31–33 Voulis St., Tel: 3232727 and 3249104) is not just a *find*—it's a gold-plated pricebuster for anyone who has surveyed these fashions in the U.S. Due to the dramatically lower labor costs in Greece, a mink that might sell for $14,000 in New York can be found at Dora's for between $5000 and $6500. Still, no expenditure is worthwhile unless the quality is top-grade. Hence, Dora usually stitches between 50 and 55 Emba females together for a major full-length garment and employs the latest colors such as luxuriant Azurine, pale Apollo, or dazzling Autumn Haze—a choice of about a dozen hues in mink alone! Other eye-poppers include jackets, smartly tailored car coats in leather and Persian lamb (roughly $2000), and fabulously chic reversible rainwear (close to $850) with lynx, lamb, beaver, Swakara, or whatever pelts you select. Classic stylings, fun furs, and a bedizening variety of vibrant innovative combinations contribute to the amazing versatility of her inventory. The shop itself is fresh and attractive; moreover, it is conveniently located in the midtown shopping district, within walking distance of the major hotels surrounding Constitution Square.

Greek Fashions: **Yannis Travassaros** has showrooms in the Athens Hilton featuring a range of stunning Greek styles (some with old embroidery), raw silks, vivid handworked peasant blouses, costume jewelry in ceramics with brass inserts, and a few antique silver pieces. There's inexpensive folkwear at a shop in the Plaka at 107 Odos Adrianou. **Nikos and Takis** (10 Panepistimiou St. and branches in *Rhodes, Corfu,* and *Delphi*) interprets the latest trends from France and Italy for the home market. **Polatof** (Voukourestiou 25 and Pindarou 26) is, by local standards, the hottest talent around. **Tseklenis** (Haritos, off Kolonaki Sq.) follows suit. **Contessina** (Voukourestiou St. at Venizelou Ave.), popular among local circles, is unquestionably sound—but much of its merchandise is imported. This is the case with the multitude of new boutiques that have sprung up recently, especially in the Kolonaki area. An international chic is now in evidence. **Tsantilis** (23–25 Ermou St. and 4 Stadiou St.) sells yard goods as well as clothing and accessories with moderate price tags. There are numerous men's shops along Akadimias St.

Greek Gold Jewelry: Two exponents have captured the world market and the imagination of women who prize this distinctive medium. **Zolotas** (10 Panepistimiou St.) retains exclusive Greek rights to Hellenic reproductions found in the finest museums. Both classical Greek and Byzantine creations abound. **Lalaounis** (6 Panepistimiou St.), a neighbor and relative, is another titan in this competitive field.

For delightfully unusual regional-style rings and other jewelry, you might try **Voulgaridis** (6 Voukourestiou St., directly behind the Grande Bretagne). We like this one a lot.

Sterling Creations: The **4 Lamda** (Tower of Athens) is another showcase for Greek themes in jewelry, this time less costly and combined with crystal, plastic, and semi-precious stones.

Handicrafts, Souvenirs, Needlepoint, Paintings: **Attalos** (3 Stadiou St.) is the *only* midcity collection worth drawing your attention or your drachmas. It has the tops in these specialized arts. You might also like to browse through the permanent exhibition of **Greek Folk Art and Handicrafts** (9 Mitropoleos St.).

Pandora, in the courtyard directly behind the Athenee Palace, is a small enterprise where unusual gifts may be found.

The National Welfare Fund (24a Voukourestiou St. plus Boutique in Hilton) offers additional lovely handicrafts—needlepoint, woven or Persian rugs, pillowcases, cocktail guest towels, beads, necklaces, and other selected items. Worth a stop. Again, when it comes to embroidery you might find what you're looking for at **Erghohiro** (Voulis St. 18).

Jewelry (Unique Creations):   **Petradi** (Voukourestious 20), though a shop in Athen's finest commercial district, is more like a petit and exquisite museum—the perfect showcase for the bold and lovely personalized art of Kate Tasedakis. If you are island-bound for Mykonos, visit her branch in the Matoyannia area, a pedestrian lane near the well-known Pierro's Bar.

Luggage storage: **Pacific Ltd.** (24 Nikis St. near Syntagma Sq.) is truly a god-send—Greek style, of course. If you've done a lot of shopping and put your purchases into suitcases that you don't want to be burdened with while island hopping, these people will care for your excess baggage on a daily (Drs 100 per piece), weekly (Drs 350 per piece) or monthly (Drs 1000 per piece) basis.

Music: **Music Box** (2 Nikis St. and 52 Panepistimiou St.) will have you dancing like Zorba. Inexpensive cassettes (around $3.50 of *bouzouki, sirtaki,* and other traditional rhythms.

Pistachio Nuts: If you have a weakness for this delicacy, street vendors proliferate like the seeds themselves at harvest time; fresh or roasted, in little sacks, they make wonderful and packable gifts for friends. The cost is considerably less than what you have to pay at home.

Raw Silk: Although **Argalios Brailas** (7 Filellinon St.) makes up dresses, slacks, and other garments, the styles are not exciting, in our opinions. We'd prefer to buy this unusual fabric—rougher and of a heavier texture than we've seen in other lands—by the meter.

Rugs: **Karamichos-Mazarakis** (31–33 Voulis St., near Constitution Sq., with one branch on the harbor road on the beautiful island of *Mykonos* and a second branch in the lobby of the Apollo Palace Hotel in Athens, currently used by U.S. Forces as their Officers' and N.C.O. Clubs) is by far the best supplier of superior quality traditional Greek carpets including the world-famous Karamichos handwoven *flokati,* the creation of which has been a Karamichos family tradition for at least 400 years—probably 1000! These gorgeous, fluffy, 100% virgin wool *flokati* rugs have adorned the homes of people from every walk of life the world over who have recognized the value of craftsmanship, quality of materials, and love put into every one produced. The extra thick ''Anniversary Flokati'' are the Rolls-Royces of the art. Chris Karamichos is so justly proud of their creations that, as far as we have learned, here is the sole dealer in the land who actually gives a money-back guarantee to last a lifetime. (The ones in our home have given daily service only for about two decades, but they look better today than when we bought them. Bred in water, literally, they have improved with both washing and wear.) Karamichos Flokati was also the sole representative selected by the Greek government to exhibit officially at the Olympic Games and at various national exhibitions around the globe. Now Karamichos-Mazarakis have expanded their line to include a wide range of unique handcrafted Greek carpets such as kilims, minoan, fur, and rag rugs. All of these carry the K-M label of quality and durability. You can hardly be expected to carry one of these in your luggage (although we have) so there is an excellent facility for mailing and for reordering once you have seen how they complement your home. On *Mykonos,* at their store on Harbor Rd., you'll find the same terrific inventory and a friendly staff. If miracles could happen, Karamichos-Mazarakis would be the only place we know where you could buy a magic carpet. Just plain wonderful!

Shoes: Thanks to the Italian-induced know-how and flair for fashion, the footwear industry is flourishing here in Greece. If you find them comfortable, then you can be shod stylishly and inexpensively. Some of the better shops along Ermou St. are **Bournazou, Petrides,** and **Mouschoutis,** and on Stadiou St. there's **Perla** and **Mouriades.**

Sports Apparel: Our best find was **Voulgaridis** (Voukourestiou St. 6, behind the Hotel Grande Bretagne). Excellent selection of straw-soled lounging shoes, men's shorts, and caps. No slacks or shirts, however.

NOTE · · · Avoid local items such as ready-made dresses or suits (inferior quality) and all imported merchandise except books, regardless of classification. (Taxes and Customs duties add 200%

extra to all foreign-made cosmetics, as an extreme example. However, a recent survey conducted by an arm of the Consumers Union came up with the startling fact that perfume purchased at the duty-free shop of Athens Airport was the cheapest in Europe—beating out Amsterdam and Brussels. So, if you're heading that way come armed with input as to the prices of your favorite scents back home for some comparisons.) The regiments of "soovineer joints" that now brassily overcrowd the center of the city are a waste of time—and money.

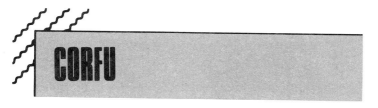

CORFU

Four compelling choices—all of them in the capital—are handicrafts, handpainted dresses, ethnic and Byzantine silver, and Greek music (tapes mostly). Otherwise the island is quaking from souveniritis.

Handicrafts: **The National Welfare Organization** (8 Kapodistriou St.) is another link in this fine chain where quality predominates.

Handpainted Dresses: **Aris** (74 Nikiforou Theotoki St.) is explosive with rainbows, novelties and ultra-bright ideas for summerwear. The prices are unbelievably low. You can hand- or-machine wash everything. A bonanza.

Jewelry: **Spilia Oro** (Nik. Theotoki 119) draws disciples from all over Europe for his silver and gold. The shop is in the Old

Town. Be sure to ask for Proprietor Lakis Manolitsas. **Costas Marollas** (Evieniou Voulgareos 61) is the silver king, especially for fine antique pieces. It is here that you can find the rare *prosfora,* a special jam vase with 6 or 16 attached spoons used to demonstrate the ultimate in hospitality.

Music: **Irene Kefalinos Music House** (a few doors from Aris in the arcades) offers a vast choice of tapes, so overwhelming that you probably should ask Nasos to guide you in your selections.

MYKONOS

Since shops are scattered everywhere along the winding pedestrian lanes of Mykonos town, part of the island spell is to thread among the narrow alleys and look into doorways of whitewashed houses, many of which serve double duty as both boutique and dwelling.

Ceramics: **Kouros** (N. Polykandrioti St. and Matoyanni St.) couldn't be more on-target for inexpensive souvenirs and copies of icons.

Handweaving: **Panos** (Matoyanni St.) boasts memorable designs based on his own mother's traditional work. Their looms produce a soft material or subtle tones that is then made up into table mats, bags, shawls, ponchos, bedcovers, and cushions. Open April to end-Oct. from 10:30 a.m.–2 p.m. and 6–10 p.m. Joan

Kousathanas, the owner's American wife, is usually available to help with your purchases. It is, without a doubt, the finest shop of its type on the island.

Jewelry: **Lalaounis** (see "Athens") has a branch here at 14 N. Polykandrioti St. run by Mr. and Mrs. Stamoulis. **Petradi** (see "Athens") can be found doing its unique thing near Pierro's Bar in Matoyanni St.

Photographs: **The Little Venice Gallery** is dedicated to the sensitive camerawork of owner Bo Patrick, who spends his time capturing the endless beauty of Mykonos. He snaps about 50 new pictures every year and sells them from postcard size ($2) to large copies appropriate for framing ($100–600). Open evenings only.

Rugs: **Karamichos-Mazarakis** (see "Athens") is located at Harbour Rd., and their *flokati* are tops if not legendary.

SANTORINI

There's really only one center for shopping and that's Santorini village itself, which sprawls over the cap of the cliff and ambles with the staircase down to the lighter landing at the base of the mountain.

Antiques: **Athanasios Papatheodorou** is a short stroll from the Atlantis Hotel. The collection is varied—from authentic ikons (costly) to decorative architectural finials called *akrokeramo* (very inexpensive) which make unique gifts.

Carpets: **E. Youkas** is on Step 566 just below a colony of charming terrace restaurants which edge toward the sea. He also carries wall coverings and pillow covers; everything is hand-loomed; low price tags.

Clothing: **Robos,** also on the Steps, stitches together summerwear mostly: floppy shirts, handwoven dresses, vests, and even bedspreads (if you're extra-large). **Aris** is a high-fashion palace by comparison, doing handpainted dresses in zesty colors.

Jewelry: **Greco Gold** in midvillage seems to have the best reputation in a commodity which should always provoke caution in tourist centers. Yanis and Stefanos Keramidas know the business well, carry a varied selection of quality goldsmithery, and are cordial in dealing with visitors.

There are literally scores of souvenir and junk shops pretending to be up-market emporia. We've been through most of them and the above appear to be the most reliable, with the fairest prices.

SHOPPING HOURS

In Dublin, generally 9 a.m.–5:30 p.m., Mon.–Sat. In most other parts of the country, 1 p.m. closings are made on Wed. or Thurs.

PUBLIC HOLIDAYS

New Year's Day, Mar. 17 (St. Patrick's Day), Good Fri. (not official but generally observed), Easter Mon., June Bank Holiday (first Mon. in June), Aug. Bank Holiday (first Mon. in Aug.), Oct. Bank Holiday (last Mon. in Oct.), Dec. 25–26.

MAIL ORDERS

After centuries of a bucolic commercial culture deeply rooted in cottage-produced commodities, hundreds upon hundreds of modern, airy factories and other fabricators have sprung up as vibrantly as shamrocks. With this, of course, merchandising techniques took a giant leap forward. The following stores are typical of the larger retail establishments which are sophisticated in the processing of international shipments and mail-order inquiries.

Postal transactions automatically yield substantial savings to you through total escape from the pestiferous Value Added Tax (V.A.T.) outlined directly below.

Kevin & Howlin Ltd, with the choicest stocks of hand-woven tweed suitings and other wearables in the nation, will dispatch samples to you which will make their closest match to your requirements. **House of Ireland** offers almost the entire nation between leaves; they are preparing a brand-new catalog, too. The great bookbinding authority, **John F. Newman and Son Ltd.,** welcomes queries from all over the globe. The forwarding services of the **Switzer** department store does a landslide business. **Heraldic Artists Ltd.** answers all queries for blazonry. Finally, the **Shannon Airport** complex prints and distributes a hefty and excellent catalog. You may obtain it by sending $2 to Michael O'Gorman, General Manager, Shannon Mail Order, Shannon Airport.

VALUE ADDED TAX

A number of countries charge a Value Added Tax. Although the principle is basically the same, sometimes it has a different name. The version in Ireland requires that you pay 10% on clothing and 25% extra on all other purchases *if used within its borders*. To avoid this levy, instruct the merchant either to (1) arrange delivery to your departing aircraft or ship, or (2) forward the goods unaccompanied straight to your home. For mail-order customers, of course, no VAT problem exists.

DUBLIN

THINGS TO BUY

Donegal tweeds, Waterford glass, antique silver, lace, linen, riding, hunting, and fishing equipment, haute couture, your coat of arms, men's accessories, Aran Islands fishermen's sweaters, Belleek ware and Connemara marble products.

SHOPPING AREAS

Grafton St., Nassau St., Kildare St., and Dawson St., are more up-market hubs. Henry St., Mary St., Talbot St., and South Great George's St. are less costly addresses. All major hotels also feature boutiques or arcades for ardent browsers; Jury's would be our first choice, followed by the Burlington and Berkley Court hotels.

Antiques and Bric-a-Brac: **Butler** (14 Bachelor's Walk) and **Naylor** (Liffey St) are tempters. Should luck with these be poor, roam at random along Bachelor's Walk and Ormond Quay. Other possibilities include **R. McDonnell** (16 Kildare St.), **Dillon Antiques** (27 South Anne St.), **Mitchell's** (40 Clarendon St.), **Saskia Antiques** (43 South William St.), and **T. J. Mitchell and Malcolm Alexander** (Lr. Pembroke St.), **Orkens** (33B Mill St.) is in the old part of the city and you'll need a taxi. A stroll along the North Quays starting at O'Connell St. Bridge or Francis St., again in the old part of town, might turn up a treasure or two.

Aran Islands Handicrafts: **Cleo Ltd.** (18 Kildare St.) in its below-street, premises, has a surprisingly large and interesting collection of this woolen specialty.

Art Reproductions: The **National Gallery** (Merrion Sq.) provides framed prints in a range from $20 to $60.

Blackthorn Walking Sticks, Spectator Stick-Seats, Umbrellas: **H. Johnston Ltd.** (11 Wicklow St.) is the traditional pacesetter (sitter?).

Bookbinder: **John F. Newman and Son Ltd.,** at its very difficult-to-find headquarters in Belvedere Court, is a joy for the aficionado. Much time is devoted to the preparation of Governmental gifts and invitations. These craftsmen work on valuable first editions, special presentation books, old manuscripts, and other *rara avises.* The bindings range from nigers, moroccos, calfs, and vellums to gold-leaf, handmade papers for specially selected endpapers. Most operations take about one month and mail orders are welcomed. A find!

Bookshop: **Eason & Son Ltd.** (40–41 Lower O'Connell St.) is a haven for browsing and buying. It has 3 floors of books, stationery, records, maps, dictionaries, and similar supplies. **Fred Hanna Ltd.** (27/29 Nassau St.) is strong on Irish ethnic themes.

Crafts: **The Kilkenny Design Workshops,** underwritten by the government (Setanta Centre near Nassau St.), is far and away the leader in presenting the best of Irish workmanship and design: Graphics, Simon Pearce's lovely hand-blown glass, bedspreads, ceramics, leather, Luma rugs, pipes, home boutique, toys, candles, and much more. Its namesake headquarters is opposite the gates of Kilkenny Castle. Upstairs is the Kilkenny Kitchen cafeteria and tearoom. This attractive purveyor fulfills a need in the capital. **Powerscourt Town House Centre** (South William St., off Grafton St.), is a lively complex filled with shops, restaurants, boutiques, and antiquaries. Its Georgian precincts date back to 1774. At **IDA Enterprise Center** (Pearse St.) craftsmen busily ply their trades in full view of the public.

Fergus O'Farrel has attractive premises at 60 Dawson St. Everything on display has been formed, molded, printed, or painted by this shop's 25 artisans, who work in a 10-thousand-square-foot private factory 16 miles from Dublin (visitors welcome). Ask for Mrs. O'Farrell herself. Far, far superior to the usual.

Department Stores: Historic **Switzer & Co. Lt.** (Grafton St.), with over 70 shops on 5 floors, is one of the liveliest and savingest anywhere abroad. Good merchandise galore, in a refreshingly sensible approach.

If you can't find what you're after here, try **Brown Thomas & Co.** almost directly opposite, which is also excellent and evokes a tone of rich Irish elegance.

Duty Free Shop: **Dublin Airport** has one. Shannon (see later) used to siphon off most of the last-minute buying, but now that the Dublin springboard is useful to international travelers it is attracting more attention.

Equestrian Needs: **The Stirrup** (60 Dawson St.) is a small but chic specialist which should please even the most avid devotee. Managing Director Mrs. Claire Hickey will tend to your needs.

Handwoven, Hand-Knit, or Hand-Fashioned Wearables:
The **Dublin Woollen Co. Ltd.** (Halfpenny Bridge) stocks Irish
handcrafts and tweed. Ask for Mr. or Mrs. Noel Roche, who
are also sterling folk. Historical note: Joycean scholars will remember that he was an agent for this firm in Trieste before
W. W. I, although not one of their most successful representa-
tives.

Haute Couture: **Pat Crowley** (14 Duke St.) Here is the hottest Irish designer on the international scene. Her celebrity collection of gifted and beautiful people is almost as stunning as
her two full wardrobes per year: spring-summer and autumn-
winter. And while the shop retains a goodly in-house stock, special orders, naturally, are inevitably the order of any normal day.
If you are housebound, write to Pat (or telephone Dublin 710219)
and ask her when she is coming to the United States. (She makes
frequent missions of mercy to socialites on this side of the Atlantic as needs require.)

   Thomas Wolfangel (99 Lower Baggot Street) offers chic
designs and well-cut day suits, evening suits, coats, dresses and
dresses-and-coats at tariffs well below those of Ib Jorgensen.
Ready-mades from his boutique are about half the price of his
custom-made creations which require 2 fittings within 3 days.
He is expert, gentle, and very eager to satisfy.

Heraldry: **Heraldic Artists Ltd.** (3 Nassau St.) is a hive of
expert scholarship, a welcome change from the cheap-jack operations that have exploited this field so depressingly. Apart from
their obvious dedication to authentic research, they also can produce plaques, scrolls, family histories, and other documenta for
your office, library, or home. Martin O'Beirne is the master of
this hunt; write and ask him about the mail order and other services.

Hunting and Fishing Supplies and Arrangements: **Garnets & Keegan's Ltd.** (31 Parliament St.) are *the* Emerald Isle purveyors and seers. Meet Directors Hanlon and Harris. Great store, enchanting people.

Irish Harps and Bagpipes: **Waltons** (2–5 Frederick St.) beckons sweetly to anyone with music in his or her heart. Within these 4 lovely old red-fronted shops which have rambled into 1, prime harps may be had from $500–$2500, including packing case and shipment to New York (more westerly destinations slightly higher). A good assortment of sheet music and records is also on tap.

Irish Jewelry: **Rionore** (38 Molesworth St.) designs and fashions Emerald Isle gems into rings, brooches, pendants, earrings, and cuff links. They're uncommon, beautiful and impressively unusual.

Irish and International Products: **House of Ireland** (Nassau St. 37/38, alongside Trinity College) brings together the superlatives that this nation creates. Tax-free shopping for both take-away and shipped goods makes the hunt at House of Ireland trouble-free. Whether it's a Waterford decanter, hand-knit Aran sweaters, or Belleek Parian China, a delicate piece of Irish Dresden, or a fine item of Royal Tara China, together with a connoisseur's selection of exquisite luxury goods from Europe—Wedgwood, Spode, Lladro, Swarovski, Anri carvings, Border Fine Arts—all at incredibly low prices. Admire the hand-embroidered linen tablecloths, rich woollen throws from Donegal, Tipperary and Avoca, a fascinating tableau of Collector Dolls depicting the social history of Ireland and the jewelry collection of Claddagh rings and Celtic crosses in sterling and gold. The Fashion Room is a brilliant oasis of color with kilts and co-ordinated knitwear and scarves, cashmere and wool caps, classics in Donegal tweeds, children's kilts and tartan dungarees. Ask for Directors Eileen Galligan or Catherine Cullen.

Jewelry: **Weir** (96–99 Grafton St.) is such a marvelous period piece itself that it deserves a casement display. Even if you don't buy, look into its Old World windows with the antique Irish silver, Tara brooches, Claddagh rings, and traditional arts of the nation's greatest craftsmen. You'll also see the finest in gold, china, glass, binoculars, timepieces, and leather goods. **H. & E. Dander, M. Samuels** and **T. W. Weldor** (all along South Anne St.) have collections of antique silver and jewelry.

Tweeds: These are the best buy in Ireland—in fact, one of the greatest shopping bargains abroad today. Every inch is handloomed, much of it in the country cottages. The varieties of patterns and shades are truly astonishing, each seeming to develop out of the mellow hues of the rugged terrain from which they come—reds of mountain ash, or bramble, grey of peat smoke, and changing casts of the moorlands. The handwoven cloth is rugged, too, but provides a supple comfort and soft tactile sensation that is always friendly to the wearer. Now there is a new lightweight tweed, a meld of wool, cashmere, and mohair which has the flexibility for warmer climates and the body of traditional Irish materials. These, together with the heavier nobbier tweeds, are handwoven in Donegal. The process of weaving, incidentally, in this district is very similar to the way it was done before the building of Donegal Castle—something you must see when you visit the region. You may also have an opportunity to view this pure new wool being worked on wooden handlooms in the snug little houses. **Kevin & Howlin Ltd.** (31 Nassau St.) is the unquestioned leader in tweeds for men. It carries all of the above products and is forever experimenting with new subtleties in the cozy realm of Irish textiles. You'll find a superb and variegated range of jackets in sizes 36 to 52 inclusive. You can figure on paying about $184 for these. Handsome suits and dashing comfort-plus topcoats also are in the Kevin & Howlin cupboard. To Complete your wardrobe for the great outdoors we'd also suggest a matching tweed cap and walking hat at $25 and $38 respectively. These will become familiar chums on drizzly days or when the autumn leaves begin to fall.

NOTE · · · The Irish Tourist Board produces a useful little booklet entitled "Craft Hunter's Pocket Guide." More than 250 craft workshops and 350 shops throughout the country are listed.

SHANNON AREA

Fashions for Ladies and Gentlemen: **Avoca** is _the_ place for serious shoppers in this busy market station. Avoca is in easy walking distance of the famous Bunratty Castle (County Clare) which you'll surely want to visit. Its housed in a two storey thatched building where the focus is on woven tweeds and clothing in the distinctive Avoca colors. Don't bother with any other copyist; prices are honest for every item you'll see.

Shannon Airport Duty Free Shop: This spacious handsomely appointed facility is—as you might expect—extremely popular with world travelers. They have come to know Shannon's eye-popping range of merchandise—both Irish and international. The values are great, too, and there are services galore. Packing and stowing facilities, gift schemes, special mailing ar-

rangements and a Shopper's Help Desk are all designed to provide an added tingle of excitement. Among the superb Irish
products that are Shannon favorites are linen, crystal, Belleek
and Dresden china, exclusive knitwear and Donegal Tweed jackets. Yves St Laurent and Chanel perfumes, Pringle and Alan
Paine cashmeres, Raymond Weil and Citizen watches, Wedgwood and Royal Doulton English china, Spanish Lladro figurines and leathergoods by Gucci and Fendi are only a few of the
world-class names in prestige merchandise that are so affordable
due to the built-in Duty-Free prices. Shannon Mail Order is the
perfect answer for the armchair traveler as well as shopping between journeys. The exclusive catalog ($2) is available to you
by writing to Michael O'Gorman, General Manager, Shannon
Mail Order, Shannon Airport Irland. The same Duty-Free advantage is woven into these prices as well and what an attraction
that makes.

NOTE · · · Watch out for (1) gimcrack souvenirs (Ireland is
flooded with atrociously made mementos at the $2 to $5 level);
and (2) most imported luxuries such as perfume.

ELSEWHERE IN IRELAND

Ireland being such a small country, you probably will have your
own transportation and won't want to miss some of the "hidden
corners" where talented artisans are at work producing some of
the products on display in Dublin and the Shannon area as well
as all over the world.

Handweavers and Irish Crafts: **Avoca** has woven a spell of magic through its worldwide reputation for handmade textiles. A quartet of ateliers and studios appears on the Irish tableau but the nearest to Dublin, set in 11 acres of woodland, is 14 miles away at *Kilmacanoque, Bray (County Wicklow),* on the main Dublin-Wexford pike. You don't have to merely see these luxuriant handweavings to believe them, you must touch and fondle them (or better yet, let them fondle you) in order to sense the cuddling finesse of textures, natural warmth, and subtle vitality. In stark daylight or in the intimacy of evening's tapers, the colors are simultaneously bewitching and flattering. The artisans—you may watch them—employ the same techniques and processes as were applied in the 18th century; hence, your purchase will be a prize that modern machinery could never duplicate. Here you will also discover regional pottery with its highly localized identity, woodwork, leather silk, and even Irish ballads (tapes and discs). Lunch and tea available; open every day year round. If you are in Galway's *Letterfrack* region, don't miss the **Avoca Handweavers** charming cottage set on the shores of Ballinakil Bay, 6 miles north of *Clifden* on the Westport road. It's filled with craft items—some exclusive—plus their own Avocations. Upstairs tearoom for sustenance after browsing; open 7 days a week mid-Mar.—end Oct. The picturesque original mill and craft shop are in the hamlet of *Avoca* (45 miles south of the capital) in the Waterford-Wexford area. Since 1723 in the Valley of Avoca handweavers have been practising their trade. Here you can meet today's skilled workers and watch them at their fly-shuttle looms. Homemade refreshments are available. The good news is that now they've opened an English branch at *Bath* (17 New Bond St.). Don't miss this one either. They're wondrous!

SHOPPING HOURS

Enormous variance, even within each city. In general, *Rome:* 9:30 a.m. (meant to ease rush-hour traffic)–1 p.m., and 4–7:30 or 8 p.m. (summer); Mon. from 3:30–7:30 p.m. only (winter). From June to Sept. stores close Sat. afternoons rather than Mon. mornings. April 21 is a Roman holiday. Some establishments shuttered in Aug. *Florence:* 9 or 9:30 a.m.–1 p.m., and 3:30–7:30 p.m., but in summer 4–8 p.m.; most currently open Sat. mornings (summer), and closed Mon. mornings (winter) and Feast Days (June 24 honors the city's patron saint). *Milan:* 9 or 9:30 a.m.–12:30 p.m., and 3:30–7:30 p.m. (winter); 9 a.m.–1 p.m., and 4–8 p.m. (summer); closed Mon. mornings all year-round, too. Many take a break for part or all of Aug. Dec. 7 is their patron saint's veneration day. *Venice:* In summer, 9 a.m.–1 p.m., and 3–7 p.m. or 9 a.m.–6:30 or 7:30 p.m. (without the noon closing), both including Sat.; many shops also open on Sun. from 9 or 9:30 a.m.–12:30 or 1 p.m. and 4–7 p.m.; and keep functioning all day Mon. too; in winter, most often 9 a.m.–1 p.m. and 3:30 p.m.–7:30 p.m.; closed all day Sun. and Mon. mornings. In any case it's best to check with your hotel concierge. Nov. 21 is the Festa della Salute, a very local holiday that commemorates the city escaping the plague. Only a few diehards stay open. In addition, the merchants here often go on holiday after Christmas.

PUBLIC HOLIDAYS

Jan. 1, Easter Sun., Easter Mon., April 25 (Liberation Day), May 1, Aug. 15, Nov. 1, Dec. 8, Dec. 25–26.

VAT REBATE

There's a 19% levy, but few people attempt to get it back because the process can be more trouble than it's worth—in this country, at least. The system is so informal that information varies as to the minimum purchase that must be made—anywhere from 525,000 lire to 650,000 lire *per item*—to be eligible for a refund. In any case, after the paperwork is done you might receive 15¼% if you've had the stamina to persevere. Nevertheless, *always* inquire.

MAIL ORDERS

Because of casual attitudes in some quarters of Italy, it's best not to initiate ANY transaction by post with ANY merchant save for those who, with their addresses, follow in these pages or any of the legions of others whom you KNOW take pride in their traditions of impeccability. Should you seek information from the sharpies—some of which have deceptively large and convincing fronts—you'd probably get a s-m-o-o-t-h reply which would promise you the moon at cut-rate prices. But once they have your money, the scenario normally ends with (1) a blank wall of silence forevermore or (2) receipt of a shoddy, sleezy, nonreturnable article which bears little or no relation to your much more expensive original order. Over nearly four decades, several hundred victims of fly-by-night shops *not* known to or recommended by our guide books have implored our intercession in attempting recoveries from these swindlers. Sadly, we could offer only sympathy; we were and are completely helpless in all such cases. So are the local American Chambers of Commerce, the local American Clubs, and, most discouragingly, the diplomatic officialdom of our United States Embassy and Consulates. Hence, if you're gulled, you're gulled without hope. There is absolutely no means of redress.

The plea: As amplified at the end of this chapter, the Italian postal system is so disastrously chaotic that it is the worst in the Western World—perennially a disgrace. Add to this the immense backlogs piled up at the Italian *and* North American customs' dock facilities and you'll realize that usually the deliveries of your purchases are subject to long (sometimes horrendous) delays. None of this is the fault of any of these dependable purveyors. First be CERTAIN that everything is insured at full value. Then exercise your patience for weeks or even months—and don't worry. At least 19 times out of 20, they will eventually show up in perfect condition.

Although all of the carefully selected houses covered now have tons of experience in international and intercontinental shipping, almost none of them offers catalogs or brochures. Sometimes the natures of their commerce rule out viable possibilities for these.

Catelo d'Auria in Rome will be happy to send you a color brochure of a selection of their gloves along with a price list. **Armando Poggi** has no catalogs for the vast stocks of china, crystal, and silver that fill this Florentine treasure house, but welcomes and willingly expedites all postal requests. From the forests upon forests of exquisite Venetian glassware so lovingly designed and produced by the **Pauly** and the **Salviati** artisans; both companies have on file hundreds of thousands of sketches of individually created patterns. Nonetheless *each of the above*

handles inquiries which are narrowed down to specific terms—
so please don't hesitate to contact them.

A. Garguilo Jannuzzi in Sorrento (86 different types of inlaid masterworks in furniture and accessories) will send their literature without charge.

For more than a half-century famed **Nardi** has been the undisputed global center for superbly traditional Venetian-style jewelry in gold and precious stones and will also cooperate on your individual queries. **The Artistic Venetian Handicrafts "Veneziartigiana" Consortium** does have a catalog and a flourishing mail order arm. **Jesurum's** enchanting baby linen is also yours for the asking by perusing their publication.

NOTE · · · Every major tourist center in the nation is now plagued by armies of "steerers." If any well-dressed, charming, suave man or woman of *any* nationality (some even pose as Americans!) strikes up a conversation with you on the street, in a cafe, or elsewhere—and then smoothly suggests that you accompany them while they pick up a purchase, be measured for a fitting, or similar dodge—BE ON YOUR GUARD IMMEDIATELY. There is at least a 98% chance that, in gambling or carnival argot, they are "shills" whose game is to sucker innocent travelers into dishonest establishments which give them a commission on everything that their victims can be high-pressured into buying. One common ploy is to introduce themselves as a "Count," a "Countess," or a similarly phony title. Their fields of operation cover virtually every type of merchandise favored by outlanders. If you fall for their honeyed pitch, 50 gets you 1 that you'll be sorry.

▪ Be careful when you buy tortoiseshell objects. There is a clever plastic imitation in many supposedly reputable shops. The test is this: When held up to the light, portions of the plastic are nearly transparent, while the genuine article is always uniformly opaque. Neither material burns, although unscrupulous merchants will tell you that plastic *is* inflammable—and then apply a match to "prove" that you're getting the real McCoy. (Important reminder: Most tortoiseshell is made from either the hawksbill turtle or the green sea turtle. Hawksbill turtle products may not be imported into the U.S., and green sea turtle products are prohibited by several states, including New York and California.)

ROME

SHOPPING AREAS

The **Piazza di Spagna** and all the streets off of it such as **Via Condotti, Via della Croce, Via Bocca di Leone, Via Frattina, Via del Babuino, Via Due Macelli** and **Via Borgognona.** The last has now been transformed into the most aristocratic pedestrian mall in the city. Motor traffic is suspended. At intervals along its center are huge wooden tubs bursting with flowers and it bristles with colorful umbrellas. While the price tags in the chic boutiques and other stores which line each of its sides climb to rarefied levels, just plain window shopping can be a treasure hunt. Here's a delightful departure from the mad hurly-burly of the Piazza di Spagna, only a block away. At the top of the Spanish Steps the **Via Sistina; Via del Corso** (running from Piazza del Popolo to Piazza Venezia); **Via Veneto** and the many streets that criss-cross it on either side; **Via Barberini, Via Bissolati; Via Cola di Rienzo,** which runs from the Vatican to Piazza del

Populo, is relatively so little known to foreigners that its tariffs are often appreciably less and some of its purveyors are very good. Also for good hunting at lower prices, a leisurely stroll along **Via Nazionale** might yield dividends. The **Campo dei Fiori,** near the Piazza Navona, is a colorful open-air food market that teems with the activity of housewives Mon.–Sat. from 9:30 a.m.

NOTE · · · The center of Rome has been barred to traffic Mon.–Sat. from 7–10 a.m. and 3–7 p.m. on an experimental basis. This was instigated in order to reduce the horrific pollution. Shopkeepers squawk, but environmentalists applaud.

THINGS TO BUY

Silk, men's and women's wear, gloves, knitwear, leather, jewelry, furniture, silver, glassware, art and other treasures for the home, religious items, sunglasses, cameos, textiles, wrought iron, toys, antiques, antique jewelry, *haute couture*—then more silk.

Antiques: Be cautious! You'll find no recommendation in this text of any individual antique vendors in Rome. **The Flea Market** (Mercato di Porta Portese), stretching ¾th of a mile along the banks of the Tiber, is the biggest open-air trading center of merchandise in the Western world. More than 800 hucksters display their wares on tables, counters, stalls, boxes, wagons, blankets, carpets, and spread-out newspapers. It is patronized by an estimated 100,000 people from its opening at sunrise to its closing at 1 p.m. As famed Author-Correspondent Nino Lo Bello, an old friend who has long been a resident of the capital, has put it, ''In Rome it is wisely said that anything stolen during the week is bound to turn up Sunday (the only day it is open) in the ocean of bric-a-brac. . . . You can buy anything and everything here, (including) a zillion weatherbeaten items the exact purpose of which sometimes defies guesswork. . . . You must learn first the price the sharpie shopkeeper asks and second the price he will sell for. To purchase anything you must engage in a seesaw contest, which is invariably synchronized with facial movements, shoulder undulations, arm and hand motions, stagey protestations and frequent appeals to God, the saints and your mother—not necessarily in that order." Right on! Thank you, Nino, for this irresistible quotation. (The adjoining ½-mile strip of automotive parts might sell you YOUR missing hubcaps, because most of its articles have also been plundered.) If you absolutely *must* see it, go very, very early, as the dealers do—and don't buy any "genuine Etruscan" articles, because they're fakes. Via Giulia, Via Margutta, Via del Babuino and Via dei Coronari are good streets for general browsing; there's a twice yearly *Settimana dell'Antiquariato;* Piazza Fontanella Borghese also offers jewelry; the same plea for caution applies to all. So watch out for counterfeits, *always* haggle and, if you can, always take along an Italian friend to protect your interests.

Books: **The Lion Bookshop** (Via del Babunio 181) has large stocks of reading matter in English. Look for the Lion Rampant outside; then go through the door and search hard for the showroom. Or try the **Anglo-American Book Company** (Via delle Vite 57), which is also versatile. **Economy Book and Video Center** (Via Torino 136) specializes in paperbacks, and will even purchase your used ones. If it's the limited edition art books with the Franco Maria Ricci stamp you're after go to the **FMR** library (Via Borgognona 4/D).

Boutiques: Dozens upon dozens.
      La Mendola (Piazza Trinita dei Monte 15) has long been one of the fashion titans of Rome, located at the top of the Spanish Steps—highest of the high-style districts in the Eternal City.

Administration today is by **Albertina** (Via Lazio 20), known globally for her knitwear creations. (Some of the latter appear as part of a permanent collection in New York's Metropolitan Museum of Art.) Hence, La Mendola augments its beautiful silks, and elegant day and evening wear with the exclusive knits, suits, dresses, coats, and even embroidered specialties of the Albertina wardrobe. Incidentally, there is a weekly fashion show at the nearby Hassler Hotel Roof Restaurant. Closed Mon. mornings but normal hours are from 10 a.m. to 1:30 p.m. and 3:30 p.m. to 7:30 p..m. Anyone who has an eye for quality will immediately appreciate the distinction of hand-loomed and hand-finished garments. The courteous staff are bi-lingual and are willing to handle air mail postage service for you or transport by Federal Express—that is if you can resist not wearing your selections immediately.

Miranda (Via della Carozze 22b), which draws a discerning type of our roving country-women, comes up with coats, suits, and dresses in interesting hand-woven materials. The pendulum starts at about $175 and climbs upward. Also good. The previously mentioned **Brioni Boutique** (Via Barberini 75-77) has long been one of our compulsory drop-in stops. **Elizabeth** (Via Veneto 128) offers an appealing versatile stock. **Blanka & Berta** (Via Sistina 76) carries very smart suits, blouses, printed velvet skirts, lots of silks for spring and summer, stylish sweaters, and handsome accessories. **Borgognona 22** (that's also the address) has exceptionally chic models at exceptionally high prices. So does **Beltrami** (Via Condotti 19). **Beatrice** (Via Francesco Crispi 80) is a fashionable magnet for both custom-mades and ready-to-wears.

NOTE · · · Don't waste your time visiting an operation called Il Discount dell'Alta Moda (Via di Gesu e Maria 16 A). In my opinion it's grim and of dubious value.

Cameos, Coral, and Related Items: **Giovanni Apa Co.,** (Piazza Navona 26-27 and another branch on the Tiburtina Road to Tivoli) once recommended, is no longer considered reliable by us.

Children's Clothes: Try **La Cicogna** (a chain called ''The Stork,'' Via Frattina) or **Casa dei Bambini** (Via della Maddalena 27); **Benetton 0–12** (Via Frattina 44–45) paints a color palette of trendy togs for youngers; **Lavori Artigianili Femminili** (Via Capo le Case 6) has the most enchanting handmade, dainty garments. Their layette sets and baptismal robes are exquisite.

Department Stores: **La Rinascente** (Via del Corso at Piazza Colonna and Piazza Fiume) is the leader. **Coin** (Piazzale Appio), **Standa** (branches all over the city), and **Upim** (Piazza S. Maria Maggiore and others) follow. None is really special. It's far more amusing to do your buying in individual shops.

Duty-Free Shop: Rome's airport sells only tobacco, spirits, and wine tax-free to international passengers.

Florist: We happen to like **Italflora.** Two addresses: Via Lombardia 21 and 59/61 Via Emilia.

Glass: We strongly recommend that you wait until you get to *Venice* to do your buying at either Pauly or Salviati, but if your itinerary doesn't include a stop there then **Vetreria Murano Veneto** (Via Marche 13) might satisfy your cravings.

Gloves: We've long believed that the small, old-line specialist called **Catello d'Auria** (Via Due Macelli 55) does the best job on the Italian Peninsula. It's about 2 blocks from the foot of the Spanish Steps near the American Express office and facing the

"Salone Margherita" theater—and be sure to double-check the name over the door, because confusion with several inferior shops in the vicinity would be easy. All that the d'Auria family has cared about since 1894 is making finer gloves than any other craftsmen. In the same ambiance of comfort and courtesy as when the shop opened at the end of last century, you will be able to find a variety of the best possible leathers (kid, doeskin and wild boar); wrist-length, 4-inch, 6-inch or 8-inch long elegant models either unlined or lined in silk, cashmere, pure wool, fur, or sheepskin. There are even 16- to 18-button kid gloves for debutantes which, on request, can be made up in sky-blue, pink, or beige; marvelous sport gloves for both genders and extra warm gloves for cold climates—you will find practically anything you could wish for, and what is more at very fair prices.

Haute Couture and Deluxe Ready-to-Wear Designers and Labels: Valentino (with 200 employees and a reported annual turnover of $120 million overall, is Italy's most important; branch in Paris), Fontana, Mila Schon, Princess Irene Galitzine, Lancetti, Riva, Fausto Sarli, Rocco Barocco, Tiziani, Versace, Missoni, Mariuccia Mandelli who is the genius behind Krizia, Biagiotti, Ferre, Armani, and Abini have the most exalted reputations; Capucci, Olivier successor to Andre Laug, Soprani (Basile is an off-shoot of this talent), and Balestra are names to be reckoned with. Both the Genny line and Mario Valentino's leatherwear are created by Versace. Complice and Byblos are in great demand, too. Emilio Pucci is now being rivaled.

Home Furnishings: Italians are leading style setters in this genre. Ample evidence of their imagination and versatility can be found at **Valentino-piu** (Via Condotti 13), **Richard-Ginori** (nationwide, with branches at Via Condotti 88, Via Cola di Rienzo 223, and other locations in the capital), and **Fornari** (Via Frattina 71). This trio is very, very fine—but very, *very* expensive.

Taitu (Via Sistina 94) features the imaginative dinnerware of designer Emilio Bergamin. It makes great table talk; high-tech geometric patterns as well as more traditional stylings; lots of gift ideas, too.

If your tastes run to Scandinavian design, have a look at **Bottega Danese** (Via della Scrofa 96) which brings its nordic notions to Latium.

Jewelry and Objets d'Art: **Bulgari** (Via Condotti 10) has established itself as Europe's leading dynasty in this field—known to monarchs for decades and collected by many of the leading families on the globe. Its name and now-familiar logo are symbols of absolute status in discernment. Items of great value are their stock in trade. On the other hand, shoppers of our bracket meet a vast selection of things that are within almost everybody's price range—all in the exquisite Bulgari taste. And here is a curious and interesting fact: The Bulgari styling is so distinctive and the hand-workmanship is so special that each of its creations (even a modest $150 piece) is instantly recognizable—as legibly as an Old Master's signature. The showcases are so lavishly set that they'll make you catch your breath: Unique collections of diamonds, rubies, emeralds, and sapphires are profusely displayed together with superb pearls, in a series of pieces that are unbelievably glorious. Wander at will among the biggest private assemblage of English and continental antique silver in Europe. Take your choice among the very rare old Chinese jades and hard stones, the Renaissance jewelry and 16th-century rock crystals, the fantastically crafted, historic, one-of-a-kind boxes and watches—enough to dizzy even the most experienced connoisseur. And that's always our problem: Whenever we make our frequent tours of these glittering premises, as we stroll, every successive island of beauty, cabinet by cabinet, seems to sit up and beg, ''Look at ME next!'' Such wonders are here that Maestro Sotirio Bulgari, who founded the firm in 1881, would surely thrill at his monument. The great, universally beloved Giorgio Bulgari has died, but his handsome, urbane, carefully trained offspring, Paolo, and Nicola, will greet you with traditional Bulgari warmth, patience, and expertise. There are aristocratic branches in *Milan* on Via della Spiga, in *New York's* Hotel Pierre, in *Geneva's* rue du Rhone, in *Monte Carlo,* and in the Hotel Plaza Athenee in *Paris* in *Tokyo, Osaka, Singapore, Hong Kong* and *London.* Your browsing is welcomed in all establishments, even if it is only to feast your eyes. So have a look—and we envy your dreams.

Lesser Antique Jewelry and Objets d'Art: Manasse (Via Campo Marzio 44), while a large step down from Bulgari, has a very good assortment of antique jewelry, cigarette boxes, opera glasses, and other fine wantables. Gold earrings; prime Russian icons; choice antique silver trays and ewers; more. Authenticity and originality are guaranteed. At **Siragusa** (Via delle Carrozze 64) archeological treasures are incorporated into inspired designs to make priceless finds even more desired and dazzling: 3rd–4th century B.C. coins, beads from Asia Minor, museum-quality artifacts—these are the basic elements. The workmanship that goes into making the pieces is pure artistry. The prices are deservedly high—rings $2000–$15,000, earrings $4000, necklaces up to $50,000. Extraordinry, but then you are wearing history. There are also several interesting antique jewelry dealers along the Via dei Coronari which might be worth your investigation.

Smaller Jewelry Items: Fornari, mentioned above (Via Frattina 71), has a very large selection of stunningly creative articles in gold and silver. Reliable and recommended.

Knitwear: Missoni (Via Borgognona 38/B, just off Piazza di Spagna) is smashingly attractive but costly. It is particularly well

known for its subtle winter colors—pale ochers, lavenders, and
grays among them. **Laura Biagiotti** (Via Vittoria 30) does wonderous things, especially with cashmere. **Trico** (Via delle Carozze) has a fine name in the field, too. **Albertina,** see under
Boutiques—La Mendola,'' (Via Lazio 20) ranks very high in our
estimation.

Leather: **Skin** (Via Due Macelli 87 and Via Capo le Case 41/
44) is one of the zestiest stylemasters on the Italian scene today—a name that is not only fun-for-the-pun, but is also sending
goosepimples over the pelts of some of the nation's biggest designers and prestige producers. Materials are butter-soft, the cuts
are generous and beautifully finished, the dyes are the latest in
hues and the fastest for your security in all weather conditions.
Substantial investments (even in the fickle realm of fashion) should
be backed with a confidence in their durability. These are. And
in comparison with U.S. costs, Skin's skins are a bargain for
top-of-the-line quality. Its both-gender repertoire includes leather
suits, jackets (some with fur trimming), skirts, pants, shoes,
handbags, plus an expert service for custom-making your exact
garment in the precise shade, cut, and style for you. If you want
to be hidebound, then by all means do it in the most modish
fashion—at Skin. For similar items at a lower price, check out
the sister operation called **Renard** (Via Due Macelli 53). There's
yet another Skin-graft on the same street. It's called **XL** and it
caters for young people. There are bomber jackets, skirts and
pants, extensive use of shearling, metal studs and printed leathers and suedes. ''With it'' all the way. Here's a truly innovative
house that is fleshing out in every direction, but especially in the
Via Due Macelli and Via Capo le Case areas. Also on the Via
Due Macelli at **Bizan** (#49/51) the fashion-building Gabizon
brothers have created a showcase for ultra-exclusive leather ready-
to-wear along with stunning silhouettes in silks and woolens.
The accessories to go with this apparel are the keynotes which

make Grand Opera out of Italian design. Here is where that shopper "who has everything" will find a little something extra with the added dash of sophistication and taste that makes Bizan garments conversation pieces in any community.

Gucci (Via Condotti 21) is still very plush. Its 2-floor premises are rich, its stocks are elegant but stratospheric in cost. **Fendi** (Via Borgognona 36A, 36B, 4L) has skyrocketed to fame along with its prices. About 2 dozen different models of suit-cases visibly status-symboled by the house's trademark; selection of ladies' handbags in an assortment of skins; restored and authenticated antique beaded purses (dating back to 1835). **L. Righini** (Via Condotti 76) and **Pier Caranti** (Piazza di Spagna 43-45) are equally inviting. **Bottega Veneta** (Salita San Sebastianello 16) is its own exclusive representative in town for that distinctive woven effect using lether strips. **Mila Taeni** (Via Lazio 8) has tiny premises but it's a powerhouse. This tasteful lady has selected handbags from Laura Biagiotti and Mila Schon's lines, Diego Della Valle shoes, La Matta leather and suede suits and trousers, plus dozens of other chic wardrobe pick-me-ups. **Giuseppi Belmonte** (Via Emilia 36) is definitely worth a look, too. **Maurizio Righini** (Piazza di Spagna 36) is excellent.

Linens and Lingerie: **Cesari** (Via Barberini 1) carries fabrics, but the socko items here are the table linens, the unusual towelings, and glamorous lingerie. Then after we'd started congratulating ourselves upon "discovering" the great allure of the latter, we gulped when the first price tag we picked up read $650! Upstairs you'll find a pleasant but (to us) not outstanding boutique with daytime outfits, sporty evening wear, and poolside garb at far less lethal tariffs.

Pratesi has been creating boudoir magic for decades and whether you order the delicate pastels of long-staple Egyptian cotton sheets which are moderately pricey or go for striped satin and cashmere quilts for just a shade under $10,000, you will know you have slumbered in the best circles possible. Pratesi's Rome address is Piazza di Spagna 10–11 (see also Florence).

Frette (Via del Corso 381 and Via Nazionale 84) will also cosset you in bed and bath and the tariffs aren't as steep either. The people in **Trepiedi** (Piazza Lucina 36) proudly boast that they make bras for Elizabeth Taylor and Sophia Loren. Since they also stock girdles and bathing suits, perhaps these also find their ways into various stars' wardrobes. This place bustles and again you'll have to s-t-r-e-t-c-h your bankroll to buy anything here.

La Perla lingerie is internationally famous. Their styles are sexy and sophisticated and you'll love them. The label is sold all over—for all under.

Men's Silk Suits and Specialties: **Brioni** (Via Barberini 79, Tel: 485.855—TLX 622125 Brioni) has created a unique world of its own—very, very special stylist known globally as the king of masculine fashion. The secret (not at all well kept) is that Brioni makes clothes for people who love fine attire. That means taking advantage of your own physique and giving it a distinction that others will recognize wherever sartorial correctness and flair are appreciated. His clients include noted actors, international personalities, diplomats and tycoons. They have been coming back enthusiastically for years realizing that the Brioni style has become their own best trademark. Available to you at their handsome showroom and tailoring center are creations made to measure in the finest soft-spoken woollens, silks of many textures, luxurious cashmere and fine-grade mohair that is as light as a zephyr. Brioni shirts are created in their own exclusive materials, revealing the state-of-the-art in both design and color. To support all this, the *Italia Style* shoes finish off the image with modish pleasure and supreme comfort. To extend these talents to a wider market internationally, Brioni has expanded to include a ready-to-wear wardrobe that is finished by hand and available to devotees at their exclusive shops in Rome, Costa Smeralda (Sardinia), New York and other important metropoli throughout the U.S., Europe and Japan. At the Rome headquarters, confer with Dr. Ettore Perrone Brioni as well as his friendly staff who include Sergio Vanni and Romeo Civili. The distaff sector comes in for lucky treatment as well. There is a fabulous ladies boutique where the well-dressed woman can find a vast assortment of clothing—either sporty or elegant. Mrs. Gigliola Savini Brioni, daughter of the founding maestro G. S. Brioni, is also available to point out the feminine superlatives; she has her own assistants to augment her careful attentions and kindness. If you want to expand your collection—male *or* female once you are back in the States, the opportunity now exists at Brioni's splendid New York establishment, 55 East 52nd St., at Park Avenue Plaza, Tel: (212) 355–1940.

Angelo (Via Bissolati 34, next to Pan Am) is also magnificent, founded by the talented Angelo Vittucci who became a legend in his own lifetime. With his equally gifted and personable partners, Aldo Uggeri and Carlo Ilari, he timorously opened their spacious and beautiful premises—to be bowled over by instantaneous success. And, with the peerless taste, imagination, and own special magic, how well his successors deserve it! Distinctive handworked suitings in silks, worsteds, tropicals, and others at competitive tariffs; striking sport ensembles; our latest one-of-a-kind dinner coat and trousers with foulard lining. Finished delivery in 3 full working days from one of the last existing workshops with more than 40 skilled craftsmen. Fashionable custom-made shirts; exclusive tie patterns; all other haberdashery imaginable. Mr. Aldo, Mr. Carlo, and their key assistants are bilingual. Second to none in the world.

Cucci, Caraceni, and **Cifonelli** are all master cutters, too—but Brioni and Angelo have U.S.-style savvy.

Elsewhere in this league, *please exercise utmost care*. Move warily among the smaller, less famous, less costly cutters, because they're all too apt to victimize you.

In all custom-made garments, always find time for 3 fittings. A minimum of 2 fittings normally does not work to perfection; YOU would be the one who takes this chance. Never accept 1 fitting with subsequent forwarding to your home, because automatically you would be buying disappointment and grief.

In the realm of ready-to-wear the Versace, Armani, Barbas, La Matta and Zegna lines reign supreme. Their strength is in their difference—textures and fabrics that are seldom seen together on the western side of the Atlantic.

Numismatics: **Soria** (Piazza di Spagna at Via Frattina corner) is world-revered by coin collectors. You can even buy a denarius of the precise vintage as the 30 pieces of silver for which Judas betrayed Jesus Christ. Soria has them all—and scores of other rarities.

Paintings: **Gallerias Schneider** (Robert Schneider) is owned and operated by Americans; **l'Obelisco, Barcaccia,** and **Il Camino** are well known. Don't let yourself be suckered by the fast operators in dozens of lesser galleries. Italy crawls with phony Renaissance "masters" and many an unscrupulous dealer will break his neck in eagerness to "certify" them.

Fantastic Pawnshop: **Monte di Pieta** ("Mountain of Mercy," popularly called "The Mountain," at Piazza Pieta) is the biggest in the world. More than 3000 people per day line up at its estimators' windows to take advantage of the low interest rates charged by this 4-century-old institution; 99% of its pledges are redeemed. Its showrooms are a bonanza of silver tea sets, jewelry, fine watches, and other luxury items jumbled among faded sheets, battered suitcases, toys, and a wild assortment of other objects. Each is tagged with the estimated value and the day it will come up for auction. Poking for bargains here can be amusing.

Perfumes, Cosmetics and Beauty Accessories: **Estivi** (Via Vittorio Emanuele Orlando 92–93) across from the Grand Hotel is the make-up artist who tops them all.

Pipes and Smoking Accessories: **Carmignani** (Via della Colonna Antonia, off the Corso at Piazza Colonna) is the Dunhill of Italy. Here you will find not only their own handmade pipes but those of other famous makers, plus everything related to smoking.

Prints and Drawings: Totally through accident—but with what good fortune!—we stumbled across **Fine Arts G. Panatta** (Via F. Crespi 117). With courtly courtesy they invited us to putter through their print and drawing collections at our own pace. Q.E.D.: We walked out with about a ½-dozen honeys for gifts, all within the limits of their extremely moderate price range. The premises are small, but such a wide variety is on display that we hope that here you might also find some happy memories of Rome. **Alinari Brothers Ltd.,** the well-known Florence specialist, has a branch at Via del Babuino 98.

Religous Articles: **Al Pellegrino Cattolico** (Via di Porta Angelica 83) offers complete stocks for the devout; they'll have your rosaries blessed by the Pope and delivered to your hotel without extra charge. Honest, 100% dependable, and fine; highly recommended.

Shoes: **Raphael** (Piazza di Spagna and Via Veneto) and **Fragiacomo** (Via Condotti 35) are pacesetters. **Tanino Crisci** (Via Condotti) is a classicist. **Ferragamo** (Via Condotti 73–74) has also been forever. **Grilli** (Via del Corso 166) and **Giust** (Via Sistina 79) are somewhat less costly. **Santini e Dominici** (Via Frattina 120) has trendy, off-beat models. For ladies, **Lily of Florence** (see *"Florence"*), at Via Lombardia 38, is the exclusive purveyor of the famous Amalfi line; Mrs. Powers, herself an American, is the warm-hearted Director of the branch. *Salutes!* **Tradate** (Via del Corso) isn't too costly and keeps in step with the times. **Sore** (opposite Trevi Fountain at No. 97) and **Cardinali** (Via di Propaganda Fide, near the Spanish Steps) are not as a la mode but are more popularly priced.

Silks and Piece Goods: **Galtrucco** (Via del Tritone 18/23) has scads of assorted materials. **Lisio** (Via Sistina 120) stocks glorious handwoven velvets, brocades, and damasks, used more for upholstery and curtains. **Polidori** (Via Borgognona and Via Condotti) and **Bises** (Via Fleming 53, Via del Gesu 63 and at "Valentino Piu" Via Condotti 13) are other top firms.

Sporting Goods: **Giusti** (Piazza Trevi) is it. Four floors of equipment and clothing for just about every sport or game imaginable; not much English spoken. **Zucchi & C.** (Via Bissolati 31) is an agent for Beretta armaments. Field and stream are its elements.

Stationer and Gift Items: **Ditta Francesco Pineider** (Via Due Macelli 68 and Via della Scrofa 7/A) has a fine line of the former, and **Taitu** (Via Sistina 94) of the latter. **Papirus** (Via Capo le Case 55a) is a branch of the *Florence* shop Il Papiro (see following section for full description). It's lined with items executed in the *papier a cuve* technique. Its sister shop **Sezione Aurea** (Via Capo le Case 20) has jewelry with the same finish, but in this case it's frozen in plexiglass. Bracelets and earrings from $20, necklaces around $90; most unusual.

Sunglasses: **Ottica Bileci** (Via Due Macelli 83) has one of the largest high-style selections under the—sun! For outright chic Italians have always considered this the final touch of refinement in apparel as well as for comfort.

Sweaters: A flock of inexpensive sweater places are on tiny Via Gambero. Root through here as the locals do.

Ties: **Giofer** (Via Frattina 118) has an endless supply in *crepe de Chine,* wool, silk twill, reps, and jacquard silk. Most cost between $12–$25. **Roxy** (Via Frattina 115 plus other branches here and in *Florence, Milan, Naples, Venice,* and *Bari*) is really running neck and neck with its neighbor; similar in all respects.

Toys: **Al Sogno** (Piazza Navona at the top of the square) is proudest of its deluxe and costly assemblage of stuffed animals. While it offers a run-of-the-factory line for reasonable tariffs, the beguilingly attractive originals run from $60 to $2,000. Wow! **Giocattoli Girotondo** (Via Parigi 7), behind the Grand Hotel, will come to the rescue of doting relatives, too. **E. Guffanti** (Via Due Macelli 59), with its representative international display, is more down to earth. **Porta Pinciana** (Via di Porta Pinciana 6) is literally a doll house where doting elders can discover a wonderland of toy figures ranging from pocketsize to colossal. All of the critters are extraordinarily lovable.

FLORENCE

SHOPPING AREAS

Via Tornabuoni is the Fifth Avenue, **Via Calzaiuoli, Via Strozzi, Via Vigna Nuova,** and **Via Por Santa Maria** are the equivalents of 34th Street, and the Madison Avenues are **Via Porta Rossa, Via Calimala** and **Borgo San Lorenzo. Ponte Vecchio,** the dramatic little shop-lined bridge, is limited to silver and gold jewelry and objects, plus specialty items. Up from there, the **Lungarno Acciaioli** and **Lungarno Corsini** hug the north bank of the river. Lots of browsing along here, too. The **San Lorenzo "Central" Market** and the even more charming **"New" Market** (Porta Rossa and Santa Maria) are also good for casual shopping. The rather poor **Flea Market** (Piazza Ciompi) is likewise open from Mon. through Sat.

NOTE · · · Since your chauffeur or guide will get a 10% rake-off (if you don't) on nearly everything you buy in Florence, *always shop alone, and always demand this gravy discount for yourself.* This does NOT apply in such top-drawer establishments as Lily of Florence and Salvatore Ferragamo (ladies' shoes), Sonya (knitwear), Balatresi (alabaster), John F. (leather), Libreria BM (books), and a few other major places. Always bargain, too, when you buy in quantity.

THINGS TO BUY

Florentine gilt and silver, inexpensive art reproductions, Florentine jewelry, knitwear, ladies' shoes, leather, mosaics, glassware and china, ceramics, embroideries, antiques.

NOTE · · · A knowledgeable source tells us that here the silver standard is different from that of the U.S. and England. "Sterling" is silver 800 while outside of Italy it is silver 925. For the most part only jewelry contains the higher weight. However, silver 925 is used for objects destined for export only.

Alabaster, Mosaic, and Semi-Precious Stone Oeuvres: **Balatresi** (Lungarno Acciaioli 22R) is so fascinatingly different that it shouldn't be missed by a-n-y-b-o-d-y. Lots of their treasures are 1-of-a-kind. Its creations in alabaster, including unusual boxes ($15 to $100), are a Klondike for seekers of strikingly unusual gifts. Those who wish to splurge will find gorgeously hand-carved articles in rare varieties of this gleaming mineral—dishes, vases, boxes, animals, ashtrays—all wrought by skilled craftsmen exclusively for them. From all the supplies dug from rich veins in their own mine, talented artisans fashion the celebrated brown onyx of Tuscany into contrasting types of trays, boxes, vases, and animals ($12 to $100). Also importantly featured are magnificent pieces in hard stones such as malachite, lapis lazuli, rodonite, and other specimens, as well as exquisite enamelware including the famous Faberge reproductions ($26 to $140). The crown jewels of their vast array are the gorgeous original works of art which are sold only here; a pair of prime examples are the striking ceramic sculptures by Giannitrapani and the 1-of-a-kind virtuosities of the last of the great Florentine mosaicists alive today, Maestro Marco Tacconi, whose brilliance in understanding the selection, cutting, polishing, and creating such magic art forms of stones is unrivaled in the world. Three more honest human beings than Proprietor Umberto Balatresi, his lovely wife Giovanna, and his sister Daniela do not exist. Their guarantee is their bond. As a bonus, these experts take delight in giving geology lessons on whatever objects intrigue their customers. Safe shipment assured to anywhere in the world; naturally no discounts. In this intricate field, it is reassuring to buy from a house and family of such established integrity.

Antiques: **Via de' Fossi, Borgo San Jacopo,** and **Via Tornabuoni** are the most expensive; we found more elegant selections, better displayed, on **Via Maggio.** Right on the Ponte Vecchio (at #42) **Pacci** is sure to catch the eye of anyone with a scientific bent. The old-world instruments are fascinating for collectors.

Inexpensive Art Reproductions: **Fratelli Alinari** (Via Strozzi 19R) has everybody licked on prints, paintings, picture frames, etchings, and related lines. You can spend 10¢, $1, $5, or more.

Belts and Accessories: **Infinity** (Borgo SS Apostoli 18 R) Florence has always been the inspiration for fashion leadership in accessories; here at this handsome 14th century tower—and only a short hop from the Ponte Vecchio—is one of the finest ateliers in the craft. It is the magic of Enio Provaroni, a Tuscan, and his Bostonian wife, Jane Dengler, who combine their talents to produce bold new ideas—even zipping into high-tech spheres. In their classical orientation they feature beautiful leather goods in natural hues, some with braidwork, some polished and burnished or simply rubbed to a fine tactile glow. A belt, a bag, a bracelet, a buckle that you can't forget, shoes, or even original leather clothes—these are the temptations at Infinity. Then, if you wish to design your own creation please help yourself to their collective willingness. Unique leather and metal midriff masterpieces (some with sterling buckles, fittings or nature's materials) might begin at about $60. Isn't that a great way to belt up?

Books in English: **Libreria BM** (Borgognissanti 4R) is a fine, versatile enterprise. Proprietor L. F. Batazzi and his staff are Americans. Another crackerjack source is **Seeber** (Via Tornabuoni 68R), which is the oldest in the city. It also offers large stocks in English and other languages.

Boutiques: **Raspini** (Via Calzaiuoli 70-74R, Via Martelli 5–7R and Via Roma 25–29R) and **Beltrami** (Via Calzaiuoli 44R and Via dei Pecori 16R) and **Beltrami Junior** (Via Calimala 9R) can dress you from head to toe in the latest chic and trendy Italian fashions. **Benetton** (Via Calimala 68R) is just one link in the enormous network of shops by that name that blanket Europe (and the USA, as well). Slacks and sweaters are their game; bold, intense, primary colors are their trademark; not expensive.

Crystal, Porcelain and Sterling: **Armando Poggi** (Via Calzaiuoli 105R and 116R). Here is where you can save from 30% to 50% of U.S. prices for world-class shopping items. These include the stellar products from such houses as Waterford in Ireland, Baccarat and Lalique of France, Wedgwood of England, Herend of Hungary, Lladro of Spain, Bing & Grondhal of Denmark, Hummel of Germany and Richard Ginori of Italy. Along with these porcelain and crystal specialists you will find the incomparable sterling of Buccellati and the distinctive line of silver created by Armando Poggi itself—a name which has been revered for more than half a century. Space prevents us from describing the full range of stemware, table-settings and accessories, but don't miss an opportunity to be dazzled by the Poggi ensemble. The two stores face each other in the same smart shopping district. All employees speak English; parcels are carefully packed on request and shipped worldwide; moreover, the Poggi services include prompt attention to mail orders.

Embroidery: **Industrie Femminili Italiane** (Lungarno Corsini 34R) follows the seasons. In springtime there is an explosion of mimosa-inspired table linen: Autumn is made for chestnuts and where the mushroom is king there are *funghi*-shaped placemats. The scent of flowers is everywhere in summer and the strawberry motif is extremely popular. There are delicate sheets and pillowcase sets for infant's cribs ($55), bibs ($10), hand towels (from $15)—every stitch done by hand. Let Mari show you the extensive collection. **The Instituto Donalici** in the Rifredi district (Via Carlo Bini 29) a 10-minute ride from town is a favorite with U.S. visitors.

Florentine Leather Fashions: **John F.** (Lungarno Corsini 2) is mecca for the greatest values in the specialty of this Tuscan capital. The leathergoods are smoother than a ruby Barolo . . . and so are the prices; you'll be underwhelmed by them because seldom have we witnessed such fine products for such low outlays. Although the magnificent frescoed 15th-century ceiling and statuary in its section of the historic *palazzo* are ornately Florentine, it is small, intimate, and convivial. Every member of the John F. clan seems to have a "try-harder" attitude to please. You'll find a broad and fashionable range of classical evening and sport handbags from $30 up, attache cases, briefcases, legal document cases, large envelope cases, hardtop cases, overnight cases; in other words, cases for every need or profession. We've recently purchased a luxurious multi-pocketed, soft-sided leather executive satchel that not only keeps our papers sorted efficiently but can also double as an overnighter. (We won't even tell you the price because after being accustomed to Stateside whammys, you'd only laugh and not believe us.) In the modest end of the stock, items such as eyeglass holders, key pouches, belts, wallets, and change purses are beautifully crafted by expert hands and sold for about a third the cost of back-home fare. And what a variety of skins you will find—in all styles and finishes. There are also racks of gorgeous coats and jackets in the most modish cuts which are fashioned exclusively for John F. For gift ideas— leather desk sets, pads, or more personal selections—here's an idea-factory you can't afford to miss. Then, if you really yearn to be wowed, smartly dressed women will want to try on the temptations in the neighboring **Mariposa** (''Butterfly'') boutique which doesn't simply stop at suede and leather, but also does wondrous things with pure silk, wool, cotton, linen, and other fabrics. They also carry the Poi line designed by Krizia as well as the trend setting styles of Titolo di Basile. Ask for Elio or any of the John F. family in either of these tandem shops. They'll stitch yards of elastic into your travel dollars.

Florentine Paper and Stationery Items: One of the beautiful rarities at **Il Papiro** (Via Cavour 55R, Piazza Duomo 24R and Lungarno Acciaiuoli 42R) is its *papier a cuve,* a delicate 17th-century process which has been almost lost. To each sheet is applied a stream of droplets of a variety of herbs in water with combs, brushes, and scribes until the desired design has been achieved. It is impossible to produce two sheets which are exactly alike. They make strikingly unusual coverings for books, boxes, telephone directories, and the like. Artistic cards and related products are also offered. **Giulio Giannini & Figlio** (Piazza Pitti 37R) and **Pineider** (Piazza della Signoria 14R) both display a delightful assortment for correspondence, gift wrapping, lining drawers, and having fun, as well as album folios and standard stationery stocks. In addition, at **Bottega Artigiana del Libro** (Lungarno Corsini 40R) there are decorative masks in the tradition of the *Commedia dell' Arte* and Venetian carnival.

Made of papier mache or leather, models include Bacco, Guto, Pulcinella, Japanese and the sun. Prices anywhere from 10,000–40,000 lire.

Galleries: **Masini** usually offers the best selection of paintings. Other choices include the **Florence Art Gallery, Michaux,** and **Vaccarino.**

Gifts: **Ducci** (Lungarno Corsini 24R) has a fascinating collection. There are the artistic creations of Alinari—those distinctive boxes with reproduced paintings, lampshades, platters, trays and fine decoration for the home or office. Florentine handicraft reaches its zenith here in such materials as wood, stone and leather. You could spend anywhere from $1 to $3000 (for stone tables and panels), but the average gift will probably be close to $50. Ask for Director Damiano Colonna. Very unique and quintessentially Tuscan.

Tarzia (Piazza dei Pitti 32R) possesses a decorative flair seldom seen in the field of artisanware. The tables, bamboo integrated with brass, the bronze ducks, penguins, turtles, butterflys, the ceramic pigeons and a zoological pantheon of friendly critters will surely coax you to buy some momento. Newest line of critters executed in a combination of ash and ebony with movable parts. We can't describe everything, but ask the charming Vicente Tarzia to show you the range, a joyful effort he makes for any visitor who requests his aid. **Piera e Bruna** (Via Guicciardini 6R) for scarves and covered boxes; **La Botteguccia** (Lungarno Corsini 16R) for small trinkets; **Volpi** (Via Panzani 16R) for modern woodwork; and **Emporium** (Via Guicciardini 122R) for some very original high-tech, state-of-the-art designs for home and office.

Gloves: **Madova** (Via Guiccardini 1R) and **Chris Gloves** (Por Santa Maria 42R) are local favorites.

Jewelry: **Aurum** (Lungarno Corsini 16R) In the world of jewelry Florence has become almost synonymous with the word "gold." Indeed, it has given its own treatment to this element and craftsmen for centuries have been copying the distinctive Tuscan technique. Aurum is Latin of gold and certainly you will find the classic Florentine workmanship here as well as the contemporary extension of this art. Fine quality jewels are incorporated into many of the designs. I was especially impressed by the Etruscan motifs. There are scores of stylings in gold chains for a multitude of purposes. You'll find bracelets, earrings and necklaces, all of them in 18-carat, the apogee of the goldsmith's art. If you have any questions or special requests Managing Dirctor Domenico Palomba is the soul of helpfulness. He can also arrange to refund immediately the 19% IVA tax for purchases over 650,000 lira. In summer business hours are from 9 a.m.–9 p.m. with no midday closure. In winter it is closed both Sun. and Mon. **Buccellati** (Via Tornabuoni 71R) and **Settepassi** (Via Tornabuoni 25R) are distinguished for conventional gems. **Gustavo C. Melli** (Ponte Vecchio) handles antique types. These can be numbingly expensive.

Knitwear: **Romei Boutique** (Lungarno Acciaiouli 32R) is the enormously successful showcase for talented, bright and effervescent Lori Romei. This radiant young lady is already establishing herself as the "Queen of Knitwear" in possibly the world's most competitive marketplace for this expression of apparel. Lori not only will serve as your consultant for clothing, but since she has no branch operations and exports only to stores within Europe, your purchases will automatically receive the benefit of wholesale pricing—a savings which no other retailer can begin to compete with on the continent. Also since she is her own in-house designer and she is always on the leading edge of fresh concepts, you will be receiving the styles of next year today. Color choices, too, are vitally important and here again you receive the fact of tomorrow's fashion rather than the prediction. Sizes available from 2 to 22 not only in knits but in wools, silks, cottons, linens, plus an exciting line of accessories. Ask Lori for her assistance or amiable Patricia or Franca, all of whom speak English perfectly. Today this is Number One in Florence. At **Poletti** (Via Parione 22R) they hand-crochet dresses out of cotton and silk thread—even luxurious cashmere, too. The resulting effect is like gossamer spider webs. Made-to-order in 15–20 days; very expensive ($1,200) but exquisite. Branch in *Rimini* (Via IV Novembre 13).

Ladies Shoes: **Lily of Florence** (Via Guicciardini 2R) is one of the best bets—and best bargains!—of its type anywhere on the Continent. Gifted artisan Lily Power, who learned the craft in Seattle, finally became so distressed by the rarity of moderate-cost odd sizes (she wears an AA) that in the late 1960s she pulled up stakes and founded her own dream business here. The happy combination of her Italian ancestral heritage and her American savvy quickly established her as a dynamic and innovative leader in the field. Sole distributor of the equally famous Amalfi and dressier Lily of Florence lines; Switzerland's celebrated Bally assemblage for men; all U.S. sizes; many thousands of North American customers annually, including our military stationed abroad; tariffs which always run 30% to 50% less than you'd pay back home. Now she has added an extremely chic line of ready-to-wear leather wearables. Mrs. Power is concentrating on her Rome branch (Via Lombardia 38); her son Lynn, her daughter Maria, and her daughter-in-law Rosemary will welcome you with grace. Terrific! **Salvatore Ferragamo,** at Palazzo Feroni 16R, is the only Florence outlet of some of the most renowed craftsmen globally in this field—but is it *e-x-p-e-n-s-i-v-e!* **Romano** (Piazza della Republica) is another alternative. **Mario Valentino, Tanino Crisci** and **Quinto Casadei** are to be found along Via Tornabuoni. **Pollini** (Via Calzaiuoli 21R) and **Carrano Maraolo** (Via Roma 6–8R) are less costly.

Leather: **Silvio Luti & Figlio** (Via Parione 28–32R), with its wide and fine selection of Florentine stylings, attractive handbags, plus other fetching articles, is one of the local arbiters; the able direction and staff here are suavely equipped to handle its deservedly brisk trade. **Fraro's** (Lungarno Acciaiuoli 36–38R) is the only place in town where you'll find the cut-velvet bags of Roberta di Camerino along with her distinctively patterned silk scarves and umbrellas. Franca and Rosy are most helpful and will show you the raincoat line, too. **Cellerini** (Via del Soel 37R) specializes in handbags and luggage; revered by their peers in this highly competitive field. Also try **Bojola** (Via Rondinelli 25R, opposite the C.I.T. office) where a blend of canvas and leather has become the trademark and a stamped leather seal the mark of authenticity. **Franco Pugi** (Via SS Apostoli 42–48R) is also worth scouting out.

Lingerie and Linens: **Romei Boutique** (Via Porta Rossa 77R) Do you want to become an undercover agent, *Signorina?* Romei can put you in the last word of fashion slink—temptations which are either dainty or daunting as well as many moods (and purposes) in between. The big names are here: Valentino, Versace, Armani, La Perla, as well as stockings by virtuosi of sheer grace such as Pierre Manteaux and, of course, the ever-present Versace. In addition to undergarments and top-of-the-line hosiery and tights, Romei stocks some of the most exquisite, languorous and utterly luxurious robes, nightgowns and pajamas to be found anywhere after midnight. The summer collection adds a rainbow of pool and beach attire which are guaranteed to turn interested eyes your way. If you've got the shape for it—as well as the nerve—give some consideration to the combination bra and shorts made in one piece. The lace is also a talking point. Summer hours are from 9:30 a.m.–7:30 p.m.; winter schedule is 9:30 a.m.–1 p.m. and 3:30 p.m.–7:30 p.m. Miss Patricia will show you all the Romei secrets. At **Loretta Caponi** (Via Borgo Ognissanti 12R) patrician lingerie, other intimate apparel and boudoir pillows are the specialities. Much of this is handmade or hand-detailed. Her shop across the street is devoted to children clothes (newborns to 10 year olds). Needless to say, they are ravishing, too. The well-known Pratesi (which was next door) had closed on our latest visit and there were conflilcting reports about its re-opening. Please check locally. **Cirri** (Via Por Santa Maria 38–40R) also has fetching finery for infants and children, smashing lingerie and lots of beautiful handkerchiefs.

Majolica Ceramics and Miscellanea: **Soc. A. Menegatti & Co.** (Piazza del Pesce 2R) and **S.E.L.A.N.** (Via Porta Rossa 107-113R) offer good browsing for Florentine, Faenza, and Deruta kiln-work. **Galleria Machiavelli** (Via Por S. Maria 39R) specializes in wonderful large platters and table or garden items. **A. Carnesecchi** (Via Guicciardini 4R) does more of the same.

Pewter: **Giovanni Del Bono** (Ponte Vecchio 2–6R) Don't miss an opportunity to visit the upper floors of this shop where items for a museum are on display.

Silver: **Sacchi** (Lungarno Acciaiuoli 82R) is the silver king of Tuscany and what a distinctive hallmark to take home! The sparkling inventory includes marvelous silver frames ($15–100), pillboxes (in about the same range of prices), silver animals, keychains, bracelets, silver cameos ($12–50), trays and candlesticks. You won't want to miss the unusual statues, too, to add a special artistic touch to your tablesettings. While silver is the mainstay, Sacchi also is noted for its goldsmithery as well as articles made of malachite, lapis lazuli, tiger's eye and other semi-precious and rare stones. All styles are represented from classic bottle coasters to art-deco mirrors; I was particularly betaken by the wine glasses and pitcher bearing a grape motif. Ask for Patricia, Lakis, Luca, Corrado or Franca who seem to know every knickknack in the house. Summer hours (April–Oct.) 9 a.m.–7:30 p.m. with no break, winter 9:30 a.m.–1:30 p.m. and 3:30 p.m.–7:30 p.m.; closed Sun. and Mon.

Trimmings: **Valmar** (Via Porta Rossa 53R) Tassels, bell pulls, materials for edging, dressy belts in jet, you name it and they've got it. Always crowded with locals.

Wrought Iron: **Certini** (Via Guicciardini 60R) has flower bedecked wall sconces ($50), candleholders ($15), picture frames ($25), boxes ($20), lamps ($90), and chandeliers ($400) that are painted. The garden has come indoors and they are graceful decorative touches that would fit in most anywhere.

Yachting: **Marina Yachting** (Via Porta Rossa 23R) is great for reefers, outerwear, sweaters, sea jackets and accessories. Chiefly for women.

SHOPPING AREAS

First find the *Duomo* on your map. Then draw a circle within a radius of one mile from the cathedral. Virtually all the important shopping for this most fashionable metropolis falls within this orbit. The following contain shops offering exceptional merchandise particularly in regard to clothing, handbags, belts, shoes, gifts, antiques, art and specialty foods: **Via Della Spiga, Via Sant' Andrea, Via Montenapoleone, Corso Vittorio Emanuele II, Galleria Vittorio Emanuele II, Via Manzoni, Corso Venezia (near Piazza San Babila), Via Durini, Via Brera, Via Solferino, Via Fiori Chiari,** and **Via Madonnina.**

NOTE · · · In the Via Montenapoleon and Via Spiga district some shops don't take the long lunch break and close either between 1:30–2:30 p.m. or remain open throughout the entire day— a typically enterprising attitude for this north Italian city.

THINGS TO BUY

Leather goods, menswear, shoes, ladies' high-fashion readymades, bolt silks and materials, gifts and boutique items, ceramics.

NOTE · · · Milan spells fashion! Along the Via S. Gregorio (between the Piazza della Republica and the Central Station) you'll find store fronts which announce *"solo grossisti."* This is the wholesale district for the rag trade. Many manufacturers are producing knockoffs of the hottest designers of the moment from Paris, Milan, and Rome. If you have cash in hand and determination, look in the windows, take your pick, walk in and ask if you can buy. They might say "no," but it's likely, if they aren't terribly busy, that they'll say "yes." You'll probably try the garment on between packing cases, but the savings will be worth it.

Antiques: **L'Oro dei Farlocchi** (Via Madonnina 5) displays quite an unusual collection with special emphasis on wood and *objets d'art*. **Decomania** (Via Fiori Chiari 7) puts its focus on the art-deco craze but also carries additional noteworthy stock.

Books: **The International Bookstore** (Largo Cairoli). The name speaks for itself—the best selection of English-language publications. **Libreria Bocca** (Galleria Vittorio Emanuelle II) is for art tomes and first editions.

Children's Shop: **Meronisi** (Via Madonnina 10) is a wee place for wee people, particularly one-of-a-kind items for infants.

Costume Jewelry: **Angela Caputi** (Via Madonnina 11) is extremely creative in this specialty field of Milan. Stunning and oh-so-inexpensive for the rewards. **Sharra Pagano** (Via della Spiga 7) is another one with up-to-the-instant styles.

Delicatessens: **Peck** (Via Montenapoleone and Via Spadari 9) is the Italian answer to Fauchon and we still salivate as we recall the l-u-s-c-i-o-u-s food displays at **Di Gennaro** (Via Agnello 12).

Department Stores: **La Rinascente** (Via San Raffaele 2) and **Coin** (Piazzale Cinque Giornate).

Designer Clothes (Men): **Barba's** (Via S. Andrea 21) is one of the trendiest. They feature their own private label as well as merchandise from other collections. **Gianfranco Ferre** (Via S. Andrea 10A) A stylist well known to male connoisseurs. **Giorgio Armani** (Via S. Andrea 9) The Armani touch first blessed men, but now extends to women's ready-to-wear as well. **Missoni** (Via Montenapoleone 1) Again, here's a designer who originally focused on the male sex but who now has broadened the scope to include women—and even matching ensembles for both sexes. **Versace Uomo** (Via P. Verri, at the end of Montenapoleone) An outstanding collection of insuperable Italian taste.

Designer Clothes (Women):   **Versace** (Via della Spiga 4) needs no introduction. This is the main attraction for women; please note it differs from the boutique for men. **Fendi** (Via S. Andrea 16 and Via della Spiga 11) These sisters need no special spotlighting for anyone who respects fine Italian design and uniqueness. Both shops are superb. **Krizia** (Via della Spiga 23) sweeps in with a fantastic collection, especially the sweaters, from the meticulous hands of Mariucca Mandelli. **Mila Schon** (Via Montenapoleone 2) offers wide variety and top quality with a strong element of elegance. **Mario Valentino** (Via Corso Matteotti 10) provides a split personality at the same address: one boutique for women and the other for men. *The* **Valentino** (Via Santo Spirito 3) is a one-and-only. Don't confuse 'em. **Enrico Coveri** (Via S. Pietro all'Orto 9) also tends to be rather bisexual—from a purely artistic point of view, naturally. His clothing and accessories for men and women are exceptional at this address very near to the Duomo.

Florist: Rightfully, the name and colophon of **Ditta Angelo Radaelli** (Via Manzoni 16) registers the most strongly among Milanese recipients.

Furniture: Milan is Italy's leader in designing home furnishings. Wander along the Corso Matteotti, Corso Europa, Via della Spiga, Via Montenapoleone, Corso Monforte, Via Manzoni, Via Brera, Via Solferino and Corso Garibaldi and you'll get so many ideas you'll want to begin redecorating your home immediately.

Gifts: **L'Utile e il Dilettevole** (Via della Spiga 46). Here's a browser's paradise! Chiefly there are items for the home, many of them antique or with a special regional personality that you will cherish as a souvenir of your travels. **Valentino Piu'** (Via S. Spirito 3) has an expensive line of serendipity from the famous clothing designer.

Hats: **Borsalino** (Corso Vittorio Emanuele II, 5, Galleria Vittorio Emanuele II 92 and Galleria Caffe-Moda Durini 14) has been covering heads almost since before the invention of hair. The greatest fedoras in creation, a topper's world of styles—from winter felts to stylish Panamas. A cap for all seasons—for men as well as for ladies.

Leathergoods and Handbags: **Eve** (Via S. Pietro all'Orto 9) offers a well-chosen collection in bags, wallets and belts. **Gucci** (Via Montenapoleone 5) carries on its relentless selling spree here. A song without end—and very lyrical. Prices, however, are worthy of grand opera theatrics. An open secret, however, is **Gucci Liquidazioni** (Via Corridoni 13). Up to 50% savings; no seconds just unsold merchandise in all their ranges. **Trussardi** (Via S. Andrea 5), to my taste, offers similar quality at more reasonable levels. It also specializes in gift items and clothing. **Prada** (Via della Spiga 1) is the lead-off candidate if you begin your investigation of this street from its source at Corso Venezia; handbags and shoes provide the bulk of its wonders. **Fratelli Prada** (Galleria Vittorio Emanuele II 63–65) is the *original* Prada store founded in the 1800s; go here if you are looking especially for a valise or attache case.

Linens: **Pratesi** (Via Montenapoleone 21) is one of Europe's greatest. Their delicacy and splendor has been gracing noble homes in Europe for eons. **Jesurum** (Via Montenapoleone 14) has an enticing selection of dentelle and an exciting assemblage of original beachwear; please turn to *"Venice"* for more details.

Market: **Via Fiori Chiari** is the Milanese site of the flea market which occurs on the third Sat. of each month. The **Fiera di Senigallia** (Via Calatafimi) is rather second rate; it occurs every Saturday morning.

Shoes: **Ferragamo** (Via Montenapoleone 23) is, of course, famous for elegant and expensive footwear. Probably the most revered cobbler in the world for the well-shod woman. **Fausto Santini** (same street at number 1) has a younger look; prices are considerably lower too. **Divarese** (#12) is an off-shoot of the Benetton empire. **Tanino Crisci** (#3) is a classicist. **Beltrami** (#16) adds accessories. **Pollini** (Corso Vittorio Emanuele 30) is amusing and trendy. **Diego della Valle** (Via della Spiga 22) works closely with many of fashion's top names. **El Vaquero** (Via S. Pietro all'Orto 3) creates boots unlike any you've seen before. And this is just a small sampling of what you'll find, so be sure you're comfortably shod for your foray.

Silks and Materials: **Galtrucco** (Via Montenapoleon 27 and Piazza del Duomo 2) is the combined Saks-Bergdorf-Macy's for dress silks, suiting silks, upholstery silks, velvets, cottons, linens and other cloths by the piece. Branch in *Rome*. None more versatile. **Naj Oleari** (Via Brera 8) is a household name all over Italy and the word is spreading. All cotton fabrics in lighthearted designs for clothing and home furnishings. **Lisio** (via Manzoni 41) is another good choice.

Silver: **Bernasconi** (Galleria Vittorio Emanuele II) has been polishing up its image since 1872. What a fabulous collection!

Stationery: **Albrizzi** (Via Bagutta 8, behind Montenapoleone) is a tiny boutique for hand-printed and antique papers. A jewel for collectors of the unusual.

NAPLES AND CAPRI

SHOPPING AREAS

Naples has limited pickings. While **Via Roma** and **Via Chiaia** are the most popular shopping stems, you'll find higher quality around **Piazza dei Martiri** and along **Via Calabritto.**

Antiques: **Galleria d'Arte** (Piazza dei Martiri 32) interested us the most; even an elaborately rococo sedan chair was at hand. All prices are fixed here. Aficionados should start at the National Museum and walk up Via Constantinopoli or Via D. Morelli and pick from the holes-in-the-wall. No guarantees on reliability; occasional values; always bargain your head off with these smiling sharks. **Il Portico** (Via D. Morelli 32 plus Capri branch) is owned by Annamaria Coronato. Choices are taken chiefly from distressed estates in the region and these are magnificent. **Bowinkel** is considered tops for antique prints.

The Flea Markets (Corso Malta and Corso Navara near the Railway Station) in the main are wretchedly junky.

Boutiques: **Mario Valentino** (Via Calabritto 10) for fashionable shoes and bags; the **Ricciardi Boutique** (across the street at No. 15), which exclusively purveys the Micmac, Christian Aujard, and Aqualo lines; **Spatarella** (at No. 1) for bargain purses.

Buttons: "Button, button, who's got the button?" **M. Tramontano** (Via Chiaia) does—more than 125,000 of them, plus a big choice of buckles and brooches, too.

Gifts: **L'Angolo** (Piazza dei Martiri) has an attractive and unusual selection.

Prints: **Alinari** (Via Calabritto) is THE place!

Capri

Most shops offer the same merchandise and the same high prices—with several conspicuous exceptions.

Antiques: **Il Portico** (Via Camerelle 37) which operates in Naples, too, has a loyal following among the *cognoscente*. Sales of the beautiful furniture, prints and paintings and other bibelots are so brisk that the contents of this shop disappear just as quickly as new lots are brought in.

Boutiques: **La Parisienne** (on the Square) is the acknowledged fashion arbiter for ladies. Matching shirts, skirts and pants at 50% of their Fifth Ave. price tags are perhaps its best-known feature. **Yves Dupuis** (Via Camerelle) is a designer in his own right and his styles have captured the relaxed, chic mood of the island. **Capri Sport, Sheba Sailor, Adrian's** and **Ribot** are other good bets. **Russo Uomo** and **Chantal** (via Camerelle 10) have great clothes for HIM.

Ceramics: **The Sea Gull** (Via Roma 25) Here's a place that's as joyful as the Italian sun—full of color, cheer, style and decorative fun. Many of the ideas spring from Paolo and Agnese Staiano who are assisted in this store by Angela and Bruno. The big items include both indoor and outdoor all-weather ceramic furniture: hand-decorated tables with matching benches, urns, columns and fountains which can turn any breakfast room or patio into a showplace. Of course, there are wonderful take-away items (from $10 up) which can be tucked into your luggage or mailed home to yourself or friends. These might include cold buffets, intimate coffee and tea sets, some splendid wall masks which are really talking points, plates, birds and animal ornaments as well as those spectacular ceramic fruits which Italians seem to have patented in the world of home furnishings. Photos are available for new and important pieces. This shop is affiliated with Masterpiece Bijoux Vogue (Via Roma 33) specializing in costume jewelry and antique Italian ceramics. Maria will help you at this address.

Jewelry: **Alberto e Lina-La Campanina** (Via Vitt. Emanuele 18) is probably more well known to the Caprese than Times Square is to the average New Yorker. You can't help becoming familiar with these lovely people since the shop is on the *only* cross-village lane that goes to everywhere. Naturally, you will window shop with every passing and, just as naturally, you will be relentlessly tempted. But wait until you meet Alberto and Lina themselves and their charming children Marioli and Filippo. These are the creators who have adorned some of the world's most attractive celebrities, shared a Peace Bell (La Campanina) with President Reagan and count among their friends who are regulars on the island such personalities as Agnelli, Niarchos, Chandon and just plain folk from all over the globe. They are so casual and warmhearted that you will immediately fall under their spell. Needless to say, the gems, pearls, the precious stones and the exquisite goldsmithery are as legendary as this Golden Couple of Capri. Open every day in summer from (9:30 a.m. to 10 p.m. Creatively they are among the jewelry titans of Europe. Incidentally, in honor of their great affection for Americans they always provide a Fourth of July celebration which is a festivity you must not miss!

Perfume: **Profumi di Capri** How would you like to have all of the haunting aromas of the Mediterranean in a bottle? It's almost a possibility. Moreover, floral elixirs are brought in from other exotic gardenspots to complete the spectrum, utilizing the very same distilling methods employed by Carthusian monks of the 16th century. It is very important that you go to this perfumer only, as there are other parvenus who are trying to exploit this historic and esteemed name. (One even has the nerve to label itself "Profumi Originale di Capri." Distilled nonsense!) This exclusive house, run by the charming Gilberte De Meyer, offers three shops, decorted whimsically in Italian ceramic gaiety. One is located in Capri itself on Via Camerelle 10, another is only a short stroll away (including the fascinating laboratory which you are invited to visit in its lovely parkland setting) at Via Matteotti 2/B, and a third up at Anacapri on Via Capodimonte which is also known as Via San Michele. Have a whiff of captivating *Caprissimo, Aria di Capri, Fiori di Capri* or the noble *Carthusia Lady*. There's also a line for men.

Sandals: **Canfora** (Via Camerelle, opposite the Hotel Quisisana) is a real family operation that has garnered fame locally.

Anacapri

Up here in this lofty tier of the island be sure to visit **Mariorita International Shop,** located within the embrace of the floriant Hotel Europa gardens and at the beginning of the path which everyone must take who wishes to visit Villa San Michele. It has a spacious, modern, open-plan effect which encourages casual browsing by the consummate shopper. There are many attendants but you are not bothered or pressured by any of the staff.

All the great names are here including such luminaries as La Perla, Valentino, Fila, Pancaldi B, Les Copins, and Capo di Monte. There are beautiful scarves, ties, handbags and a fine selection of cameos, too. And, in spite of the fact that Capri caters primarily to warm-weather trade, you will also find leather, coats, jackets and umbrellas for the cooler months. The range runs from sportswear and beach attire all the way up to sequins and glitz for sophisticated evenings. A unique item which Americans love is an ingenious gaming table (plus chairs) in inlaid mahogany or cherry which incoporates almost every known gambling pastime; this takes two months to make and costs approximately $2,500 delivered—a converstion piece for a lifetime of enjoyment.

Remember, too, the previously mentioned **Profumi di Capri** which is nearby.

NAPLES—POMPEII HIGHWAY

Cameos, Coral, Handwrought Jewelry: The world center of these first 2 specialties is concentrated along the Naples-Pompeii Highway. Try **M. & G. Donadio** first, the most popular, and avoid another purveyor in the district called Giovanni Apa which now seems to be unreliable in our estimation.

SORRENTO

Sorrento is the largest, greatest, and most celebrated center in the world for inlaid furniture and similar artistic accessories. The scope and range of its products is astonishing. Literally they run into the hundreds. Utilizing skills which flowered here ages ago, every single piece from the most modest fruit basket to the most elaborate baroque highboy is 100% inset by hand. To see these displays is a unique shopping experience.

The cornucopia of exquisite, exclusive masterworks in the enormous 3-level showrooms of century-old, 400-employee **A. Gargiulo Jannuzzi** (hub of Main Square) stops us in our tracks. After watching its maestros ply their complex crafts while articulate Libby Gorga explains their cunning techniques, this introduction better prepares visitors to ''oh'' and to ''ah'' as they roam through the monumental collection of everything from dining sets to chests of drawers to ladies' desks to 3-table nests to cigarette, music, jewelry, and cigar boxes to a plethora more; 86 different items run from $8 to $50. Beautiful, moderately priced convent or orphan-children handmade embroidered tableware, blouses, handkerchiefs, and the like, a strong alternate magnet. Statues by such famous sculptors as Borsato, Cappe, Galli, and Merli; porcelain department; free brochures; worldwide shipment; guaranteed delivery; continuously open 365 days (summers until 10 p.m.). We admire Matriarch Gargiulo and sons Peppino and Apollo. Wonderful!

At smaller **Notturno,** nearby, there are interesting bargains.

More limited but also excellent. **Melanie** and **Cuomo** are dependable but even less versatile establishments which in general seemed to be costlier.

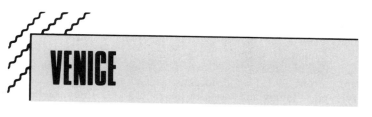

VENICE

THINGS TO BUY

Venetian glass, handbags, silver, lace, handmade and hand-printed papers, and jewelry.

NOTE · · · This city teems with guides, concierges, gondoliers, and other steerers hungry for the 15% to 25% commissions on your purchases. As in Florence, (1) shop alone, (2) don't even tell your hotel people where you're going, (3) don't buy on Murano Island, and (4) ask for a minimum of 15% off the list price for yourself (except in the leading shops such as the ones listed below). To counter the fringe operators, the Chamber of Commerce and the legitimate old-line merchants set up the Venetian Crafts Association to attest both product-quality and business ethics among its members; be sure to look for the Association's 4-leaf-clover symbol display.

Arts and Crafts: **Veneziartigiana—Union of Venetian Artistic Artisans** (Calle Larga San Marco 412/13 The secrets of artists from bygone centuries are revealed in the products of more than 60 workshops located here at *Al Redentor,* one of the oldest pharmacies in the Republic, and once defined by Lorenzetti as a "stupendous example of an 18th century setting." The consortium includes the exotica of gold- and silversmiths, engravers, glass blowers, chandelier builders, lace makers, embroiderers, bronze fashioners and even china doll creators. You will also find costumes and fancy dress from the past as well as the distinctive Venetian papier mache, leather, bronze and feathered masks. As a few examples from the splendid collection, don't miss Countess Foscari's frames tipped with silver or brass and her other inspired *objets d'art* which range from $20–200. There are mirrors, gilded-wood decorations, and even exclusive cameo-type glass lamps and vases in the motifs of Tiffany, Galle and Daum. All information as well as a magnificent color catalog (which you would be proud to have in your library) available through Suzanne Margherita at the above address. She can tell you about the 15% discounts for export purchases as well as further reductions for wholesale. Closed the last three weeks in Jan. and most national holidays.

Books, Prints and Photographs: **Osvaldo Bohm** (S. Moise 1349/50) is a firm that has specialized, for many years, in photographs of Venice and its art. Their archives are vast and scholars consult with them constantly. They are the publishers of "Venice, The Naya Collection" which is a must—a classic example of the magic of Venice as captured through a lens. Original framed or unframed etchings, lithographs and antique maps abound—even simple postcards. A purchase here will keep the memory of this unforgettable city always alive. For bibliophiles, **Filippi** (Calle del Paradiso 5762), **Libreria Cassini** (Via XXII Marzo 2424) and **La Libreria La Fenice** (S. Marco 1850) are tops. A shop at Calle del Canonica 337A carries the Studium series on Venice.

Boutiques: **Krizia** can be found at Calle de la Ostreghe 2359 **La Couple** (San Marco, Frezzeria 1674 and Calle Larga XX

Marzo 2366) carries some choice labels and at **Draganczuk** (Calle XXII Marzo 2288) there are hangers of Ungaro, Complice and the eye-catching Iceberg sweaters designed by Castelbajac.

Ceramics: **Rigattieri** (S. Marco, Calle dei Frati 3532/35) The fruit of Bacchus and Eden are manifest in this orchard of Italian pottery. They'll bring sunlight to any home, garden, poolside or office.

Children's Clothes: We were very pleased with what we bought at **Maricla** (Calle Larga XXII Marzo 2401) and we also liked its embroidered lingerie for grown-ups.

Creative Jewelry: **Paolo Scarpa Primitive Jewelry** (San Marco-Merceria San Salvador 4850) is a small but fascinating showcase on the main street running from St. Mark's Square toward the Rialto Bridge. Its name derives from the warm-hearted and artistic couple who discover distinctive items from their global travels and create out of them some of the most striking ethnic ornamentation to be found anywhere. The unique quality that draws so many film luminaries, artists, archaeologists and collectors to this petit museum-like boutique is that the origins of the rare and mystical ingredients are intentionally eclectic. Not being constrained by the conventions or lore of one nation alone this talented team might assemble the beads, stones or talisman of ten nations or regions and form them into one necklace—each piece, of course, being exclusive. Prices fun from $100 to $10,000 and are free of purchase tax because all are classified as antiques. Both Paolo and Francesca enjoy explaining the backgrounds of their adventures in remote outbacks of the world. Closed on Sun. and Mon. as well as from Nov. 1 to Mar. 1 when you might find them searching the fringes of forbidding deserts or the forgotten trade routes of Central Asia.

Fabrics: Few things are more sumptuous than the silks, damasks, velvets and brocades of Venice. **Luigi Bevilacqua** (Campiello Comare 1320 near Campo Zandegola in Santa Croce), **Lorenzo Rubelli** (Campo San Gallo 1089–91) and **M** (San Marco 1651) have brilliant arrays of all of them. **Salvatore Trois** (Campo S. Maurizio 2666) is dedicated to the fabulous Fortuny. This quartet goes unrivaled and is world-famous.

Florist: **Colleoni Marco** (Frezzeria S. Marco) assembles lovely bouquets.

Glass: Venetian glass needs no introduction to any connoisseur old enough to lift a milk goblet, because it's probably the most renowned and eye-appealing variety blown today. But the traveler must choose his merchant with utmost care in this racket-infested industry here. That's why we suggest that you avoid the Island of Murano and the swindlers or fringe-dealers throughout Venice itself and do 100% of your buying only in the 2 oldest, largest, and soundest houses—**Pauly & Co.** (Ponte dei Consorzi, Piazza San Marco) and **Salviati & Co.** (San Gregorio 195, across the Grand Canal from the Gritti Palace and Campo S. Maria del Giglio 2461, adjoining the aforementioned hotel). These 2 establishments are impeccably honest and reliable; both are such fairylands of glittering beauty that they shouldn't be missed by any sightseer. Actually, they're as much a part of the Venetian spectator's scene as the Square, the gondolas, and the cathedral.

We list them in alphabetical order because of their equal ranking. The venerable Pauly Co. supplied most of Europe's Royal Houses before the war. Their Golden Book contains the signatures of ex-President Nixon, ex-President Gustav Heinemann of West Germany, ex-President Podgorny of the U.S.S.R., Margaret of Savoy, the King of Afghanistan, d'Annunzio, Marconi, Princess Stefania, Eleanor Roosevelt, and hundreds of similar distinction. Their products have won 25 Gold Medals, 16 Notable Award Prizes, 33 Award Diplomas, the French Legion of Honor, the Crown of Leopold, and the Crown of Italy. In their archives, you'll find 800-thousand one-of-a-kind sketches of antique, classical, and modern patterns. A team of celebrated Glass Masters produces exclusively for them. Even though Pauly has 3 retail branches on Piazza San Marco, don't miss a tour of its Ponte dei Consorzi headquarters. There's a demonstration furnace and budget shop on the ground floor; upstairs, you may wander at will through perhaps 30 glorious rooms full of treasures for the table, the home, and the eye. Now you'll also have the chance to admire the highly recommended Limoges Porcelaines table sets and the famous collection of bronzes made exclusively for Pauly by the most reputable foundry craftsmen of Italy.

Salviati, dean of the field, reached its centennial in '59— and in '63, it captured the celestial "Golden Compasses" award, the biannual "Oscar" presented for Italy's most noble designs in manufactured products. Salviati-developed techniques have long since surpassed the most exquisite artistry of the Renaissance masters. Their pioneering has had a profound influence on the evolution of glass all over the world, thanks to a team of designers and glassmakers to whom we owe the most select production of Murano riches in the fields of tableware, vases, candelabra, lamps, and architectural lighting. Salviati mosaic panels or murals have been commissioned by such widely scattered places as the Vatican, the Royal Palace of Siam, Windsor Castle, and California's Stanford University. The President of the Italian Republic has presented to the Emperor of Japan and his Family a 270-piece Salviati-crafted glassware set. This company also maintains 2 retail outlets on Piazza San Marco, but it would be a pity to miss their magnificent display mansion. In addition to 2 of the most exciting museum collections of ancient and modern glass in existence, as well as a glass and metal sculpture exhibition by American Claire Falkenstein, you'll find a demonstration furnace, and you'll also revel in chamber after chamber which shimmer like the Pleasure Dome of Xanadu.

Both firms guarantee safe arrival to your home of everything they ship—and you can absolutely trust them on this. As we stressed in the earlier "Mail Orders" section of this chapter, *have limitless patience about shipment delays* (months are par for the course, due to Italian export red tape and the logjams at U.S. piers)—and be sure to find out approximate delivery costs to your area, because port brokers' fees are sometimes wicked through no fault of these good artisans. Please remember, also, that NOBODY (not even you!) is permitted to pay U.S. Customs duties and handling before our American officials can examine and evaluate all foreign purchases upon entry into our country— so sometimes it is impossible for these companies to guesstimate this particular levy with accuracy. Whether you spend nothing, $1 for a string of beads, or $4000 for a set of spiderweb-and-thistledown champagne glasses, a visit to both these institutions is a must for any American shophound.

Gifts: Try **Decor Art** (Calle Larga XXII Marzo, near the Square) for small but unusual articles or nearby **Alibaba** for larger pieces particularly suitable for wedding presents.

Jewelry: In quantity, in fame, in the distinction of its worldwide clientele, the unchallenged King of this City of Palaces is **Nardi** (Piazza San Marco 68-71, in the Arcades). Since 1920 it has specialized in designing and creating treasures in gold and precious stones, all handmade and signed as originals with the Nardi name. Today 2 Nardi pieces at first glance are recognized and envied virtually everywhere: Its fabulous "Othello, The Moor of Venice" pin (from $1000), and its ingenious triple-tiered ring which forms a bouquet of tulips. Its current fashion innovations are in enamel or "Angel Skin" (rose coral) surrounded by diamonds. Full line of gems, including antiques; new shop adjacent at No. 68 with exceptionally fine rarities; and now, at No. 71, Nardi presents a special line in hard semiprecious stones and watches; no purchase tax ever; open all year. Expert guidance from Sergio Nardi himself or from Messrs. Gebbani or Zambon.

Knitwear: **Missoni** (S. Marco, Calle Vallaresso 1312/B) casts its stylish purls into sleeveless sweaters (from $180), cardigans (about $380) and jackets ($800 range); umbrellas begin at only $40. So popular that it is often hard to get through the door.

Lace and Refined Linen: **Jesurum** (Ponte Canonica 4310) run by Mario and Alessandro Levi Morenos, is virtually a treasury of spectacular and delicate fashions for table, boudoir and bath as well having such specialties as baby linens, fine embroidery, wedding veils, christening dresses, lingerie and a long line of Jesurum-inspired styles and fresh new explosive color innovations. (You can even ask one of the shop managers to show you the rarest "jewels" of Jesurum—an antique lace collection kept in a strongroom.) The building itself is a collector's item from the 12th century; it is located behind Saint Mark's Basilica and beside the famous Bridge of Sighs where it has pampered the great families of Europe since 1870. Though certainly awed, you shouldn't be frightened by the prices because the inventory is broad enough to accommodate any budget, whether you're shopping for a unique $4.50 pin-cushion, inexpensive cocktail napkins for friends back home—or splurging on custom-made personals where cost is no object. Naturally, in a house like this only the finest cottons, silk and other natural fibers are employed. Branches in *Milan* at Via Leopardi 25 and in *Parma* at Via G. Tommasini 6.

Leather Goods (Men's and Women's): **Luigi Vogini** (S. Marco-Ascensione 1291, 1292, and 1301) has a trio of splendid shops, all within a ducat's throw of each other. There are shoes and boots for your foundation, luggage for your journeys, attache cases for your business, purses for your fortune, accessories for your whimsey, clothing for your warmth and in all products there is that special Vogini fashion for your ego. A bonus: apart from regular hours this foursome remains open from 11 a.m.–7 p.m. on Sun.

Masks and Carnival Attire: These are synonymous with Venice. They have their origins in the *Commedia dell'Arte* (leather was the traditional material for the theatre) and the feverish 18th century when the world went wild during carnival. And here it still does. Out of a glorious past come personages such as Arlecchino, Tartalia, Brighella, Pantalone, Pulcinella, Columbia, Isabella and Smereldina. At **F. G. B.** (S. Marco-Frezzeria 1581 and S.M. del Giglio 2459) fantasy and a highly developed artistry are combined to produce extraordinary pieces. They range in price from $25 to $360. The suns and the moons and the double-faced inventions are masterful. **Laboratorio Artigiano Maschere** (Barbaria de la Tole, Castello 6657) and **Arte Giano Maschere** (Calle del Ridoto) are two other local favorites. **Il Prato** (S. Marco-Frezzeria 1770/1) can add any manner of fancy dress.

Paper (Handmade, Handprinted) and Fine Bindings: **Legatoria Piazzesi,** (Campiello della Feltrina 2511, near the Gritti) offers a fascinating parade from file folders to address books to pen trays to wastebaskets to many other choices. **Ebru** (S. Marco-Calle della Fenice 1920) has, in addition, marvelous animals, candlesticks and geometric forms, all in marbleized paper.

Pastries: Oh, those heavenly sights and aromas which so deliciously advertise **F.lli Milani** (S. Marco-Frezzeria)!

ELSEWHERE IN ITALY

These values we consider extraordinary: In *Como,* it's silk, silk and more silk by the sail-length. Three landmarks vie for the leadership. Proprietor Ercole Moretti of **Seterie Moretti** (Via Garibaldi 69) is assisted by 10 designers in the creation of his specialty of strikingly original prints; each pattern is limited to a maximum output of 10 pieces. At **Rainoldi,** proprietoress Giovanna Rainoldi and her nephew Antonio offer wearables at their Piazza Cavour headquarters, plus bolt silks, sheets and linens at their other 2 branches. The latter firm is closed Mon. **La Seta** is a factory outlet off the *autostrada* coming from *Milan.* As you pay at the toll booth, you'll see its large building on your left; clearly marked signs direct you to its enormous parking lot. Owner Mantero sells his own production by the yard or already made up into shirts and blouses. Since the tariffs in all are virtually at wholesale levels, identical purchases cost appreciably more elsewhere. Recommended. In *Genoa,* **A. Alioto** (Via Ippolito D' Aste 7-5) is a superstar. The craftsmanship and quality in fashion jewelry are enormous, but the prices are startlingly low. Everything hand-designed and handmade; stunning bracelets, necklaces, brooches, earrings, chains, charms and more in both classic and modern, each bearing its own unique flair. Private 3rd-floor studio-apartment (No. 5) with door marked **"A. Testa";** difficult to find, but not to be missed under any circumstances. Also in *Zoagli,* a small town about 18 miles south of Genoa near to Rapallo, you'll find the **Seterie di Zoagli** (via Aurelia 104). This factory weaves antique silk fabric and turns it into ties ($5–12), scarves ($7–18), and foulards ($15–25). In *Ischia,* the **Dominique** chain (6 stores) carries outstanding boutique items at stiff quotations; **Filippo** (on the main street) is also expensive and fine for men's and women's slacks. The flock of others on Corso Vittoria Colomare "import" their wares from Florence, Sorrento, and other mainland hubs. Sadly, this island has no significant specialty.

NOTE · · · Watch out for (1) Bag snatching and pickpocketing which have become so rife in Rome that the U.S. Consulate has had to prepare a printed fact sheet on how to obtain assistance in case you become a victim of this wave of petty crime. Another handout outlines ways to avoid the loss of personal papers, identification and credit cards, money, traveler's checks and other valuables. It even suggests how a woman should wear a shoulder bag. We wonder if they distribute aspirin, too? (2) The "egg-on-the-head" gambit. Resourceful Roman rogues are now fleecing ladies of their fur coats by breaking eggs over the victims' heads. As the goo oozes slowly and decidedly downward, the startled women remove their wraps with the gallant aid of "innocent by-standers"—whose records in the 100-yard dash would be the envy of any U.S. track coach. So *please* hang on to your valuables—and send that coat to the cleaners! (3) Export license requirements on antiques, paintings, china, tea services, and similar goods (enlist your dealer's help). (4) Mechanical gadgets (too often they break), some cottons except handblocked prints (they shrink), imported perfumes (too high), counterfeit paintings and numerous imitations of brand-name products such as "Swiss" or "Cartier" watches, "Clark's" shoes, "Gucci" and "Louis Vuitton" leather goods. These copy-cats earn an estimated 2-to-3-billion dollars a year and create Dolomite-size headaches for the honest manufacturer who has spent his own fortune making his product synonymous with quality. Antiques also are questionable, so approach this field with utmost caution. Ski boots should be tried on with icy calm since 90% of the Italian ones come from non-factory moonlighters. Finally, (5) the Italian Postal Service. We suppose that *somewhere* on the globe there might be a mail carrier that is as complete a disaster and as total a disgrace; based on our own dismal experience, however, we doubt it. Hard-pressed Italians and savvy visitors use commercial couriers such as Rome's Missori and Tavani (Viale M. Gelsomini 14) to deliver anything of the slightest importance. If you have absolutely no recourse but to use the mails, please *be sure* to register your letter or package before affixing the stamps. Keep a duplicate, if possible. Better still, save the item and drop it into the first mailbox you spot that is not on Italian soil.

NETHERLANDS

SHOPPING HOURS

Complicated as all get-out. Department and durables stores open
on Mon. at 10:30 a.m.; otherwise open 9 a.m.–5:30 or 6 p.m.,
including Sat. Hairdressers pull their blinds Mon. afternoons in
some towns and Tues. afternoons in others; shops featuring con-
sumer goods generally close Wed. afternoons. Many continue to
9 or 9:30 p.m. on Thurs. and Fri. with resorts and seaside spas
functioning almost at their own whimsy. There's a flock of other
variables—so check before leaving your hotel.

PUBLIC HOLIDAYS

Jan. 1, Good Fri. (most shops open), Easter Sun., Easter Mon.,
April 30 (Queen's birthday), Ascension Day, Whitsunday, Whitmonday, Dec. 25–26.

PURCHASE TAX DISCOUNT

VAT is 18½% here. Merchants may refund this amount by fill-
ing in an OB 90 form, or if they are participants in the Holland
Tax Free organization they'll issue a special check. They will
inform you as to just how you go about receiving the rebate.

Goods purchased in each shop must be valued at over 300 guilders to qualify but remember, there is no law 'that requires all shopkeepers to offer such benefits. In addition handling charges take a 3% bite out of the final amount you'll get back.

MAIL ORDERS

What a curious and puzzling paradox! In this midget nation of giant sinews which was long the seat of a colonial empire perhaps 20 times larger than its own area, organized international and intercontinental mail-order trade is virtually nonexistent. Many firms are experienced in prompt and flawless shipping to foreign countries, and yes, all of the top-quality merchants are pleased to apply their famed Dutch efficiency to individual inquiries or orders from abroad, but virtually none of them is disposed to develop this channel of business which could be so profitable to them. Although catalogs and brochures exist, with the exception of the Amsterdam Airport Shopping Center's presentation (see below), we've never run across any in English. They, by the way, mail over 360,000 catalogs a year!

The world-famous house of **Bonebakker** is uneasy about selling its diamonds and other luxuries by post; for the customer's satisfaction and theirs, they prefer on-the-spot viewing before purchase. But for its existing clients all services regarding mail orders will be accomplished with pleasure. **Focke & Meltzer,** the most modern china-and-crystal shop on the Continent, has long operated a mail service with excellent results. If you wish to subscribe to it without charge, this prime house will regularly forward inside word concerning new articles and special offers to you. Daily it receives a score or more of requests for information about its fairyland of hand-painted Blue Delft, imprints and other china, hand-blown and hand-cut crystals, Christmas plates, faiences, earthenware, and similarly noble offerings; when you fine-target what you seek please write to **Focke & Meltzer**

(P.C. Hooftstraat 65–67, 1071 BP, Amsterdam, Holland). Your reply should come in a jiffy.

Thus, if you should be interested in ordering by mail from any establishment we mention you must initiate the proceedings by writing a carefully detailed descriptive letter of your requirements.

AMSTERDAM

Shopping Areas: **Rokin, Heiligeweg, P. C. Hooftstraat, Van Baerlestraat, Beethovenstraat, Nieuwe Spiegelstraat** and **Spiegelgracht** are Amsterdam's prize shopping streets; **Kalverstraat** and **Leidsestraat** aren't what they used to be.

THINGS TO BUY

Diamonds, Delft ware, flower bulbs, crystal, silver, handicrafts, miniatures, fine art, maritime gear, Indonesian bric-a-brac, tea tiles, duty-free articles.

Antiques: The **Nieuwe Spiegelstraat** and the adjoining **Spiegelgracht** are famous for their cluster of perhaps 30 dealers, most of them featuring different specialties. Both are across the canal opposite the Rijksmuseum. Good hunting! Every Sun. from 9 a.m.–4 p.m. at the **Nieuwmarkt,** vendors put out their wares.

For indoor antique markets when the weather is inclement:

try **De Looier** (Elandsgracht 109) which can be reached by hopping on Tram #17; open Mon.–Sat. 11 a.m.–5 p.m.

March is the month for The Amsterdam Art Weeks, and two of its most ambitious events are the Old Art and Antiques Fair held early in the month at the New Church (Dam Sq.) and the Antique Books and Prints Fair in the Marriott Hotel.

Arts and Crafts: **Galeria-Atelier Voetboog** (Voetboogstraat 16, off the Spui) is a confederation of about 45 artists. Several are present daily, working on the spot; very creative and tasteful textiles, ceramics, drawings, jewelry and painted silk; open Tues.–Sat. 11 a.m.–5 p.m.

Bulbs and Seeds: **J.B. Wijs & Zoon** (Singel 508-510) are the specialists who cut through all the red tape of shipping and exporting those marvelous Dutch bulbs. Canalside site in the heart of the flower market; it couldn't be more atmospheric or appealing. Remember, most countries—the USA included—prohibit their importation unless accompanied by a health ceritificate issued by the Plant Disease Service—so leave it to the experts.

Chocolates: **Fa. W. Berkhoff** (Leidsestraat 46) will lure you off that diet—but fast!

Cigars: Regiments of tobacconists all over the city specialize in the famous Dutch cigars. The venerable **P. G. C. Hajenius** (Rokin 92-96) puffs up a large variety; it also offers imports and serves every smoker's needs. The redecorated store is most impressive. They recently put a cigar on the market called Grand Finale, which is the first "wet" Dutch smoke and requires special humidors. It is meant to appeal to those who hanker for a more Cubanlike blend.

Delftware, European Crystal, and China: The most famous is **Focke & Meltzer,** leader through the Lowlands since 1823 and now the most modern crystal-and-china shop on the continent. Their year-coded collection of genuine Blue Delft handpainted pieces by the true Royal Delft artisans of ''De Porceleyne Fles'' is the most complete we have ever seen. This medium is rife with so many perils for the unwary that we only put our confidence in this establishment. Proprietor Marc. P. M. Meltzer represents this family's 7th generation of crystal and china traders. Scads of claptrap ''Delftlike'' fakes are peddled all over Holland but there's no monkey business about the authentic handpainting here. You'll find Focke & Meltzer at P. C. Hooftstraat 65–67 (beautifully rebuilt headquarters 3 minutes behind the Rijksmuseum) and in the center of Amsterdam at Rokin 124 (decorated with an original Dutch oakwood interior; you can feel the rich atmosphere of the 18th-century Golden Age). The other prestige Dutch name is Tichelaar Makkum. This Frisian pottery is cherished for its deep-warm colors over a white-coated tin glaze. F & M's ''Amsterdam Museum Collection'' is so priceless that most museums cannot afford similar exhibits. Because this company was originally founded by Bohemian glassmakers it has always featured the largest collection of fine crystal in Northern Europe—Orrefors, Baccarat, Lalique, Daum, Swarovski and their own globally renowned Meltzer Kristal, the world's most expensive stemware. Possibly you'll order only 1 set priced at more than $5,000,000! The china and faience from 22 European countries is a bit more affordable. Look, too, at the very rare Russian lacquer boxes and exquisite handpainted miniatures from Palekh. To find these at all is an achievement. In Amsterdam ask for Cees Hogendoorn, Bart Hoyng or Marc P. M. Meltzer. Inquire about their tax-free services and trouble-free worldwide mailing. Their reputation stands for 167 years of excellence. The publication *Welcome to Amsterdam* is F & M's gift to you if you request it.

Department Stores: **De Bijenkorf** ("Beehive"—and that's how it feels! Damarak 90-A) is best. **Vroom & Dreesmann** (Kalverstraat) is also highly satisfactory. Both have branches in key cities. **Maison de Bonneterie** (Kalverstraat 183) has some very attractive merchandise too.

Diamonds: Be careful: Negotiate *only* with firms known for their integrity. When buying diamonds for investment, sealed or not, be well and correctly advised about future price developments and expectations for their future value. Prices can vary in both directions, of course, as they follow market fluctuations. Be satisfied by buying the right type of stone at the right time. You'll avoid disappointment by avoiding any guidance that is less than the best. (And top-quality advice is free in any case.) Consider the purchase of diamonds and jewelry in the same way as if you were buying a new car, a video recorder, or a TV. It's the pleasure or usefulness you derive that should be the prevailing factors, not primarily a matter of investment. Nevertheless, diamonds are forever—and that's the biggest difference.

In this key center of the most popular of precious stones, there are still bargains galore—but if you aren't thoroughly conversant with their technical subtleties, they can be terribly tricky to buy. That's why we suggest that you head straight for the oldest and most respected gem merchant in the Netherlands—the house of **Bonebakker** (Rokin 86-90) which was beautifully refashioned and enhanced in oak and marble as a showcase for such stunning products. On Rokin 86 an additional production and exhibition wing has been installed. A direct connection has been created with the sales center, where you can browse and shop without disturbance and in privacy. Glass doors shield you from any inconvenience while providing the intimacy desired for conversation and concentration. Rather than be steered by a commission-hungry guide to lesser purveyors (including outright tourist traps), for actual buying we'd much prefer to be advised about cut, color, clarity, style, and value by distinguished experts who lay the long history of Bonebakker's reputation on the counter every time they display a stone. The Amsterdam landmark was founded in 1792 by Adrianus Bonebakker; in 1840 King William of Orange ordered his crown to be designed and created by Adrian Bonebakker. Ask about the museum that has been initiated in cooperation with the City of Amsterdam—masterpieces of this historic house dating from the 18th century that have become a national heritage. Each purchase comes with a certificate stating all the characteristics and, naturally, the Bonebakker guarantee. You'll see how rough diamonds are transformed into dazzling gems by master craftsmen and how their jewelry is composed. There's immediate service for setting and alterations. Moreover, their diamond prices today aren't a single guilder—or even a single *kwartje* (10¢)—higher than anywhere else. And they need not be expensive because the enormous inventory provides every shopper with an opportunity to own a Bonebakker stone. Also in the collection are Patek Philippe as well as Baume & Mercier and Emile Pequinet watches, Dunhill giftware, antique silver, and other sinfully appealing luxuries. The new and innovative Gift-Products Department has exclusive presents for management purposes. In addition, Bonebakker has started designing their own signature collection of jewelry and special items which shouldn't be missed. Unlike finished jewelry and similar articles, loose diamonds are exempt from a 18½% VAT tax. To holders of an American passport, on all purchases exceeding DFL 300, loose diamonds excepted, an immediate discount of 15.6% is allowed. Simply ask for the refund form, which you'll give to a Dutch customs official when leaving the country. Closed only on off-season Sundays, April 30, Dec. 25–26, and Jan. 1. The knowledgeable English-speaking manageress is an exceptionally wise and patient advisor. Here is Bonebakker's base of heritage and experience, of artistry, taste, and technology. In this modern era it is truly rare to find direct lineal descendants of an age-old dynasty of Dutch manufacturing diamond merchants to handle your individual needs. Diamonds are both so arcane and so important a purchase that it's simple common sense to do business with a firm with such impeccable standards of craftsmanship and reliability. You'll not only feel safer but *be* safer.

Schaap & Citroen (Kalverstraat 1 and Rokin 12), founded in 1826, is also worthy.

English Lifestyle: **Mulberry** (P. C. Hoofstraat 46) is wonderful for these wearables and accessories. See under ''London'' for particulars.

Fashions: This Low Country has its own brand of haute couture as one might expect in such a liberated atmosphere. Here certainly is the nerve center where fashion statements are often the most daring on today's European scene. One of the unquestioned leaders in a controversial field is **Frank Govers** (Keizersgracht 500), the quintessential Dutch designer. His handmade pieces reflect the richesse and flamboyance of costumery. Pleats, puffs, cuffs, lace, sequins, velour, satin—the works! To us, this bizarre expression possesses a character all its own. Govers undoubtedly is a genius. Whether you admire him or not is another question. There are many zesty boutiques lining P.C. Hoofstraat. Some of the hottest names include **Tim Bonig** (#92), **Vivalei** (#94), **Max Mara** (#108), **House of Standing** (#113), **Edgar Vos,** and **Azzurro. The Society Shop,** covering a lot of real estate along Van Baerlestraat, is the target for men seeking elegant and classic stylings.

NOTE · · · Mode Amsterdam is quite a happening. Usually scheduled during the first two weeks in Sept. in the New Church; 2–4 shows daily; open to the public; entrance 5–10 guilders.

Flying Home: Bona fide nonresident departing passengers at **Schiphol Airport** (Amsterdam) *with destinations outside the Benelux countries* may save up to 60% on a raft of luxury items (liquors, tobacco, perfumes, cars, binoculars, watches, toys, tape recorders, etc.) at the largest and 1 of the 2 lowest-priced Tax Free Shopping Centers on the Continent. There are about 40 shops in the complex carrying a staggering 40,000 items. Read its free brochure before buying. Our only carp is that sometimes its stores are out of stock of exactly the listed item or items upon which the traveler's heart is set. This is a frustrating disappointment, because you may visit the area only as you leave. Be sure to look for the yellow price tags with the words "Tax Free"; the white tickets signify a levy for Common Market residents.

Fine Art: **Galerie D'Eend't N.V.** (Spuistraat 270-272) is comparatively low-priced, because it's sort of a community studio for selected painters and sculptors. Excellent if you hit the right day.

Flea Market: It's located at the famous Waterlooplein near the new semicircular Music Theater. Nothing seems out of place in this bizarre bazaar—rusty keys, orange squeezers, piles of paintings, china, corsets, cradles, books, furs, water taps, tailor's dummies, and much, much more. Mon.–Sat. 10 a.m.–4 p.m.—and haggle mercilessly on everything.

Lace and Linens: If you must, **Het Kantenhuis** (Kalverstraat 124). But to us it's so commercial, with so much machine work, that we strongly urge travelers with Belgium on their itineraries to hold off until their arrival there.

Maritime Gear: **Andries de Jong Ship Shop** (Muntplein 8) is an outstanding chandler. This colorful establishment is especially noted for its lamps, maps, and useful seagoers' fare. A versatile assemblage at relatively low costs.

Markets: Aside from the already mentioned Flea Market and various antique markets here are a few others to pique specialized interests: **Artist's Market** (Thorbeckeplein) Sun. in summer; noon–6 p.m.; painting and jewelry a la Montmartre; **Bird Market** (Noordermarkt) Sat. mornings; **Book Market** (Oudemanhuispoort) Mon.-Sat. 10 a.m.–4 p.m.; **Flower Market** (Singel) Mon.-Sat.; **General Market** (Albert Cuypstraat) Mon.-Sat. 9 a.m.–5 p.m.; **Stamp Market** (Nieuwezijds Voorburgwal opp. nr. 280) Wed. and Sat. 1 p.m.–4 p.m.; **Textile Market** (Noordermarkt/Westerstraat) Mon. 9 a.m.–1 p.m.

Shopping Center: The variegated **Amstelveen Shopping Center** is 5 minutes from Schiphol Airport.

Sweaters: **Trisha** is the label employed by **Patricia Elfring,** one of Holland's greatest (and nicest) young talents. Her handmade stylings go for multiples of her homegrown prices because by buying directly from her you eliminate mark-ups. These are exclusive creations found only in the finest international boutiques. She also does custom work. Get in touch. (Address: Katwijkstraat 19 I, 1059 XM Amsterdam; Tel: 020–141229.)

Tea Tiles: These unusual tablets which are about twice the size of this book and nearly as thick, have a history that goes back to the 4th century. Highly decorative and segmented (pieces were broken off and used as currency in the Far East), the "bricks" make marvelous inexpensive gifts (about $10). The tea is compressed into a relief that can be hung on the wall, framed, actually used to brew a cuppa or—imagine the chagrin!—placed on a coffee table. Available in the delicatessen shops at the Amsterdam Airport Duty Free Shopping Centre.

THE HAGUE

SHOPPING AREAS

Spuistraat and a second unbroken street with 3 separate names (**Venestraat, Hoogstraat,** and **Noordeinde)** are the hubs.

Antiques and Bric-a-Brac: The more affluent hunter should find the best quality of aged treasures locally on Noordeinde, with old pewter a big specialty. For items which normally cost less, the Denneweg area is replete with small shops in which copper, brass, and lower quality pewter seem to predominate. Here's a list to help you zero in if time is short.

Antique Clocks and Barometers: **ten boom en van Duffelen** (Noordeinde 132) buys, sells, and restores them.

Antiques in General: **Smelik en Stokking BV** (Noordeinde 156), **Damen** (Noordeinde 95), **Floor** (Denneweg 33), **B. van Leeuwen** (Denneweg 114 A), **In de Vergulde Tuitlamp** (Denneweg 110A).

Antique Markets: At **Lange Voorhout,** May 27–Sept. 24; every Thurs., 9 a.m.–9 p.m. and on the **Plein,** Oct. 4–May 10; every Thurs., noon–9 p.m.

Books: **De Slegte BV** (Spuistraat 9) has shelves full of new as well as secondhand volumes at low prices. There are sections for books at both the antique markets mentioned above.

Dutch Furniture, China and Delft Ware: **S. van Leeuwen** (Noordeinde 164).

English Furniture: **Spoor** (Denneweg 68).

Handicrafts: **Tesselschade-Arbeid Adelt** (Noordeinde 92) is a center for tea cozies, folkloric dolls, children's dresses, table-mats, hand-painted canisters, and other objects, toys, and Hin-deloopen painting. The *Amsterdam* branch is on Leidseplein; both are philanthropic institutions.

Silver and Jewelry: **Jeweler Schaap** (Noordeinde 86, Hoogstraat 23, Plaats 2) stocks gems, antique silver, and some modern silver. Persian Gulf pearls its pet feature; friendly personnel here. **Steltman** (Kneutikdijk 2A) is strong for traditional stones, as is **Bodes en Bode** (Denneweg 50). **In den Silvern Molenbeecker** (Hoogstraat 3) has special ornaments and other sterling pieces.

Used Clothing for Gentlefolk: Please don't scoff, because **Secondhand Rose** (Mauritskade 69-71) carries top-quality la-dies' wear "as new" at 50% or less of their original prices. The turnover of wardrobes among the diplomats' wives in this Dutch capital is tremendous, and Proprietors Steffy Rathje-Becher and Anca Struycken-Landwehr have ingeniously exploited it. Gowns to furs to shoes to mink hats to handbags to bikinis—all are astounding bargains. Cross your fingers that their stocks will be copious on the day of your visit!

ELSEWHERE IN THE NETHERLANDS

In *Delft,* **"De Porceleyne Fles"** factory (makers of the genuine Delft ware) will welcome your visit between April 1 and Oct. 31 to both their demonstration section and showrooms. Hours: 9 a.m.–6 p.m. daily and 1 p.m.–6 p.m. Sun. Tourists are now admitted in winter, but there is no action.

In *Rotterdam,* head for **De Lijnbaan,** which is a mile-long American-type shopping center. **The Beursplein Shopping Center** combines branches of large department stores, market stalls, small shops and a terrace cafe. Otherwise, the 2 most rewarding streets for prowling are Binnenweg, Hoogstraat and the Zuidplein.

De Bijenkorf (The Beehive) is the leading department store, ensconced in a handsome building designed by U.S. Architect Marcel Breuer. This operation is one of the closest to American merchandising techniques in Europe, excellent for just about anything the traveler might need. **Vroom & Dreesmann,** the runner-up, is also highly satisfactory. Both have branches in the key cities.

Although antique hunting isn't as exciting here as The Hague or Amsterdam, you'll discover a mixed-bag of stuff on Tues. and Sat. from 10 a.m.–5 p.m. in the Binnenrotte and Hoogstraat areas as well as on the Grote Kerkplein by the St. Laurens-church. There's a stamp exchange Wed. from 2 p.m.–5 p.m. and Sat. from 10 a.m.–5 p.m. on the Schouwebergplein.

In *Utrecht,* the one place not to miss is **Jeweler Schaap** (Steenweg 63). In this branch (headquarters in The Hague) you'll usually find the most desirable secondhand silver in the nation— because here's where the lion's share comes when big estates are broken up for taxes. Most of it is hallmarked.

NOTE · · · Watch out for the previously mentioned Delft imitations, furs (only rabbits are raised), routine costume jewelry (expensive and dull), gloves (heavy types okay, but dress-ups dowdy and costly), perfumes and fine wines (taxed to death).

NORWAY

SHOPPING HOURS

In the larger cities (*Bergen* excepted): On weekdays normally 9 a.m.–5 p.m. in winter, sometimes to 4 p.m. in summer, and 9 a.m.–2 p.m. on Sat. Thurs. most shops remain open until 7 p.m. and some of the larger stores repeat this on Fri. as well.

PUBLIC HOLIDAYS

Jan. 1, Maundy Thurs., Good Fri., Easter Sun., May 1, May 17 (Constitution Day), Ascension Day, Whitmonday, Dec. 25–26.

PURCHASE TAX DISCOUNT

Here 16.67% is tacked onto the price of all goods. You can get that back (less a 4.5% service charge) on your purchases (we understand a minimum of 300 NOK must be spent in each store) at all departure points. Under a new streamlined system shopkeepers who display the sticker bearing the legend ''Norway Tax Free Shopping'' will issue you a Tax-free Shopping Cheque and your cash refund will be forthcoming upon leaving the country. This is the case even if you have paid by credit card. Be sure to have your packages ready for inspection if called upon to show them. Don't forget to have your passport handy on all shopping forays.

MAIL ORDERS

In addition to the expensive bijoux which anyone would expect to find in **David-Andersen,** Norway's number one jeweler, it is full of knockout exclusive creations at encouragingly modest prices. Please read our following report on this landmark for a general idea of these unbeatable bargains. Then if you're as intrigued as we think you might be, handsome, foldover brochures (most of them in color) with price lists are yours for the asking. Their subjects: Gold Plated Sterling Silver Enameled Flatware, Saga Silver Flatware (24 different utensils), Silver Enameled Jewelry, Uni David-Andersen's handmade jewelry with Norwegian Stones, Pewter, and Cast Pewter. They're great.

William Schmidt & Co., where nothing is ever mass produced, has been for over 2 decades our unchallenged favorite for wearables and souvenirs of authentic Nordic flavor. Deeper in this chapter some of its prize original specialties are listed. It has a tremendous export business to North America. Your inquiries would receive warm and efficient attention from the proprietary Fretheim clan.

SHOPPING AREAS

The prime target is definitely along **Karl Johans Gate** and the side streets radiating from it. The **Aker Brygge** complex is an absolute *must*. It has become a local landmark. Another venue could be **Hegdehaugsveien/Bogstadveien** which starts behind the Royal Palace going toward the Majorstua district. **Markveien** and **Thorvald Meyers gt.** in the East End are at the lower end of the market.

THINGS TO BUY

Norwegian enameled silver and jewelry, hand-knit sweaters, regional furniture, hand-loomed textiles, glass, and other handcrafts, maritime art, sports equipment, antiques.

Antiques: **Kaare Berntsen** (Universitetsgaten 12) leads the pack in quality and price; smaller **Wangs Kunst** (Kristian IV den Gate 12) and **Hammerlunds Kunsthandel** (Tordenskjoldsgate 3) sometimes offer good hunting. We're particularly fond of **Bergfjerdingen** (Damstredet 20); it has 2 elves' rooms with copper molds, wood, glass, pottery, and a single big fireplace.

NOTE · · · Personally, we didn't think the **Antik-Brukt Markedet** (Trondheimsvn. 13) was worth the $6 cab fare.

Arts and Crafts: **Norway Designs** (Stortingsgaten 28) is just opposite the Continental Hotel in midcity. (Please check the address because there was talk of them moving and we'd hate you to miss the experience of a visit here.) Descend one flight to its large, well-lit showroom and *what* a parade of merchandise you'll see; good taste is manifest even down to the smallest eggcup cover. You'll delight in the pottery, glassware, ceramic sculptures, candles, clothing, woven shawls by Sigrun Berg, throw blankets, wooden trays, wrought-iron candelabra, kitchen equipment, place mats, wool tinted with natural dyes and knitting patterns, hand-carved replicas of Viking motifs, and more. Director Per Lippestad is most helpful.

Husfliden (Den Norske Husflidsforening, Mollergaten 4) has an old name. There's a whole section devoted to looms and weaving materials. Yards of fabrics, rugs, embroidery, pewter, and other artisan work fill their shelves. Among other things there's a good selection of painted or paint-it-yourself furniture. **Heimen** (Arbeiderg.—corner Kr. IV's gt.) offers yet another intriguing collection of handicrafts, textiles, hand knits, and various kinds of national specialties including made-to-order models of the Norwegian National Dress (around $1600).

Marjatta Butikk og Galleri (Kongensgate 14) is charming. Dresses, candles, glassware, materials, sweaters, shawls, and ceramics are among the choices available.

Bazaar: The butchers' stalls in the historic brick firehouse behind the Cathedral (Church St. near Market Place) have been rebuilt into enchanting little shops. It's known locally as *Basarhallene*. Look for the thumbsize jewelry quarters of **Donna and Maren Ann,** the glass engraver's workshop and **Galleri Hylla,** which are under the eaves. Lots of additional attractions; just right for browsing; fixed prices everywhere.

Books: **Tanum** (Karl Johans Gate 43) is surely one of the best shops in Europe. You won't want to be rushed here.

Buttons: **Knappenhuset** (Akersgate 20) seems to have at least 2,222,222 of them tucked in its drawers. Traditional silver clasps for sweaters very inexpensive.

Candy: The **Freia** brand satisfys many a sweet tooth in these parts. They have their own retail outlet at Karl Johans Gate 31.

Coins: **Oslo Mynthandel** (Kongensgate 31) is both heads and tails for collectors.

Department Stores: **Steen and Strom** will give you a fine cross section of Norwegian retailing.

Enameled Silver and Viking-Style Costume Jewelry: Scandinavia's largest jewelry store is **David-Andersen** (Karl Johans Gate 20). The size and elegance invite shopping curiosity and assured fascination for such variety. Moreover, these air-conditioned premises never wreck our budget; prices are really modest. Their irresistible enameled demitasse spoons ($25–$50), their enameled costume pieces (from $25), dessert spoons or cake forks ($63), sterling salt-and-peppers, vases, plates, and other fired items are equally tempting. A second feature here are the exquisitely handworked "Saga" trinkets—brooches, rings, earrings, pendants, bracelets, and cuff links, which sell in the comfortable price bracket of $19 to $109. Full line of hand-crafted sterlingware in exclusive antique and modern Norse patterns plus a collection of really old silver and antique as well as contemporary silver jewelry, and unusual forget-me-nots for gentlemen. In enameling and silver, ask for Mrs. Njoten, and in jewelry, see Miss Huseklepp; 4th generation owner, Jon Arthur David-Andersen, an alumnus of St. Olaf College in Minnesota, is also on hand.

Florist: **Hoegh** (Hotel Continental) is excellent.

Furs: **Studio H. Olesen** (O. Slottsgt. 18-20 and Universitetsgt. 20) and **Thorkildsen** (Nedre Slottsgt. 9 and Vikaterrassen) have the most exalted reputations.

Glassware: **Landsverk** (Grensen 10) contains such an inventory that it's hard to choose. **Christiania Glasmagasin** (Stortorvet 9) has three floors of china, pewter, glass, souvenirs, and more. Hadeland Norwegian glass is good—miles from being as stupendous as those fabulous Swedish products, but not as expensive, either.

Maritime Objects of Art: **Damms Antikvariat** (Tollbugate 25, Tordenskjoldsgate 6) is a nexus for old maps, bowsprit sculptures, binnacles, sextants, and wonderful prints of the historic brigs and steamers which once plied these Northern waters. Lovers of things nautical will find authentic pieces with very fair price tags. **Captain's Cabin** (H. Heyerdahlsgt. 1) has everything to do with marine lore and decorative objects. Salutes to the **Oslo Flaggfabrikk** (Stortingsgt. 6, entrance at Rosenkrantzgt.) where any flag, banner, or ensign you might wish can be made up. There's a large stock already, befitting such a seafaring nation.

Pewter: Try **Tinnboden** (Tordenskjoldsgate 7).

Porcelains: **Porsgrunn Porselen** (Karl Johans Gate 14) ranks highest. Full line, including figurines; inferior to top Danish brands, but excellent all the same.

Regional Wearables and Souvenirs: **William Schmidt & Co.** (Karl Johans Gate 41) is the nation's top center for clothing and articles of genuine Nordic flavor. Its midtown headquarters reopened in a new building is going great guns—with the standard full range of items. One of the oldest stores in Norway, established in 1853, its colorful gamut of provincial harvests includes handknit sweaters in ancient Norwegian patterns—the largest selection by far on the Continent. There are models for ladies, men, and children—all shrink-resistant, color fast, mothproofed, and wonderfully comfortable to wear. They have added a line of machine-knitted garments of the highest quality, too. Lovers of the unique may buy dramatic, long-lasting handbags, gloves, hats, ski boots, and other togs in genuine seal, as well as attention-arresting reindeer-skin hats and slippers or reindeer knives. Women will find Schmidt's famous "Vams," gay and pert ¾-length wool sports coats useful and versatile. Collectors of curiosa will discover intriguingly cute woodcut figurines and naughty trolls. Small fry delight in regiments of dolls in beautiful native costumes. For the home, you'll see hand-printed placemats in the rose pattern, silver and enamel items, handwoven mats and table runners in old Norwegian designs and a profusion of hand-made pewter vases, candle holders, ashtrays, and scads of other interesting possibilities. Flat 12.5% saving on U.S. or foreign deliveries; sizable mail-order business; all shipments totally guaranteed. Current Family-Standard-Bearer T. Fjeld Fretheim and his equally gracious daughters, Mrs. Ellen Hauge and Mrs. Elizabeth Syberg, speak perfect English; they will take care of you graciously. All major credit cards welcome. The best of its type in the Norselands.

Shopping Macrocosm: **Aker Brygge** is opposite the City Hall facing the port, the excursion boat harbor and the busy life at quayside. This is possibly Europe's most ambitious achievement in urban renewal—the rebirth of an once dreary and almost forgotten derelict into an exciting combination of shops, parlors and restaurants of almost limitless variety. A Plexiglas-covered staircase crosses the waterfront boulevard and enters the Aker Brygge zone. In summer there is an apron of tables for snacking and sipping plus 2 adjoining edifices: the Shipyards Halls and the Terminal Building. An effort has been made to create a shopping village with its own joyful personality and unique approach to innovative displays. There's an open-air theater on the pier, bands, and street artists. Many purveyors are members of the Norwegian Tax-Free Shopping Plan where you can receive a 10% to 14% reduction on purchases. Opening hours at 10 a.m. and late closings both in summer and winter; some shops open on Sundays from 1 p.m. to 6 p.m.

Other shopping centers include the **Vika complex,** 3 blocks from the Hotel Continental, which comes up with everything from couture boutiques to a laundromat. There is another shopping arcade at **Karl Johans Gate 14.** The interior patio has been fenced off and a trellis set up. Snackers sit at umbrella-shaded tables. Baker Hansen supplies the calories. Around the perimeter are various shops. **Grensenland 9,** aka ''Borderland,'' is a shopping passage in which the facades of old buildings have been kept intact. Here, too, are some boutiques for browsing and the inevitable bakery.

Sports Equipment: At **Klingenberg Reiseeffekter og Paraplyer** (Roald Amundsens gate 4), among the suitcases and umbrellas, you'll find sturdy Beckman backpacks—a *must* for any hiker or lover of the outdoors. Select from leather models and less costly synthetic materials. This is an absolutely top-quality brand. **Speider Sport** (Stortingsgata 8–12) and **Sport Co.** (near the Hotel Continental) also cater to athletic-minded locals.

Woven Goods: **Sigrun Berg's** cozy little haven, in a charming old quarter (Damstredet 20), offers original stylings in woven dresses, skirts, jackets, bedspreads, and the like. While her label is also found in a few choice shops (such as Norway Designs, if you don't want to stroll over here) this is where you'll find the greater selection, naturally.

BERGEN

SHOPPING HOURS

Slightly different here than in *Oslo*. Closings Mon., Tues., Wed., Fri. at 4:30 p.m., on Thurs. at 7 p.m. and on Sat. at 2 p.m.

SHOPPING AREAS

Midtown is the magnet. In **Bryggen Brukskunst,** the remodeled old town, artists and artisans are slowly but inexorably taking over ancient houses to ply their trades.

THINGS TO BUY

The same as in *Oslo*.

Decorative Art: **Prydkunst Hjertholm** (Olav Kyrresgt 7) is the permanent exhibition of talented young Norwegian artists and artisans of pewter, ceramics, wood, jewelry, and handwoven rugs. It's imaginative and innovative.

Department Stores: Try **Sundt** or **Kloverhuset** for widest variety; both are inferior to Oslo's Steen & Strom.

Florist: **Iris** (Markevein) is versatile and reliable.

Gift Shops: **Hogi's** (Markeveien 2A, near the Hotel Bristol) is a reflection of exceptional taste. Minor examples of what we like here are the tea cozies, the unusual candles, and the drinking cup of tin and pewter combined with burnt spruce.

Glassware and Pottery: While **Glasmagasin** (Olav Kyrres Gate 9) has limited dimensions, its stocks are large. Hadeland glass (pride of the country) and Stavangerware of both Figgoportsgrun and Figgostavanger are among its most popular specialties.

Handicrafts: Bergen's world-famous **"Husfliden"** (Vagsalmenning 3 plus nearby branch) has proudly sustained its reputation as Norway's leading center of rugs, West Coast hand-knitwear, and the like for over 8 decades.

THINGS NOT TO BUY

This nation has very little merchandise that doesn't measure up to scratch. Textiles (manufactured, not hand-loomed) still seem second-line, in general; leather goods are expensive and not worth it; the majority of the fur stylings are old hat.

PORTUGAL

SHOPPING HOURS

Normally from 9 a.m.–1 p.m. and 3–7 p.m. Closed Sat. at 1 p.m. Many shopping centers open 7 days a week until midnight.

PUBLIC HOLIDAYS

Jan. 1, Apr. 25 (Portugal Day), May 1, June 10 (Camoes Day), Corpus Christi, Aug. 15, Oct. 5 (Day of the Republic), Nov. 1, Dec. 1, 8, and 25.

MAIL ORDERS

Fashionings in gold are traditionally the most popular and rewarding type of purchase by visitors to this land. **W. A. Sarmento** is this commodity's most venerable and illustrious virtuoso. To balance its richly opulent stocks of gems, tea services, flatware, and precious bric-a-brac, many of its massive assemblage of exclusive, handwrought, gold-plated silver filigree earrings, brooches, cuff links and the like cost strikingly little. Its handmade copies of antique jewelry are particularly impressive. Splendid buys.

    Madeira Superbia, with 3 branches, is by far the leading source in the capital for Madeira enbroideries, organdies, and tapestries. This field is so crowded with second-rate would-be competitors that here is where we have long, long placed our cash and our trust. If this famed Portuguese specialty should spark your fancy, write to the director for further facts on the specific category you seek.

NOTE · · · Country markets are usually great fun and some of the most attractive regional crafts stand ready and waiting to be plucked up. Here's a short list of likely targets. **Albufeira, Algarve** (every third Sun.); **Barcelos** (Thurs.); **Cascais** (Wed. and Sat.); **Lagos** (first Sun.); **Portimao** (first Mon.); **Sintra, Feira de Sao Pedro** (every second and fourth Sun.).

Factory visits are also extremely interesting. South of *Nazare* are ceramic works at **Caldas da Rainha,** and north of Nazare at **Marinha Grande** you'll see artisans creating fine crystal. In *Ilhavo,* south of Oporto, is the **Vista Alegre** porcelain empire. Visitors are welcome.

LISBON

THINGS TO BUY

Gold and costume jewelry, woven Madeira products, ceramics, porcelains, decorative arts, and handicrafts.

SHOPPING AREAS

The **"Chiado"** section: Nova do Almada, Rua Garrett, and Rua do Carmo—plus **Rua da Escola Politecnica,** outside the

"Chiado," and the **"Baixa"** section encompassing the streets from the Rossio Sq. to the Tagus River.

NOTE · · · In August 1988 the "Chiado" district was ravaged by fire. Rebuilding in this picturesque quarter should be well underway by now. Our corrected copy is as up-to-date as possible as we go to press.

Antiques: We've seen carved wooden statuary of angels, saints, and gargoyles, stunning tiles, satiny pewter, and paintings of the highest order—a vast parade of fine arts. **Solar** (Rua D. Pedro V 68-70) is a splendid first stop for the aficionado. **Xairel** (Rua D. Pedro V) is another winner. If you don't find what you're after in either of these, browse up and down the same street through a number of interesting alternates. The only sad note is that the prices have skyrocketed.

Antique Furniture Copies and Leatherwork: For a unique experience, first tour the magnificent **Fundacao Ricardo do Espirito Santo Silva** (Decorative Arts School Museum) at Largo das Portas do Sol 2—a treasure house of perfect reproductions of 17th- to 19th-century European furniture plus Portuguese silver, tiles, Arraiolos rugs, and other masterpieces. Then walk a few steps to the hurly-burly of its workshops, which employ craftsmen who create marvelous chairs, tables, mirrors, screens, lamps, sconces, bookbindings, chests of drawers and candlesticks. (It has been whispered that most of the copies in Versailles were manufactured here.) The Order Department is on the 3rd floor. Deliveries take months; it's all high-key hustle and bustle. Here's a display that we commend to you with enormous enthusiasm.

Art Gallery: The most fashionable one is **Galerias Sesimbra** (Rua Castilho 77, behind the Ritz, and also in the Sheraton) for contemporary paintings, sculpture, and tapestries. The most choice classic works are to be found in the aforementioned antique shops that cluster along Rua Dom Pedro V.

Ceramics and Porcelains: Lovely things at **Vista Alegre** (Largo do Chiado 18); small branch in the Ritz. **Ana,** also in the Ritz, shouldn't be missed. Its ceramics are enchanting. **Sant-'Anna** (Rua do Alecrim 91A) is equally fetching in another way; more and better antique tiles are featured; at your instructions, the borders on shades will be painted to match the design on any lamps which catch your fancy. It stocks an interesting variety of plates and ashtrays at tempting price levels. **Fabrica de Loica de Sacavem** (Av. da Liberdade 49-57) offers handsome large tile pieces. **Viuva Lamego** (Largo do Intendente Pina Manique 25), routine and low-priced, has a more versatile assemblage.

Department Stores: **Casa Africana, Armazens Conde Barao** (Rua Fresca 13), **Sopal,** and **Lanalgo** (Rua de Santa Justa 42). Pretty routine.

Drugstore: **Farmacia Azevedos** (Rossio 31).

Fado Records: Best selection of these national laments at **Valentim de Carvalho Lda.** (Rua Castilho 39 and Av. de Roma 49). Amalia Rodriguez is still *the* singing star.

Florist: Flores **Romeira Roma** (Avenida de Roma 50C) draws a society clientele. Artistic arrangements; fairly expensive by local standards.

Gold Jewelry, Gold Trinkets, Gems, Objets d'Art: Portugal has Europe's biggest and finest bargains in gold. This precious metal is the best single buy in the land—and **W. A. Sarmento** (Rua do Ouro 251, foot of the Santa Justa elevator) is the nation's oldest and most respected specialist. This world-famous landmark was founded in 1870 by the original Wenceslau Sarmento; today it is operated by his brilliant namesake-grandson and his great-grandson Arthur, both of them *ne plus ultra* experts in gemology and in their own special division of metallurgy. If your budget is limited, there is an almost bottomless display of alluring, intricately filigreed earrings, brooches, cuff links, and similar items, most of them in handworked, gold-plated silver. Equally tempting are Sarmento's 19¼-carat gold charms and natural sterling "costume" creations—a huge variety of subjects and designs in a very inexpensive price range. Because every article, no matter how modest, is fashioned in the Sarmento workshops, it is infinitely superior to the look-alike junk in the jungle of flashy tourist shops which soil the main streets of Lisbon. For the beauty lover who can afford to spend more, Sarmento points with pride to (1) its very important collection of sterling silver copies of masterpieces in the Portuguese Art Museum, (2) its rare collection of antique gold and antique jewelry copies, entirely made by hand, (3) its largest stocks of flatware, tea services, and other house silver on the Peninsula, (4) its dazzling gems, and (5) its carefully selected array of decorative bric-a-brac. All major credit cards are accepted. Now the fifth generation of this legendary family assures that the great traditions of Portuguese skills will move into the 21st century.

Portuguese Handicrafts: Our leading candidate is **Casa Regional da Ilha Verde** (Rua Paiva de Andrada 4). Some Azorian creations are here. **Casa Quintao** (Rua Ivens 30) is known for its Beiriz and Arraiolos rugs. (The latter come ready-made or in weave-it-yourself kits.) **Casa dos Tapetes de Arraiolos** (Rua da Imprensa Nacional 116-E) is a viable alternate. Additional selections of regional crafts can be plucked from **Centro de Artesanato** (Rua Castilho 61), and **Avenidarte** (Avenida da Liberdade 224). The last two have the largest abundance of wares.

Madeira Embroideries, Organdies, and Tapestries:
Madeira Superbia (Avenida Duque de Loule 75A, with branches listed below) is again THE house—and we've seen them all. Every piece of their richly wrought stock comes direct from their venerable studios and "factory" in the island capital of *Funchal*. (Visitors to Madeira should ignore sleazy competitors and head straight to its Rua do Carmo 27-1 headquarters.) Four of their lures are their gay breakfast sets (1 mat and 2 napkins), ever-useful bridge sets, top-quality 8-piece lunch sets, and oh-so-luxurious dinner sets. In tableware, we are particularly fond of their delicate organdy squares (6 mats, 6 napkins). This progressive enterprise has expanded its range to include full lines in special materials of dresses, long evening dresses (all Madeira embroidered), silk and linen blouses (Madeira embroidered and appliqued), fine handkerchiefs for both genders (with or without monogram), and daintily designed children's wearables. Colorful regional tapestries, into which every thread is hand-embroidered, have long been one of Madeira Superbia's most famous specialties. Low-priced examples which await your inspection are the floral needlepoint chair covers and squares for cushions. Ladies will find flocks of evening bags in both petit point and gross point. Householders will find a wide assortment of decorative tapestry rugs. Art connoisseurs will find rugs and wall hangings which are remarkably duplicated tapestry copies of the paintings of classic and contemporary masters. Lots more, too! At the main store, ask for Miss Georgina or Miss Genovera. The Madeira Superbia branches are in *Lisbon's* Hotel Ritz (Elia Faria) and in *Estoril's* Hotel Estoril Sol (Ana Simoes). We've yet to locate anybody as fine. Highest recommendation.

Pavilhao da Madeira (Avenida da Liberdade 15) is also dependable, but to us not in the same class. **The Ann Leacock Lda. Co.** chain (Galeries Ritz in *Lisbon* plus 2 branches in the *Algarve* and 1 in *Cascais*) is now definitely second string, in our opinions; we saw every outlet. **The Madeira House** (Rua Augusta 135) impresses us as having become so commercial that we no longer like it at all.

Markets: There are a number of so-called commercial centers in Lisbon. The most grandiose scheme so far is the **Centro Comercial das Amoreiras** (Avenida Duarte Pacheco, ½-mile from the Ritz Intercontinental). It bulges with more than 300 shops, dining spots, plus the Exhibition Hall. Downstairs at the **Imaviz Shopping Center,** across from the Hotel Sheraton, you will find a complex of at least 50 different stores and boutiques—and here, among whatever else catches the eye, the visitor should buy cork products if he or she is interested. It stays open from 9 a.m.–12 p.m. 7 days a week, including holidays. So does the **Terminal Market** in the Central Railway Station, which offers in addition a 4-star restaurant, a Chinese restaurant, a supermarket, a disco, and other extras as fringe benefits. The quality is higher in the former. Finally, to us at least, both the **Lisbon Thieves Market,** at the Campo de Santa Clara in the Alfama district (open Tues. and Sat.), and the **Lisbon Fish Market** are a waste of time. Neither is a fraction as colorful or as interesting as some of their counterparts in other European cities.

Menswear: **Lourenco & Santos Lda.** (Rua 1 de Dezembro, near the Hotel Avenida Palace) is a first-rate shirtmaker. Their cloth is fine, long-staple, pre-shrunk Oxford and their handworkmanship is flawless—price tags considerably lower when compared with London and other centers. An indulgence? Yes, but at what a bargain! This establishment's better lines are carried here, with lower-grade items in its branch at P. dos Restauradores 47. **Pestana & Brito** (across Av. Liberdade from Hotel Tivoli) is also excellent. Imported Burberry, Aquascutum, M. Carven, and various Italian labels with high price tags due to

Customs; off-the-rack summerweight suits; made-to-measure jackets and suits which require 3 fittings; good selection of machined shirts. Its tailors are on vacation during most of of Aug.

Optics: **Optica Miramon** (Rua da Prata 269-271) is owned and operated by a contagiously warm and gregarious gentleman who was one of Portugal's greatest running stars in modern history. He and his staff would attend to you efficiently, deftly, and with the best of good cheer.

Port Wine: The State sponsored **Instituto do Vinho do Porto** (Port Wine Institute) displays 300 varieties for show only; now that a law to boost exports forbids the distribution of all rare or outstanding bottles within the land, it is no longer able to sell these treasures.

Stamps: **C. Santana** (Av. Liberdade 157 1°) and **Numifilarte** (Calcada do Carmo 25) are the pacesetters. The latter also deals in coins.

ESTORIL AND CASCAIS

Estoril

The selections and varieties of merchandise are still so limited that everything we saw can easily be duplicated or bettered in *Lisbon*.

Cascais

Embroidery: **Bordados de Sao Miguel Acores** (A. 25 de Abril 7, 1-D) is worthy of the Royal Warrant of any King or Queen. The specialty here is the creation in all sizes of tablecloths, napkins, and mats to match your own favorite set or sets of porcelain. Just bring a plate along with you and the wizard lady proprietor will do the rest. Fabulous! Place mats with napkins run from about $25 to $35 apiece; in banquet cloths you can go up to $1000; delivery normally takes 3 months, but it's more than worth the wait. Her apartment is filled with lovely displays.

Souvenirs: **A & C Lourenco Lda.** (Av. Marginal 31) is really GOOD and that's so rare and so hard to find. The percentage of the customary junk for tourists is minimal here. Definitely worth a visit for that Portuguese gift or memento.

Otherwise we found nothing of unusual interest.

THINGS TO BUY

Main Shopping Streets: Wander down **Camacha** and **Rua Dr. Fernao de Ornelas** for window-shopping the majority of the better establishments. All are closed during lunch hours and on Sat. afternoons.

Antiques: **Galerias da Madeira** (Rua Bettencourt) was a big disappointment to us. No longer recommended.

Department Store: The "big" department store is **Maison Blanche.** It is entirely Victorian and small-townish in tone, quality, and styling.

Embroideries, Organdies, and Tapestries: We recommend that the second stop of your shopping day be made at the Rua do Carmo 27-1 studios and "factory" of **Madeira Superbia**—and don't let that commission-hungry taxi driver or anyone else steer you to an inferior house. Up 1-flight; serene, venerable ambiance; complex of large, plainly decorated rooms in which are displayed for sale all of the scores of beautiful products made by this ranking establishment. For specific listings please turn back to the Madeira Superbia write-up in the *"Lisbon"* section. Unrivaled.

If Madeira Superbia shouldn't happen to have the item you want **Marghab** (Rua dos Ferreiros 175) might be able to come up with it. Also a top-drawer company.

Handicrafts: The very best shop in all of Madeira is **Casa do Turista** (R. Conselheiro Jose Silvestre Ribeiro 2), where you will find a living catalog of virtually all of the highest quality products created on the island. This cluster of lovely small rooms was inaugurated in '54 in exquisite taste. Here is a cross section of Portuguese handicrafts that is unequaled even on the mainland—ceramics, porcelain, pewter, brass, copper, embroidery, wickerware, vases, candlesticks, placemats, tiles, and lots, lots more. There is a wine-tasting room, reproductions of a country shop ("venda") and an old-fashioned rural living room, plus a thatched shed in the basket-weavers' tradition. The English-speaking sales personnel are specially trained not to push. Safe shipment to any part of the world is guaranteed. Owner-Manager Jose Barreto has made it better than ever. In our enthusiastic opinions, here is an absolute *must* which no traveler should miss.

Home Furnishings and a Ladies' Boutique: **Cayres** (Rua Dr. Fernao de Ornelas 56 A/B) is the pacesetter. Branches have been opened in the Sheraton, Savoy, and Madeira Palacio hotels, as well as in Vila Ramos. It is definitely worth a browse.

Madeira Wines: A call at the famous **Madeira Wine Company** used to be richly rewarding—but now that the Government has limited the domestic sale of all rare vintages of both Madeiras and ports to push the export markets, some of its former luster is gone. Nevertheless, it's still worth a visit to wine lovers.

Market: The sprawling **Central Mercado** (Rua Fernao Ornelas) is busier than the Bronx Zoo's bird cages at feeding time. Its rows of small concessionaires' booths are a riot of color and diversity. Tropical fruits, flowers, bathing caps, fish, shoestrings, junk jewelry—you name it, and it's probably here. Go as early in the morning as you can arrange. Enormous fun as a curiosity.

THINGS NOT TO BUY

Women's dressy shoes (casuals are okay); ''bargain'' local fabrics (often poor quality or not dye-fast); leather goods (not so hot); perfumes and imported luxuries (lethal import duties).

SHOPPING HOURS

Generally speaking: 9 to 9:30 a.m.—5:30 p.m., Mon.–Sat., Thursdays till 7:30 p.m. in Princes St., George St., and the Waverley Market-St. James Centre.

PUBLIC HOLIDAYS

Jan. 1, Jan. 2, April 13, May 7, May 28, Aug. 6, Dec. 25–26.

MONEY-SAVING PERSONAL EXPORT SCHEME

Please see ''England'' chapter since the system is the same.

MAIL ORDERS

The Scots have long been celebrated as one of the most upright, trustworthy, honest ethnic groups in the world.

Bonus shopping tip: The **St. Andrews Woollen Mill,** adjoining the Old Course Pilmour Links at St. Andrews (see ''Elsewhere in Scotland''), is *the* knitwear outlet for us. Packing and mailing are flawlessly provided. It's a must!

Kinloch Anderson offers a superb service. Address inquiries to Mrs. Isobel Sked. They provide full color catalogs, sample swatches of material and snippets of wool from their color co-ordinated knitwear (if necessary), and an order form with an easy to follow self-measuring system for their made-to-measure kilts and jackets, plus a size chart for the ready-made ladies' skirts. The booklet entitled *Tartans and Highland Dress* delineates their stock for men and boys, including appropriate stockings, shoes, day or evening sporrans, lace jabots and ruffles, skean dhus, plaid and sash brooches, and tartan evening sashes for women.

The Tartan Gift Shop in the capital handles requests by post, too.

EDINBURGH

SHOPPING AREAS

Princes St., Rose St. running parallel behind it and now partially a pedestrian zone, **George St., Royal Mile, Grassmarket** and the **Waverley Market.**

THINGS TO BUY

Scottish clothes, tartans, traditional jewelry, and other national items, Scottish handicrafts, silver, thistle glass, bagpipes, sheepskin lined suede coats, sporting equipment, antiques, River Tay pearls.

In '76 the weavers of Harris tweed, the vegetable-dyed, hand-spun and woven cloth known throughout the world, voted over-whelmingly to continue their age-old manufacturing methods instead of converting to mass production. In this increasingly shoddy merchandising culture, these gallant individualists demanded adherence to the venerable tradition that their product is a "tweed made from pure virgin wool originating in Scotland, spun, dyed and finished in the Outer Hebrides, and handwoven by the islanders in their own homes on the Islands of Harris, Lewis, Uist, Barra, and their several purtenances and all known as the Outer Hebrides." Salutes!

Yet another island group has been heard from: The **Shetland Knitwear Trades Association,** identified by its logo of a lady knitting. Only articles produced on these 100 Scottish rock-dots will sport the label. It is estimated that almost a half million items are produced by about 2,000 cottage "outworkers." These include thick sweaters called "gansies" as well as other accessories. Since so many low-grade knockoffs of Shetland and Fair Isle knitwear are flooding the market—the names have become generic—the islanders are now determined to protect their cherished image. Both styles incorporate patterns rooted in Scandinavia as well as in textiles found in the flotsam of the Spanish Armada. Shetlands are chiefly monotone while Fair Isles blend various hues. For a guarantee of quality look for the lady in the logo.

Antiques: **Wildman Brothers** (54 Hanover St.) is dependable for silver, china, mirrors, and the like. **McIntosh's** (60 Grassmarket) offers mixed pieces; it's small. Most zealots look for Portobello pottery jugs and brass candlesticks, reputedly blue-ribbon choices. **Alexander Adamson** (48 St. Stephen's St.) specializes in Georgian furniture among other things. **Cavanagh-The Collector's Shop** (49 Cockburn St.) has oddments of coins, postcards, medals and other militaria. **Dunedin Antiques** (4 North

West Circus Place) is known for its furniture, metalwork and antique fireplaces. **Whytock and Reid** (Sunbury House, Belford Mews) can supply church furnishings, rugs, carpets and British 18th- and 19th-century furniture. **Carson Clark Gallery, Scotia Map Sellers** (173 Cannongate) speaks for itself.

Antique Fairs: One takes place at the **Roxburghe Hotel** July 26–30 and Nov. 18–22 (these dates could differ slightly from year to year). Another venue is the **Assembly Rooms** (June 20, and 27, July 4, 25, Sept. 5, 26). The annual **Antique Dealers Fair of Scotland** is in full cry Oct. 9–11. We recommend you check all these dates beforehand.

Bagpipes: **Clan Bagpipes** (13 A James Court, Lawnmarket) announces its skirl on that most Scottish of Scottish real estate, the Royal Mile. The basic model sells for about $350, puffing on up to the finest silver and ivory adornments which command around $2000. Make your neighbors into enemies with the $55 kit, providing a practice chanter, an instruction book, a cassette but, alas, no earmuffs. Joseph Hagan is the clan master here.

Brass Rubbings: **Scottish Stone & Brass Rubbing Centre** (Trinity Apse, Chalmer's Close, High St., opposite Museum of Childhood) is for do-it-yourselfers. They'll show you how and equip you and then you may choose from their copies of Pictish stones, Scottish brasses, and Medieval church brasses to work on. An inexpensive way to solve the problem of a gift or enhance your own home.

Department Store: **Jenners** (Princes St.) is an all-purpose address.

Handicrafts: **The Scottish Crafts Centre** (Acheson House, Canongate) sells baskets, pottery, knitwear, jewelry, printed textiles and stone carvings; you may even have your family crest woven in tapestry here. Another possibility is the **Tartan Gift Shop** (96a Princes St.). They stock more souvenir-type merchandise much of which, in our opinion, sadly lacks in quality.

Jewelry, Gold and Silver: **Hamilton & Inches** (87 George St., an 1835 interior that itself is an architectural showpiece by David Bryce) has represented the apogee of Scottish traditional jewelry (both old and new), gem set ensembles, silverware, and globally famous Edinburgh crystal since 1866. If you're looking for Highland Dress accessories, here is probably the international center for this specific skill, following a history of distinction that is as proud as the clans they serve. **R. L. Christie's** (18 Bank St.) is also highly respected.

Pure Malt Scotch Whiskies: **Justerini & Brooks** (39 George St.) is a paradise for connoisseurs of this most glorious of national dews. As you are probably aware, while the overwhelming majority of scotches are made of perhaps thirty to forty different blends, this light, super-fine type is the product of one single distilling run. On these premises you will find what surely must be the largest assemblage in the world.

Shopping Center: **Waverley Market** spreads out over three floors. There's a craft center as well as the usual varied stores found in a mall. The lower floor is a veritable United Nations of fast-food counters. Open Mon.–Fri. 9 a.m.–6 p.m., Thurs. till 7 or 7:30 p.m. and Sun. 11 a.m.–5 p.m.

Sporting Goods: Dip your line first at **Country Life** (Balgreen Rd. 229) or at **F&D Simpson** (28 W. Preston St.), both specialists in angling and hunting.

Tartans and Tweeds: **Kinloch Anderson** (John Knox House, 45 High St.) is the venerable firm, founded in 1868, which specializes in superior quality men's and women's clothing—tartans (a range of over 400 available), tweeds, cashmere, silk, and cotton. Here, in this former house of the Scottish religious reformer, you'll find Director H. G. Lindley, who is not only an historian and curator of this institution, but probably also the world's leading authority on tartans and apparel pertaining to the clans.

GLASGOW

TOP SHOPS

While it draws far fewer travelers than *Edinburgh,* the demand for first-line merchandise is equal and the quality is identical. Within its laudable redevelopment program you'll find the former fishmarket called **Briggait** has leapt from the 19th century into the 21st, adding about 50 new shops in the dramatic transition. Elsewhere you'll find the extra-fine **Frasers** (Buchanan St.) for *furnishings and bric-a-brac,* **Burberrys Ltd.** (64 Buchanan St.) for *rainwear, sports clothes and cashmeres,* and **National Trust for Scotland** (Hutchesons Hall, 158 Ingram St.) for *gift* *ideas and myriad publications.* The headquarters store of **R. G. Lawrie** (110 Buchanan St.) is also here, for *souvenirs.*

ELSEWHERE IN SCOTLAND

Aberdeen

Antiques: **John Bell & Co.** (Bridge St.) probably has one of Scotland's most worthy collections. Six floors fully stocked; Proprietor Bell and his son impeccably candid and honest in their dealings; sometimes shudderingly costly.

Fishing Rods: **Fishing Tackle Ltd.** (35 Belmont St.) is now the acknowledged laird of the streams.

Auchterarder

Textiles: **R. Watson Hogg Ltd.** has been extoled for its top quality, guaranteed mailing, recorded updating of sizes, and a handsome variety of textiles.

Fort William

Tweeds and Woolens: **Highland Homespun** (High St.) is about the best in town, but come autumn the pickin's are slim.

Galashiels or Hawick

Mill Shops: Bargain hunters who pass through these two manufacturing centers of the well-known ''Border knitwear,'' are urged to stop at their mill shops for this specialty, as well as for fine tweed skirt lengths at factory prices.

Inverness

Knitwear: Give priority to **Hector Russell House** (4/9 Huntly St., beside the River Ness). It purports to have any registered tartan, either in-the-bolt or tailored. Ladies' knits start at around $100, "full" models are $300 or so, and children's versions are a bit less. Clan chiefs have been patrons here for decades.

Loch Lomond

Suede Coats and Jackets, Sheepskin-Lined: The well-known **Antartex** factory is located near here about 30 minutes from *Glasgow* at *Alexandria* on the Lomond Industrial Estate (Tel.: Alexandria 52393). Hand-knits are also available for both men and women.

Oban

Hand-Made Celtic Jewelry and Other Scottish Specialties: The **Iona Shop** (2 Queens Park Place) creates gold and silver Celtic jewelry with semiprecious stones in its own workshop. It also purveys such national products as Scottish horns, Sgian Dubhs (Gaelic Black Daggers), Celtic table mats, staghorn cutlery, and Celtic wall plates by Spode. Here's far and away the best of its kind in the region.

Perth

Designer Knitwear: The **Cottish Pedlar** (Mrs. Patrick Henderson, Lawton, Burrelton, Tel.: 082.15219) is a delightful lady named Morag Henderson; she welcomes visitors to her historic Perthshire home, by appointment, to see a constantly up-dated selection from both established names in this field as well as talented newcomers. She has an eye for men's and women's fashion. Due to low overhead, her prices also are low. If she doesn't have your size she'll order it and send it. Only 10 miles from Perth, this is an experience no shopper should miss.

River Tay Pearls: **A. & G. Cairncross,** the 101% reliable jewelry leader here, offers the best selection of this fascinating curiosity. This fresh-water variety is harder than the oriental type; because they're so rare, they are usually graduated. Interesting but expensive. They are genuine seed pearls, not to be confused with "seeded" pearls.

Pitlochry

Woolens: **Macnaughtons'** extra-large stocks of woolen machine-made products—skirts, coats, suits, ties, purses, and more—don't much impress us with their styling, but perhaps you'll disagree.

St. Andrews

Knitwear: The nation's best buy and most famous garment is knitwear. Of the scores upon scores of outlets we've perused, not one reaches knee-high to the **St. Andrews Woollen Mill,** adjoining the **Old Course Pilmour Links** here. Manager Jimmy Stuart warmly encourages visitors to wander through the rambling building, to view the Tartan Gallery (over 600 tartans) and the collection of Knitting stitches. Shetland pullovers in the $29 bracket; top-name cashmeres in the $235 range, dipping for special bargains to $175 or so; tartan travel blankets, $37; sheepskins, $69; mohair throws at $65 and stoles for $23; many more choices, including cut-price ends-of-batches, factory seconds, discontinued lines, and a category amusingly dubbed "Frustrated Exports." Personal dollar checks accepted; V.A.T. refunded; packing and mailing provided; closed on the Good Lord's Day (so is the Old Course). If you're anywhere nearby, *please don't miss it!*

China and Pottery: **The St. Andrews' Pottery Shop** (1 Ellice Place, North St.) features Buchan Thistleware, Dunoon Stoneware, the full Montrose line and its own historic Scottish Castles designs in fine bone china plus displays of leading British china and crystal. They pack and post to any destination. No shipping, however, from its seconds shop (South St., corner of Abbey St.). Owners Mr. and Mrs. Dennis and their helpful staff will take good care of you.

Golf Clubs: Ask the **Golf Pro** here for the Master's Maker. Many distinguished players insist that there is none other in his league.

Prestwick and Glasgow Airports

Scottish Crafts and Gifts: The Scottish Crafts and Gifts Shops at the airports now offer more and more comprehensive lines of duty-free merchandise to international travelers. Except for the perfumes, cigarettes, and spirits in both, however, we cannot believe that there are any notable variances between the prices of the merchandise here and the same articles outside the Customs barrier.

NOTE · · · Watch out for phony "white heather" (it's 10 to 1 that it has been doctored to resemble this extreme rarity), and the typical tourist claptrap (worth about half what they ask for it, if that).

SHOPPING HOURS

Since joining the Common Market regulations allow shopkeepers to decide their own opening and closing hours. It is a real free-for-all. However, as a guideline, most shops selling anything but food: 9:30 a.m.–1 or 1:30 p.m. and 4:30 or 5–8 p.m. (8:30 p.m. in summer) weekdays, with Sat. afternoon closings (usually in summer months only, but this isn't an absolute rule either). Food stores, including supermarkets: Mon. through Sat., 9 a.m.–1:30 p.m. and 5–8 p.m. Public markets: 7:30 a.m.–2 p.m. Large department stores remain open until 9 p.m.

PUBLIC HOLIDAYS

Jan. 1, Jan. 6, Good Fri. (in some provinces Easter Mon.), May 1, Corpus Christi, July 25, Aug. 15, Oct. 12, Nov. 1, Dec. 8, Dec. 25 (Dec. 26 in some areas too). There are many regional holidays so you'll have to do a bit of detective work to be sure you don't arrive some place hoping to sightsee and shop and find everything shut tight. *Barcelona* celebrates Sept. 11 (Catalan Day, province-wide festivity) and Sept. 24 (Nuestra Senora de la Merced); *Madrid* has a special fete for San Isidro (May 15) and the Patron Saint of *Palma de Mallorca,* San Sebastian, is venerated on Jan. 20.

DISCOUNT ON PURCHASES

I.V.A. is Spain's designation for value added tax, percentages which vary from 8% to 33% depending upon the category of merchandise. If your shopkeeper participates in the program and is cooperative you could receive a significant rebate. There are several provisions: (1) the item must cost a minimum of 25,000 pesetas, (2) you must receive a triplicated form from the shop, and (3) upon departure from Spain you must show Customs your purchase or purchases and leave the documents with the officials. In time the tax should be sent back to you, but as the system is so new and the nation's adjustment to this complicated commercial administration is so vexing we wouldn't rely on a rebate for some seasons to come. Other countries with greater experience and a longer history of tax-refunding are, for the moment at least, more reliable.

MAIL ORDERS

There are definitely 4 (whose addresses follow) which sit atop the catbird seat through experience, volume, and knowhow in overseas transactions with stay-at-homes.

Casa Bonet, with headquarters in *Palma, Mallorca,* and branches in *Madrid* and *Marbella,* is to embroidered linens and allied articles what Havana leaf is to cigars or what Golden Sterlet is to caviar—but at Canary Islands' tobacco or whitefish roe prices. The measurements, colors, and design patterns of close to 100-thousand special orders are individually tabulated in its files. If anything in our reports below on these 3rd-generation treasure-houses (particularly that on the Palma hub, which contains the fullest descriptions) should pique your serious thought, communicate your questions personally to the Global King of Embroidery, don Alfredo Bonet, about either his standard stocks or custommade beauties for *you.*

American operated **Galeria Kreisler** (Hermosilla 8 in Madrid) is the city's leading repository for traditional art on sale while **Jorge Kreisler** (Calle de Prim 13) specializes in modern art and **Kreisler** (upstairs at Serrano 19) is the gift shop. From any of the Kreisler locations items can be ordered and shipment is guaranteed.

The catalog of shotguns provided free of charge to interested sportsmen by **Diana Turba** is right on target.

As is stated later, there is only one—we repeat, one—founder, developer, and leader of the multimillion-dollar Spanish pearl industry. This is **Perlas Majorica of Mallorca,** whose products are sold by hundreds of authorized highest-type retailers from Madrid's Serrano to New York's Fifth Avenue to Los Angeles' Wilshire Boulevard to Paris's rue St.-Honore to Rome's via Condotti to the leading merchants in Rio, Johannesburg, Tokyo, and all sophisticated points on the compass. But if you mail order them direct from Palma de Mallorca in Spain (always best for variety of choice) your savings will be literally *huge*. Write to Manageress Antonia Girbau of the factory's direct outlet at Avenida Jaime III 11. These bluish-white, cream-rose or grayish-black *coups-de-maitre,* made by a secret process which is almost impossible to imitate, come in a galaxy of sizes and combinations of necklaces, brooches, earrings, bracelets, and rings, all with a 10-year international guarantee honored by any Perlas Majorica dealer anywhere. Specify as closely as you can what you're after.

Few other pacesetters in this country's emerging commerce are yet sufficiently alert to expand into nontraditional techniques of salesmanship. To the national loss, the *manana* psychology is still so widespread that in general most likely your inquiry would draw a reply only when the recipient would get around to it—be it the following week, the following month, or never.

MADRID

SPECIAL SERVICE · · ·

Guidelines is your friend in Madrid. Designed carefully by the Fielding guidebook team and especially for the visitor with limited time, it focuses precisely on the things that matter to you.

Finding the unusual, the finest, or having something tailor-made is facilitated quickly by having a knowledgeable and discerning resident available to help you. Art, special showings, private exhibits and locales not normally open to the public are other advantages of personalized hospitality in a strange city. Advice on purchasing, quality, fashion, furnishings—the whole range of exploiting a new capital—are achieved in one morning.

The shopping services involve introductions to designer collections, studios, ateliers, showrooms or salons.

Barbara Ham, an American with fluency in Spanish and French, will accompany you—either on a one-to-one basis or in small parties totalling no more than five persons daily. Her long residence in Spain assures you of expert guidance. Moreover, her background in European history and culture will enrich any travel experience and enhance your memories of Iberia.

Guidelines' pattern follows the Madrid custom: 10 a.m.–2 p.m. Pickup in a specially provided chauffeur-driven vehicle. Time for coffee or an aperitif at one of the capital's ''insider'' spots. Return to your hotel or lunch destination and package delivery if desired.

Details: Telephone Barbara Ham at 3084709 from 4 p.m.

SHOPPING AREAS

Calle Serrano, Av. Gran Via, and **Plaza Cortes** district.

THINGS TO BUY

Embroidered linens and needlework, *haute couture,* men's suits, children's dresses, Spanish handicrafts, Lladro porcelains, home furnishings and fabrics, leather goods, magnificent shotguns, fine art, candies, jewelry, special colognes.

NOTE · · · Two *warnings* follow. Wherever you wander in today's Iberia, please be extremely leery of most of the so-called "factories" or shops where tour guides might lead you. The commissions they collect on *your* purchases from *your* outlay normally average 25%. You'd be wise to comparative shop and then to patronize ONLY reliable independent merchants such as those listed below. Naturally, if you use **Guidelines** (described above) *no commissions are ever sought.* Only a fee for the day is paid and that varies with the number of people sharing the vehicle or the complexity of the program.

Be careful about buying Lladro porcelain from those who represent factory seconds or discards as factory firsts. The latter plainly bear a crown and a stamp saying "Made by Lladro." The others do not.

Antiques and Religious Items: We suggest **Hijos de Abelardo Linares** (Plaza de las Cortes 11) for conventional ware, and **Talleres de Arte Granada** (Serrano 56) for fine crosses, reliquaries, and other objects of an ecclesiastical nature. Calle del Prado (off Plaza Cortes) is also a good street for hunting, but use every wile to try to beat the dealers down.

NOTES · · · **Feriarte** (IFEMA Fair Installations) is the annual exhibition of Spanish Antique Dealers which takes place around the last week in November—prices range from modest to astronomical.

    Mercado Puerto de Toledo should be a reality by now. What was the Madrid central fish market was to become a center for art and design. There's space for 160 shops and its planners hoped to gather under one roof the best art galleries, antique dealers, fashion designers, craftsmen of all sorts, jewelers and, in addition, a host of excellent restaurants.

Artisanware: **Artespana** (Ramon de la Cruz 33, Hermosilla 14, Plaza de las Cortes 3 and Centro Comercial Madrid 2 La Vaguada plus branches in other key cities) displays the finest craftsmanship in media such as ceramics, hides, glass, copper, bronze, wood, cane, raffia, straw, and a wide assortment of textile hangings, spreads, and rugs. Selected Spanish masters have also applied their skills to the creation of distinctive furniture and handcrafted pieces which evoke a warm Iberian tone in any home, office, terrace, or garden. Similar items in the U.S. (if, indeed, they were available) would cost at least 4 times more. This confederation comprises a brilliant showcase of Spanish talent, obtaining its formal start as early as 1969 by the National Institute of Industry. The success was immediate and obvious.

Belts (Made to Measure) and Buttons: *Baden-Baden* (Villanueva 3) has one of the finest selections in town.

Books: **Miessner Libreros** (Jose Ortega y Gasset 14) probably offers Madrid's most versatile stocks. **Libreria del Patri-**

monio Nacional (Plaza de Oriente 6) specializes in all kinds of guides to Spain, some with unforgettable photos; lots of postcards; drawings of Royal sites.

Boutiques for Ladies: New ones are erupting all over Madrid as ubiquitously as a galloping case of acute hives. Among the most reliable are **Brizo** (Jose Ortega y Gasset 27), **Ted Lapidus** (Serrano 53), **Tres Zetas** (Jose Ortega y Gasset 17), which is really "in," **Cabasse** (Serrano 8), and **Blanco** (Velazquez 26). How they come and go!

Candies: Special, special, special! **La Violeta** (Plaza de Canalejas 6, only a short stroll from the Hotel Palace) will caress your taste buds with violet-shaped, violet-colored and violet tasting sweets for about $11 per kilo (2.2 lbs.) or about $5.50 per pound. They are *exquisite*. This is a Madrid landmark. **Santa** (Serrano 56) handsomely packages its own delicious chocolates in gift items such as vases and baskets. The best.

Ceramics: **La Tierra** (Almirante 28) has a colorful and rustic array of pots, jugs, jars and bowls from every corner of Spain. There are antique furniture and rugs as well. **Arribas** (Claudio Coello 16) is also a clearing house for these popular arts—some of smaller dimensions, a bit cheaper and more portable.

Children's Dresses: **Friki** (Velazquez 35), **Bu Bu** (Castello 35) and **Nancy** (Diego de Leon 29) are very good.

Coins: As everywhere in the world, tricky. One dealer whom we are told is eminently reputable is **Juan R. Cayon** (Fuencarral 41)—or brave souls (foolhardy?) may take their chances in the hundreds of antique establishments in the city. Please make caution your watchword.

Colognes, Cosmetics, and Miscellany: If you're not already familiar with the scents and flowered soaps created by Puig (pronounced "Pooch"), a Spanish maker, take a whiff or two—they're excellent. **H. Alvarez Gomez** (Paseo de Castellana 41, Sevilla 2, and Serrano 14) is also long-established as a local landmark with equally large and versatile stocks.

Cuban Cigars: Although their importation here has been severely curtailed, they are still available from place to place—but the U.S. Customs would confiscate them if you were to be caught taking them home. (We're not advising; we're merely reporting.) Some people feel that their general quality has notably deteriorated. But the Montecristo No. 1—WHAT a beautiful smoke!

Department Stores: **Celso Garcia** (headquarters at Serrano 52 plus several metropolitan branches) is definitely the highest-class Iberian entry. Its wares are more select and its prices are often a bit higher than those of its competitors. Excellent. **Galerias Preciados** is stuffed with happy surprises at lower-cost levels. **El Corte Ingles,** while extremely popular, is down a small peg in comparison.

Embroidered Linens and Needlework: **Casa Bonet** (see *Palma* and *Marbella*), the world's mightiest name in this field—which sells its superlative hand-worked pieces at prices so low that you won't believe them—has a branch in the capital at Nunes de Balboa 76. All its glorious Palma stock is available. (1) Make this your first stop, (2) ask for English-speaking Miss Pilar, and (3) DON'T MISS IT!!

Fabrics: **Zorrilla** (Serrano 2 & Preciados 18) is tops.

Flea Market: Go from 10 a.m.–2 p.m. on Sun. mornings to El Rastro (Plaza Cascorro), expect a Castilian stew of commodities, and bargain like hell. Its so-called antique stores are also open on weekdays, when it isn't of quite such vital interest to the pickpockets. Be sure to leave all your valuables (including passport!) in your hotel.

Flowers: **Bourguignon** (Almagro 3) caters to most of the diplomatic corps and/or rich, hot-blooded *caballeros* of the capital—but it's expensive. **Castaner** (Serrano 20) and **Maria Luisa** (Serrano 2) also have beautiful blooms.

Food and Wine: **El Gourmet de Palacio** (Calle de Pavia 2) carries *vino* from most regions of Spain as well as 48 different cheeses plus other delicacies such as sausages, pastries, pates, olives, home-baked breads, and fresh asparagus—naturally, much of this is seasonal.

Gallery and Gifts: American-operated **Kreisler** (Serrano 19 upstairs) displays, sells and will ship (all you can't carry away) some of the nation's most popular gift items from this address. You'll find Lladro and Nao porcelain figures, selected handicrafts, many of which are made exclusively for this house, such as a rich and exciting line of genuine damascene jewelry from Toledo which reveals such a historic Iberian background. You'll also discover the fabulous Perlas Majorica. (For the price—*much* less here than in the USA—they are unbeatable.) Load up, too, on Spanish soaps, perfumes, and colognes, fantasies which are increasingly rivaling their French counterparts. It's worth dropping into this fascinating complex, if only to say hello to Ohio fireball Edward Kreisler, its delightfully friendly founder.

Galeria Kreisler (Hermosilla 8) now is home to some of the finest traditional art in the land, with frequent exhibits of distinguished Spanish painters and sculptors, plus a continuing collection of graphics on hand at all times.

Jorge Kreisler (Calle de Prim 13—behind the Army Ministry) is Ed Kreisler's son and he fills out the spectrum by exhibiting on a regular basis the abstract, avant-garde creations of the leading Spanish artists. (These differ completely, of course, from the Figurative School shown in the aforementioned headquarters.) They range from the oils, graphics and sculptures of such masters as Miro, Picasso and Juan Gris, to those of virtually all talents of special note within Iberia, to those of the younger group who show exceptional promise to pay later dividends. Most are permanently represented in Madrid's National Museum of Contemporary Art and in prodigious foreign showcases. Despite the tremendous renaissance in Spanish art, it is still much less costly than French, Italian, American and other *oeuvres*. Nowhere in existence is there anything comparable.

Here are a few more to be visited as well: **Biosca** (Genova 11), **Juana Mordo** (Villanueva 7), **Antonio Machon** (Conde de Xiquena 8), **Gamarra and Garrigues** (Villanueva 21), **La Maquina Espanola** (Marques de la Valdavia 3), **Soledad Lorenzo** (Orfila 5), **Theo** (Marques de la Ensenada 2), **Olivia Mara** (Claudio Coello 19) and **Marga Paz** (Columela 13—1st floor).

NOTE · · · ARCO, the contemporry art fair, usually held during the second week in Feb. has really put Madrid on the map. Last year, out of 230 stands, 150 were galleries from abroad. It ranks in importance with Basel, Chicago and Paris. Everything exhibited is for sale; free admission; audio-visual aids; a must if you're tuned in to this scene.

Gifts: Try **Musgo** (O'Donnell 15), **Rohan** (Serrano 14), **Bagoz** (Alfonso XII 8, next to Horcher's), **Paola Bottega D'Arte** (Claudio Coello 95), or **Paulino** (Gran Via 12 and Velazquez 68).

Gloves: **Rafael Benito** (Calle de Recoletos 12) is the favorite of most travelers; it offers ready-made and made-to-order at decent prices (for Spain). Suggestion: If you're en route to Italy, you'll find far better bargains there.

Guitars: **Jose Ramirez** (Calle Concepcion Jeronima 5) is to musicians what Lafite Rothschild is to oenophiles—producer par excellence! Concert artists around the world (including Segovia and Yepes) are playing his signed masterpieces which cost about $1845 for the *Flamenco* style and $2345 for the *Clasica*. In all, his workrooms turn out no more than 600 of these rare jewels a year (eight of these being the special Centenario model; available for $6500; on special order only; 4 month wait for delivery). The *Elite* ($4500), patterned on the *Centenario* but less ornate, counts for about 14 per year. These, by the way are export prices—minus the 12% tax. Here is a dedicated and industrious genius whose family has been heightening the art of the classical guitar for a century.

Haute Couture: Today's leaders include **Felisa-Jose Luis** (Genova 19), **Pedro del Hierro** (Nunez de Balboa 13), **Miguel Rueda** (General Oraa 5), **Francis Montesinos, Manuel Pina, Adolfo Dominguez** and **Agatha Ruiz de la Prada.** If you are very high on Dollar Green, you'll get beautiful and exquisitely made creations from the big league Iberian Houses—but you'll pay almost as much as you would in Paris, Rome, or elsewhere.

Hunting and Fishing: **Diana Turba** (Serrano 68) has catered to the outdoor wishes of Iberians for more than 3 decades. Moreover, as Spain has traditionally been one of the richest and most interesting zones for aficionados of field and stream, its reputation has spread beyond the Pyrenees and to other continents. For clay-pigeon shooting, I own a Spanish-produced shotgun and have had several over the years; from personal experience, I can say that these are among the most beautiful products anywhere, with exceptional tracery, the finest mechanisms, superb balance, and lightness. While prices start close to the $200 range for a serviceable gun, a higher expenditure will reward you with something that might cost 3 or 4 times more in other countries. Spanish trout and salmon fishing also are known globally, so the equipment matches the estimable needs of the local sportsmen. Appropriate clothing as well as casual wearables are available. Consult with Mr. Jose Lopez Matilla on any hunting or angling requirements and on how to obtain the generous Spanish tax rebates for your purchases.

Jewelry: **Joaquin Berao** (Conde de Xiquena 13) designs avant-garde bracelets, earrings, necklaces, belts, and boxes. His basic materials include silver, rosewood, and *palo de santo* (a tropical American tree known as lignum vitae or "wood of life"—a hard, heavy timber), which all translate into stunning, individualistic pieces. Important one-of-a-kind creations in the $225 range; boxes from $40–150. **Jesus Yanes** (Goya 27) is in a league with the finest continental houses. Creating exquisite pieces since 1881, their collection evokes the moods and design trends that stretch back to the turn of the century and bound into the 80s with the new *Yanes Junior* line. Their creativity runs the gamut from grand gala to casual and sporty. Ask for either Mr. Jesus Yanes or his son, Juan. Their catalogs, showing some of the more remarkable treasures are, in themselves, jewels.

Leather Accessories: **Samot** (Conde de Aranda 6) and **Acosta** (Hermosilla 20) specialize in handbags. **Del Valle** (Conde Xiquena 2, Menorca 37, Princesa 47, and Orense 6) also purveys leather attire in a lower market range. **Vallima** (Ayala 42) and **Meneses** (Serrano 31) are also very good.

Lladro Porcelain: **Original Hispana, S.A.** (Maestro Guerrero 1, behind the Edificio Espana) is one of the better purveyors of this most-desired manufacturer. The demand worldwide has become so great over the years that often stocks are limited, but here you should be able to find a piece that pleases you. Talk to owner Raquel Barnatan Levyi or any of her efficient staff.

Liquors: Those distilled in Spain are yours for a song, in straw jugs, matador bottles, *senora* bottles, all shapes and sizes. Taxed imports are higher. One quart per person 21 or over is the duty-free limit for U.S. voyagers with a small levy collected for more.

Men's Suits: **Ongard** (Av. Gran Via 34), **Cutuli** (San Jeronimo 29) and **Gregorio Ruiz** (Zorrilla 23), are all well known and respected. Average suit: Around $400. **G. Cristobal** (Castellana 53) is also one of the finest. **Adolfo Dominguez** (Jose Ortega y Gassett 4) and **Jesus del Pozo** (Almirante 28) have the latest ready-to-wear fashions.

Musical Instruments: **Instrumentos de Musica** (corner Calle Mayor and Calle Bailen) is especially interesting for *aficionados* of Ibero-American folkloric instruments—ceramic pieces from Mexico and lots of unusual wooden wind pipes in varying sizes.

Porcelains: **Najera** (Plaza de la Independencia 4), aside from furniture, features porcelains made and decorated by hand in Spain, plus other bibelots.

Provencal Prints: **Souleiado** (Columela 1) is one of the Spanish links in this popular French company. Bolts and bolts of cloth ready to be cut to your own specifications are scattered about as well as already made-up cushions, placemats, bags of assorted sizes and other delightful home furnishing accessories. A Mediterranean atmosphere pervades but this breath of country air can fit into even the most sophisticated surroundings.

Shoes: **Bravo-Calzados de Lujo** has many doorsteps in Madrid—with some of the proudest footprints in the world on them. Though their products are affordable by anyone, the fashion and quality seem to attract film luminaries, aristocracy, and taste-makers from all walks of achievement. The basis is super-fine materials (*lujo* means "luxury" in Spanish) and unstintingly detailed craftsmanship. Naturally, Bravo creates its own line, but additionally you will find world-class fashion cobbling by Magli, Alexander—Nicolette, C. Jourdan, C. Dior, Bally, Sebago, Timberland, Florsheim, Paraboot, Lanvin, Moreschi, Church's and many others. Handbags, leather clothing, and accessories as well as exclusive stylings of its leather-bound realm are available in profusion. For midtowners, the following outlets are most convenient: Serrano 42, Hermosilla 12, Gran Via 31 and 68, Goya 43, and Princesa 58. Further branches in *Seville, Torremolinos, Marbella, Fuengirola, Barcelona, Valencia, Bilbao, San Sebastian, Santa Cruz de Tenerife,* and *Las Palmas de Gran Canaria.* If you are traveling extensively, ask for exact addresses at one of the Madrid establishments. It's *Bravo* every step of the way.

Smokers' Accessories: **Pozito** (Serrano 48) is loaded with pipes and lighters, if you are so inclined. Almost every brand of pen imaginable, too.

Stamp Market: Sun. mornings only (northeast corner of Plaza Mayor), but be advised that you'd better be an expert, repeat EXPERT, to prevent these smoothies from conning you to part with your shirt, pants, and shoes.

Tapestries: **The Royal Tapestry Factory** (2 Fuenterrabia) has been in existence since the 16th century and its looms have satisfied many regal tastes. No problems over patterns, sizes or colors—even the highly sought-after Goya and Bayeau reproductions are available. Delivery time is the snag—at least a year! Open daily (excep Sun. and Aug.) 9:30–12:30; definitely worth a visit.

Toy Soldiers: **Chauve** (Jorge Juan 31) has exceptionally high quality pieces with appropriate backdrops both painted or unpainted.

SHOPPING HOURS

Department stores open continuously from 10 a.m.–8 p.m., other shops from 9 a.m.–1 p.m. and 4:30–8 p.m.

SHOPPING AREAS

The most elegant is along the **Paseo de Gracia** between Plaza Cataluna and the Diagonal. The most colorful encompasses a stroll from **Plaza de Pino** through **Calle Petritxol,** around the corner of **Puerta Ferrisa** to **Galerias Malda,** and back again to Plaza del Pino.

Antiques: This city has become a *must* for collectors. It has gained a reputation for top quality and reasonable prices. Choices are far-ranging and not strictly limited to Iberian works of art, but mirror the worldly taste of the Catalans. Within the confines of the **Centro de Anticuarios** (Paseo de Gracia 55–57 which is actually El Bulevard Rosa shopping mall.) there are more than 70 dealers, including the prestigious Sotheby's of London. Outdoors, in front of the Cathedral, in the Plaza Nova each Thursday from 9 a.m. to 2 p.m. are further offerings. A stroll along the nearby Calle Paja, Calle Banos Nuevos and San Severo which are all chockablock with shops, should net you additional rewards.

Boutiques: **Choses** (Paseo de Gracia 97), and **Santa Eulalia** (Paseo de Gracia 93/95). Each beckons with its own special flair. The latter also purveys dress and coat materials. In the above mentioned El Bulevard Rosa and La Avenida (Rambla de Cataluna 21) there are scores of shops spotlighting Spanish *moda,* which has great vitality. **Groc** (Rambla de Cataluna 100) and **Aramis** (on the same street at 103) are both favored by those in the know.

Candles: Try little **Martin Mas** (Carmen 5, next door to Quo Vadis restaurant) for an unusual assortment at low, low prices.

Crystal and Glass: **Riera** (Paseo de Gracias 91) should be your first stop for these commodities.

Department Store: **El Cortes Ingles** is the best choice. Warning: **The Galleries Malda,** with their covered arches and seas of foreign bargain-hunters, are strictly Tourist Trap.

Leather Accessories: **Loewe** (see *"Madrid"*) has stunning branches at Paseo de Gracia 35, Diagonal 574, and the Hotel Princesa Sofia.

Scents: **Regia** (Paseo de Gracia 39) has an especially versatile variety of perfumes, colognes, and toiletries.

Shoes: **Yanko** (Paseo de Gracia 100) purveys some of the finest ladies' and men's shoes in the nation. While there, please be sure to stroll into the Gaudi building at the corner of that block—a bizarre and remarkable creation of this historic architectural genius.

Silver: **Roca** (Paseo de Gracia 18) is the most interesting that we have found.

Sports Clothes: **El Dique Flotante** (Paseo de Gracia 4/6 for men and Calle Rosellon 261 for both men and women) is chic and versatile in both of its establishments.

Sporting Goods: **Armeria Barcelonesa** (Fernando 23) is a Sportsman's Paradise, Iberian Division.

Stamps: **Calico** (Plaza del Angel 2) is tops regionally. Ask for Mr. Calico himself.

Palma de Mallorca
SHOPPING HOURS

Like "*Barcelona*" except that midday closings are at 1:30 p.m.

SHOPPING AREAS

Paseo del Borne, Av. Jaime III, Calle Puigdorfila, Calle Constitucion (just off the Borne half-way up on the right), **Calle San Nicolas,** and, in the district of Plaza Cort, **Calle Colon** and **Calle Jaime II.**

THINGS TO BUY

Embroidered linens, handkerchiefs, Mallorquin arts and crafts, raffia items, high-fashion accessories, Loewe leathers, ladies' and men's shoes, exotic Oriental imports (including Chinese), furniture, ceramics, hand-loomed fabrics, shoes, gastronomic delicacies, Mallorquin wrought iron.

BEST SHOPPING

Antiques: **Linares** (near the Cathedral at Pl. Almoina) rules the roost. It is a branch of the celebrated *Madrid* thoroughbred, and both its stocks and its plant are in exquisite taste. Very expensive and, in addition, frequently the sales staff are not very kind. **Gelabert** (Calle Arabi 3) specializes in furniture. Never a lot on hand, but what's there is choice. **Midge Dalton** (Pl. Sta. C. Thomas 20) has tiny premises bursting with bibelots that have international pedigrees. **Case Belmonte** (Via Roma) contains a hodgepodge—the lineage of many items could be questionable, in our opinion.

Art Galleries: **Sala Pelaires** (Pelaires 23), **Privat** (Apuntadores 38), **Nadal** (Moncadas 9), **Almudaina** (Morey 7), **Jaime III** (Jaime III 25), **Circulo de Bellas Artes** (Unio 3), **Galeria 4 Gats** (San Sebastian 3), **Galeria Ariel** (San Bernardo 16, behind the Cathedral), **Galeria Bearn** (Calle Concepcion 6), and the aforementioned **Grife & Escoda** (Avenida Jaime III 138) are typical examples. No guarantees by your reporters!

Artisan Wares: (See *"Pollensa"* Galerias Vicens.)

Delicacies: Scads of them are wonderful to take home, as long as you pick the items with which the U.S. Customs will not interfere. Saffron, which costs almost as much as gold in the States, is a Spanish product—and a local purchase at very substantially less of this exquisite aromatic would last the average gourmet for a year. A glass tube containing about half a gram of these valuable threads is around $2. Intriguing little tins of truffles are another delight; they're good gifts, too, at perhaps $4.25. Olives with anchovies—delicious!—come for about 50¢ per small tin and $3 per larger size. **Colmado Colom** (Santo Domingo 5) should be able to fill the bill.

Department Stores: **Galerias Preciados** (Avenida Jaime III) wins in a walk. Excellent. **C & A** now has a branch at the top of the Borne.

Embroidered Linens, Handkerchiefs: **Casa Bonet** is to needlework what the Rolls-Bentley is to luxury cars—except for its fantastic price values. The Spanish Art Commission permitted it to open handsome headquarters at Plaza Federico Chopin 2 in Palma's heartland of National Historical Monuments. For nearly a century, during which it was the official purveyor to the Spanish Royal Court, this distinguished house has won consistently every Exposition Gold Medal in sight and has spread the fame of Mallorquin hand embroidery all over the globe. The artistry of its 350 island specialists cannot be duplicated anywhere else today; its museum is an Aladdin's Cave of musical scores, Chinese calligraphy, and intricate etchings exquisitely duplicated by needle. The array of bridge sets, tablecloths, placemats, runners, and the

like—every stitch done by hand, in plain or colorful patterns—
is (adjective applied literally) sensational. And the monogrammed sheets—well! Newest pride of the house is its
even-lower-price, exclusive, perfectly executed line of machine-
made linens of highest qualty; as one example of this unique
Bonet process, a 118-x-72-inch tablecloth with 12 dinner-size
napkins is only $265, as well as wash-and wear from about $130
for the same size (a hand-embroidered cloth is also $265 because
even though the individual labor is more expensive the textile
used is not as costly as what is needed for machine production).
For men, one special suggestion for sartorial elegance: Class AAA
linen handkerchiefs, *with your own signature or choice of 200
monogram-styles, for around $10*—a $35 value on Fifth Avenue. Don Alfredo Bonet, the global King of Embroidery, mas-
terfully reigns over his fabulous monarchy; ask for him personally
in the Palma headquarters. Casa Bonet also has stores in Spain's
capital (see *Madrid*) and in the Costa del Sol (see *Marbella*).
Super-super.

Footwear: Ladies' and men's shoes are one of Mallorca's
biggest exports, and **Yanko** is a leader of this key industry for
all of Spain. Its boots for both genders are simply *beautiful*—
and their prices are from 35% to 50% less than the best on Fifth
Avenue! The pioneer Yanko retail store is at General Mola 3 in
Palma. At the factory outlet (along the Palma–Alcudia road at
km 27 near Inca), open April–Oct. daily 10 a.m.–2 p.m. and
4:30–8 p.m., you'll find odd lots and last season's leftovers;
25% saving on shoes, bags, jackets, and trousers.

Glass: **Gordiola** (Calle Victoria 2 and Jaime II 26) is internationally famous for its regional glassware of all types. Here is
the finest quality and most outstanding selection on the island.
As an alternate, a visit to the glass factory at *S'Esglaieta* (Vall-
demosa Road) might well be worth your time. We do not like

the prices, attitudes, or swarms of bus traffic at the much-advertised *Campanet* center.

Home Furnishings and Gifts: Try **Poker** (Moncadas s/n), **Piccolino** (Calvo Sotelo 165), and **Interior** (San Martin 6).

Jewelry: **Nicolas** (Av. Antonio Maura 14) and associates are specialists in modern stylings and are universally considered top-of-the-art in reproducing examples of the Isabeline epoch. In more than 20 years of living on Mallorca we have bought fine Swiss watches at lower than Swiss prices here. The boldly handsome Breitling Geneve, the sportsman's timepiece, is especially designed for sailors. **Relojeria Alemana** (Jaime III 26, Colon 14 and 40) is also a treasury of great timepieces, some made to their own design. The store at Jaime III is the showcase for its best mastery. **Gregory** (Constitucion 1) is inclined toward jewels, major settings and special commissions. There is a flair here that bespeaks richesse but a haughtiness that broadcasts snobbery. **Karatti** (Plaza Pio XII 9) is discreet, providing a wide choice in more general categories. The island has a history of excellent jewel crafts, with superb artisanry cultivated in the ghetto district since before the Inquisition. Prices are lower than in most other European markets for such goldsmithery and gem setting.

Leather and Suede: Chic and glamorous **Loewe** (see *"Madrid"*) has a branch at Paseo del Borne 2. **Pink** (Avenida Jaime III) and **Percay** (Constitution 5) have a large display of handbags. Naturally, however, neither its styling nor workmanship will stand one second of comparison with Loewe's products.

   None of the loudly touted factories and shops for antelope or suede in *Inca,* center of this industry, appeals to us much. Most of the cheaper lines are so poorly dyed that, after wearing, the color will stain your hands and your body. You might be the rare, rare buyer who has the luck to benefit by hitting a once-in-a-blue-moon high-quality processing run; with one exception so far we haven't. The aforementioned **Pink** (Avda. Jaime III) has a reasonably smart line of coats and suits; they make all necessary alterations. The honest people here especially advise against buying black, because they tell us that it is their only color which rubs off.

Optical Equipment: **Optica Balear** (La Rambla aka Via Roma) occupies spacious, airy quarters on Palma's most attractive avenue, the tree-lined flower market district. Examination, fitting, and repairs all can be rendered double-quick for travelers in a hurry—at prices *far* below U.S. levels! Some of the most fashionable names are represented: Dior, Yves St. Laurent, Courreges, and many new, exciting brands in sunwear; precision supplies of Zeiss, Bausch & Lomb, multifocal lenses, banks of contact lenses, light-sensitive glass for changeable conditions, and all accessories in optics from the finest houses are here or at their neighboring store, **Optica Llompart-Socias.** Ask for the kind and professional proprietors Toni Llompart or Juan Socias. Personally, we have used them for years—with pleasure. Branch at *Inca* (Calle Mayor).

Enchanting Oriental Handcrafts and Boutiques: Look first at **Manila Import** (Galeria Jaime III, corner Paseo Mallorca 4) featuring superb Philippine, Taiwanese, Hong Kong, Chinese, Indian, and Thai crafts which range from perhaps $7 up. **Rodier** has the complete Spanish-manufactured Rodier ladies' sportswear line (Avda. Jaime III 11). Worldwide shipments. Laudable.

Pearls: Caution! There is only one—we repeat, *one*—founder, developer, and leader of this industry: **Perlas Majorica,** with 1000 artisans the largest in the world. Don't confuse it with ''Majorca'' or ''Mallorca''—and be SURE to look for its ''Official Agency'' seal. Others are rank imitators whose products might (and often do!) chip, fade, and lose their luster within weeks or months after purchase. But Perlas Majorica, which has continuously researched methods of improving its secret manufacturing process since 1915, finally hit the jackpot in 1952 with a revolutionary discovery which makes them so closely resemble genuine first-rank pearls that it's difficult for anyone but an expert to tell them apart. Their iridescence and luster are perfect and unalterable. They laugh at perfumes, humidity, perspiration, and changes of temperature. They come in bluish-white, cream-rose, and grayish-black. Every individual Perla Majorica carries a unique 10-year (!) International Certificate of Guarantee which you may present in the U.S. or 50 other countries. (Curiously, its biggest market among these 50 is Japan!) Their sizes, also flawless, run from 4 to 14 millimeters in diameter—offering so many hundreds of combinations either strung or in ear-clips, pins, and rings that most U.S. pilgrims end up buying several pieces. And the prices! For *exactly* the same Perlas Majorica exported globally, you'll pay a piddling $30 to $200 here. If you're making an island excursion, don't fail to make the fascinating circuit of the factory at Via Majorica 48 or its new shop opposite in *Manacor* (beware of steerers, imitators, and fakers in this city). But if your visit is limited to *Palma,* this lovely branch is at Avenida Jaime III 11 (just off the Borne, the main street), where you should ask for Manageress Antonia Girbau. While there, please look at the new line of Joyas Majorica, semiprecious stones set in silver. But don't be a sucker for the oceans of cheap "Majorca pearls" you'll see everywhere; buy *only* Perlas Majorica to be safe.

Perfumes and Cosmetics: **Gerardo Canellas** (Borne 10) is filled with bargains in brand-name beauty products. There are always sales and offers so it isn't any wonder that you have to fight your way through the crowds that surge into its small precincts.

Porcelains: **Grife & Escoda** (Avenida Jamie III), *Madrid's* best-known source, is the headquarters for this branch. It's a highly distinguished purveyor, which is sometimes slow on special orders. Outstanding stocks.

Wrought Iron: **La Casa del Hierro** (Calle Victoria 6) has exquisite birds, angels, bottle stands, serving trays, candlesticks, flower brackets, and a host of other Mallorquin wrought-iron specialties. Ask Manageress Senorita Paquita to show you one of their all-time best sellers—the $8 musical ashtray "Do Rey Mi." In addition, ask to see their ingenious Christmas tree for $22.

Pollensa

This village, about 35 miles northeast of *Palma,* is noteworthy on several scores—its attractiveness and the existence of one of the finest artisan assemblages in Spain. The latter is **Galerias Vicens** at the crossroads to Puerto Pollensa. Decorators arrive from all over the world to purchase the distinctive "Cloth of Tongues." Apart from these cheerful and remarkable bolts, you'll discover antique treasures, cushions, placemats, napkins and tablecloths, raffia baskets, early Spanish tiles, and hundreds of excellent gift notions and items for the home. Ask for Juana, who speaks English and is so helpful. Open Mon. through Sat. Major credit cards honored. Exceptional and worth a day's excursion from Palma for viewing the town and for shopping at these unusual centers.

Spanish-Style Furniture: **Casa Paco,** en route to Formentor too, sits at the crossroads of the main highway next door to Galerias Vicens. Good selection and craftsmanship; decent tariffs; deservedly popular locally. We know nothing about its foreign shipping procedures. Ask to be taken across the road to view their antique furniture and decorative pieces—some real "finds" possible here, too.

Further along at *Puerto de Pollensa* (the coastal village before starting up the mountain to *Formentor*) drop in at **Volna** for leather and **Esa Fiorini** (both on Calle Formentor) for amusing, slightly off-beat fashions.

MARBELLA

Embroidery: Here's the best buying news which has yet added luster to this chic, blooming resort on the Costa del Sol: **Casa Bonet,** which rates in the pinnacle class on the Iberian Peninsula for the discriminating North American shopper, has a branch at Plaza de la Victoria 3. Please turn to the *Palma de Mallorca* section for background on this one-in-a-million establishment. After reading the first sentence of the Palma write-up ("Casa Bonet . . . is to needlework what the Rolls-Bentley is to luxury cars"), you'll learn why the deliciously low prices on its stunning bridge sets, tablecloths, placemats, runners, and its garden of embroideries have always thrilled customers from all over the globe. Lovely, spacious and tasteful premises; extra-handy location. Cheers to *simpatiquisimo* Don Alfredo Bonet, his Marbella-based assistant Carmen, and the other fine professionals of this store. Unbeatable.

Florist: The rich swain, errant husband, dinner guest, or gracious soul would have to go all the way to Madrid before he would find a more fashionable and expensive florist than **Martin** (Carretera General de Cadiz).

Handicrafts: The trainloads of low-quality tourist junk which passes for handicrafts all along this coast is for the birds (not Genus Skirted, but Genus Sucker).

Rosenthal China: Perhaps incongruously, this is the specialty of a mini-shop in the Marbella Hilton. Perhaps congruously, the place is doing a whopping business.

SWEDEN

SHOPPING HOURS

Standard shops are normally open from 9:30 a.m.–6 p.m. from Mon. through Fri. and from 9:30 a.m.–4 p.m. on Sat. Department stores virtually always start operating at 9:30 a.m. Their closing hours jump around on the clock, however: either Mon., Thurs., or Fri. (optional), 7 p.m.; Tues. and Wed., 6 p.m.; Sat. from early June to early Aug., 2 p.m.; Sat. during the rest of the year, 4 p.m. and, as a bonus, some are open on Sun. from noon–4 p.m.

PUBLIC HOLIDAYS

Jan. 1, Jan. 6, Good Fri., Easter Mon., May 1, Ascension Day, Whitmonday, Midsummer Day, All Saints Day, Dec. 25–26.

MAIL ORDERS

Sociologically, Sweden is more advanced than the United States, Canada, or just about any other major nation in existence today. Its living standards are so high that it is also one of the most expensive countries in the world. Even though the bulk of its retail merchandise is peak-precision produced, here is the reason why so many of its citizens load up to the limits on acquisitions whenever they travel abroad.

But foreign tourists get an eye-popping price break which is withheld from all residents of this land. Whenever certain classifications of goods are exported to individual buyers the sizable Value Added Tax is waived.

As you will find directly below, the magnificent house of **Svenskt Glas** goes even further. Each piece of its world-famous Orrefors and Kosta Boda crystal—dazzling drinking glasses of every imaginable size and type, vases, bowls, candlesticks, prisms, animals, figurines, ashtrays, candy dishes, the lot—costs about half of what any store in North America demands, delivered to your home. Additionally, shipments are guaranteed against mishap or loss in transit. Today, however, the vastly increasing trend in collecting or investing in glass involves even a greater turnover than its substantial routine mail order business. Svenskt Glas' annual series and limited editions have become an enormous success. As one example of many, the glass sculptures which it sold 10 years ago now fetch 30 times the purchase prices at auctions—and every piece sold yields a substantial contribution to such worthy organizations as the World Wildlife Fund and UNICEF. Consequently Svenskt Glas has compiled a brochure featuring the establishment's originals plus selected other limited edition items from Sweden's foremost glassworks. Those who send for it will automatically receive similar offerings in the future. In the upper bracket category, here is one of the most exciting finds in this *Guide*.

If you should be interested in learning more about the home furnishings or gifts that beckon from **Svenskt Tenn,** then write to them. The same goes for any desired article among the gay Swedish provincial handicrafts at **Svensk Hemslojd,** or whatever else may catch your eye throughout this chapter.

Mobel-Shop, which beautifully hand-crafts Swedish furniture from mellow aged logs, ships all over the world. They would be pleased to send its free brochures to you.

Your request or requests should elicit full and incisive responses from wherever you might turn, because these enterprising Nordics are unsurpassed in their professional efficiency.

SHOPPING AREAS

In the center look for **Drottninggatan** (a walking street), **Kungsgatan, Hamngatan,** and **Sergelgatan.** The open market is at **Hotorget.** In the Old Town browse around **Vasterlanggatan** and **Osterlanggatan** and visit the summer open market at **Stortorget.** The Hotorget Station (subway) and Central Station (basement) feature a cluster of stores which are all open until 10 p.m. daily, plus Sun. afternoons and evenings. Don't miss **Gallerian** on the Hamngatan. It is a very superior shopping mall.

THINGS TO BUY

Glass, silver, ceramics, textiles, furniture, home furnishings, handicrafts from Dalarna and Lapland, carpets, antiques.

TAX REFUND FOR PURCHASES

VAT in Sweden is called *Moms*. Quite a number of shops participate in the Sweden Tax Free Shopping Service or the Scandinavian Tax Free Shopping Service which allows you to recover the major portion (actually 14%) of this hefty 19% levy. You'll see a sticker that says "Tax Free for Tourists." The procedure is simple. After purchase you complete a form detailing your name, address, and passport number. This document shows what you have bought and the full supplement you have paid. There is a check attached which shows what your refund will be (minus a small handling charge). Just cash this upon departure from Sweden either at the airport or at the Tax Free office at ports or sometimes on board ship. (At Arlanda Airport remember to allow at least half an hour before boarding as a margin of safety during peak seasons because lines can be long.) We are told that officially there is no minimum amount you must spend to get the rebate. However, stores would prefer it if your purchases would total 250 Skr.

Antiques: Two giants: **H. Bukowski** (Wahrendorfsgatan 10) with its important auctions in April and Oct., and **Molvidsen** (Nybrogatan 21). Both are famous. **Beijer** (Birger Jarlsgatan 6) also has a fine reputation. Please check locally to learn when they raise their gavel. **The Municipal Auction House** (Regeringsgatan) has frequent sales in many price categories—paintings a specialty. In addition there is the **Stockholm Auction Galleries** (Jakobsgatan 10). A walk through the old streets of the Vasterlanggatan-Sjalagardsgatan-Stortorget areas should turn up anything from china to whatnots to King Olav Skotkonung's false teeth.

Artbooks: **Ko-Bi,** located in the vaulted cellar of Hemlin's Bokhandel (Vasterlanggatan 6), is exclusively devoted to the sale of volumes of modern masters, frequently together with numbered and signed prints imported from all over Europe. They are selected with exquisite taste by the friendly English-speaking owner, Stefan Schueler. Whether you want an outstanding authority on Swedish folk or Yugoslav Naive art or on postwar German or French lithographs, or are a serious collector who wants to invest in a Miro, Chagall, or Max Ernst limited edition, you will be courteously and knowledgeably advised. Closed in July.

Artisanware: **Konsthantverkarna** (Master Samuelsgatan 2) is *truly* an assemblage of prizewinners! The reason for this is that in order for the craftsmen to be selected to have their products on display and for sale, their work has to be passed by careful judgment of a jury. There are expressions in glass, ceramics, silver, brass, and wood; you'll also find colorful textiles in Scandinavian tones, leathercraft, and pure sculpture. If you have any special needs or wish to be informed concerning the rich lore and origin of each individual piece, be sure to speak to Kristina Durchman.

"Bits and Pieces:" This is the translation of **Tyger och Tidlosa Ting** (Kopmangatan 1)—and it's a fun place to buy. Pillows, dolls, music boxes, fabrics, dresses, shoe bags, and other widely assorted stocks in small quantities are scattered about. Different and amusing.

Books: **Akademibokhandeln** (Master Samuelsgatan 32) and **Hedengrens** (Kungsgatan 4) have endless selections.

Boutiques: **PQ** (Smalandsgatan 2) is one of the latest and is handsomely chic; it has many imports; the accents are on casuals and sports. Around the corner, along Nybrogatan, are more of this ilk such as **Madame** and **Black & White. Amorina** (Vasterlanggatan 23) specializes in sweaters and skirts. **Beatrice** (at #30 on the same street) dresses some of the smartest ladies in town. Any of the following are also worth scouting out: **Williams** (Kungsgatan 24) **Valdy's** (Norrmalmstorg and Kungsgatan

7), **Plaza Boutique** (Engelbrektsgatan 12) and **YSL** (PK Shopping Center, across the Hamngatan from Gallerian).

Cameras: **Hasselblads** (Hamngatan 16 and Drottninggatan 35) and **Wiberg** (Karlavagen 61) are the nation's leading purveyors of the interspatial Hasselblad brand—the famous Swedish camera that American astronauts took with them to the moon. The first sells only new equipment; the latter stocks both new and used ones and accessories.

Ceramics and Glass: **Galleri Birger Jarl** (Birger Jarlsgatan 2) Here at this epicenter of the Swedish capital you can find some of the most tempting shopping and gift items of your nordic travels. Five exceptional companies are represented: famous Gustavsberg and Rorstrand (both ceramics) of Sweden, the beautifully designed Arabia ware (ceramics) of Finland, and the inventive Finnish glassmakers Iittala and Nuutajarvi.

Chandler: **Skeppshandel AB Gunnar Gordon** (Osterlanggatan 19, in the Old Town) is permeated by the unique, pungent odor of tarred rope. Flotsam and jetsam from the seven seas has found its way into these crowded precincts.

Department Stores: **NK** (Hamngatan 18-20) is the leader. **PUB,** a cooperative, is lower-level but also interesting; **Ahlens** (Klarabergsgatan/Drottninggatan) is one of the biggest and very modern. **Bredenberg** (Normalstorg) is a woman's specialty shop on a large scale.

English Lifestyle: **Mulberry** (Birger Jarlsgatan 10) There is a distinctive quality to English design that comes to its clearest definition through Mulberry. This company does not seem to be constrained to an ordinary stock, but does things in its own inimitable way whether it is producing a brass pen, hardy Scotchgrain luggage, handbags, a waxed cotton drover coat, cavalry twill trousers, a linen skirt or cotton shirts. Mulberry as easily designs duster raincoats as it does leather riding boots or reefer jackets. For ladies or for gentlemen, the key is that quintessential British mood that makes you cherish a garment or accessory for years—chiefly because its character is everlasting and the quality is unimpeachable. The amiable, English-speaking couple who are responsible for this exclusive assemblage are Conny and Eva Lindstrom. They can show you the variegated Mulberry collection, inspired by Roger Saul, the designer and founder of this global organization. The atmosphere—an enchanting precinct of polished wood, rich leather and tasteful textiles—is a reminder of Great Britain's finest hours for town and country.

Flea Market: (otherwise known as the *Loppmarknaden* by the syllable-loving Swedes) is located in the parking garage of the Skarholmen Shopping Center, a 20-minute haul from the center on Subway 13. In our estimation it is a complete waste of time.

Furs: **Ivan Petersson** (Kommendorsgatan 32) has a distinguished name locally. This gentleman is a judge at mink auctions and specializes in this fur. However, we still prefer Birger Christensen in *Copenhagen* (see ''Denmark''), but this is a matter of individual taste.

Furniture: **Mobel-Shop** (Renstiernasgatan 24) has a full and handsome line which is hand-fashioned from old pine. Because they only work on logs which have aged on forest floors, it takes on a lovely sheen in the Nordic 16th-to-18th century manner. There are tables ($120–700), chairs ($80–120), 3-seat sofas ($850–1850), and bowls ($85–154). Especially fine for summer homes. **Nordiska Galleriet** (Nybrogatan 11) is also a furniture specialist. There is a small section here of unusual gift items. **Artema AB** (Stora Nygatan 46) up in the Old Town is just the

place for finding special antique painted pieces. Its limited opening hours (Mon.–Fri. noon–6 p.m., Sat. 11 a.m.–2 p.m.) should
not dissuade you in the least. In this rustic motif the selection of
clocks, cupboards, tables, chairs and other items is small, but
very, very choice. **Draken** (Kopmangatan 2) speaks the same
vernacular.

Gifts and Interior Decoration: **Svenskt Tenn** (Strandvagen
5) occupies a beautiful 2-tiered establishment in one of the finest
shopping districts of Stockholm. The moment you step inside
you might think you had mistakenly walked into a museum of
Swedish and international design. Displays are not only enchanting but are also instructive in demonstrating how you can create
a similar mood in your own home. You'll find a bewildering
variety of gifts from all over the world: *tenn* (Swedish for pewter), English plate, china, Swedish crystal and fashion jewelry.
But most dazzling for their uniqueness are the hand-printed textiles. More than 100 different motifs with exotic and warm colors—exclusively created for Svenskt Tenn by Josef Frank, a
professor of architecture in Austria who devoted most of his life
to interior design for this house alone. Frank also designed furniture of distinguished quality inspired by 18th-century English
styles as well as by Far East traditions. The mail order service
is superb—a tremendous asset since once you buy or see these
articles you'll certainly wish to order again. **Royal Gift Shop**
(The Royal Palace South Wing) has recreated princely collections in gold, silver, brass, pewter, textiles and glass. The location, too, couldn't be more provocative—on any Tues.–Sun. from
10:30 a.m. to 4:30 p.m.

Glassware: The leading purveyor of Orrefors and Kosta in
the capital is appropriately named **Svenskt Glas** (Birger Jarlsgatan 8). It is a small, exquisite, Tiffany-style establishment which
has supplied the Royal Families of Sweden, Denmark, and the

United Kingdom for more than 60 years—as well as tens of thousands of discriminating Swedish families, plus regiments of foreign guests such as you and us. The dazzling advantage here for all North American shoppers is that with ALL costs included—purchase, shipping and insurance—*you'll still pay about half of the American retail price for precisely, identically the same articles*. This is also why so many U.S. and Canadian executives are ordering so heavily here for their *business* gifts. What fantastic bargains!! Since the factories nudge up the tariffs all too often, the figures quoted below might not be to the penny—but the differences would be too slight to vex you. The most popular category among our overseas pilgrims is their tableware: 4 types of glasses, 12 of each shape, from $800 to $3200 complete. Engraved art crystal runs from $60 up. Colored, multilayered, one-of-a-kind pieces start at $135 and they're gorgeous. Highball, Old Fashioned, Martini, and other barware can be had from $200 per dozen up. Again this year, in collaboration with the World Wildlife Fund, Svenskt Glas is producing a limited line of animal sculptures of endangered species—and a hefty portion of each purchase is contributed to the W.W.F. (How typical of this fine forward-looking house!) And how beautifully they will monogram or crest your crystal! Export packing by carefully trained specialists; Mail Order Department (ideal for gifts); 19% discount on all foreign shipments. Excellent English spoken by the entire staff.

Handicrafts: **Svensk Hemslojd** (Sveavagen 44) is the marketing center for the handwrought creations of Sweden's best artisans. Mrs. Gunnel Hannell is its highly capable Director. Look for the painted wood Dalarna horse hanging over the entrance. **Hantverksbutiken Klockargarden** (Kungsgatan 55) has, among other things, a whole room devoted to brushes—at least 60 different kinds for home use in all sizes and textures. They are both functional and handsome. **Brinken** (Storkyrkobrinken 1) means "hill" and, here in the Old Town, in cozy surroundings, you'll discover an alluring array of wooden objects, brass, pewter, crystal, ceramics, lighting fixtures, jewelry, sweaters and textiles. Ask Evy Norin for a catalog and price list. We rate this one very high on the hill. **Stockholms Lans Hemslojdsforening** (Drottninggatan 18–20) is a regional branch of the abovementioned National Handicrafts Society. It draws off the talents of artists domiciled in the area. Additionally, here's where you can order the fresh-as-spring Swedish National Costume. This was originally designed in 1903 and much of its embroidery is *jugendstil* inspired. Fully clad—from headdress to shoes—a ready-made outfit costs approximately 6000 Skr. ($950); or, if you do-it-yourself, materials should run around 2300 Skr ($360); either can be gotten by mail in blue-yellow or red-blue-yellow. They are so popular that there's even a 6-month wait for the ready-made version! **De Fyras Bod** (Birger Jarlsgatan 12), also a good bet, is run for the blind. In addition, there are pillows ($18) and tablemats ($6–12) here for you to embroider that are especially handsome. **Panduro Hobby** (Kungsgatan 34) stocks the raw materials from which you can create your own Scandinavian artistry. **Kerstin Adolphson** (Vasterlanggatan 44) up in the Old Town can offer handknit sweaters, leather bags, embroidered blouses and Lapland creations. Not far away is the realm of **Kerstin Allena** (Kopmangatan 1) where you must see her flights of fancy—handbags adorned with raised birds actually composed of feathers. See if they still have the haunting postcards by Beng Eldes with their mystical trees, dreamlike landscapes and forests.

Hunting and Fishing: **Wildforss** (Fredsgatan, corner of Drottninggatan) has all the gear and clothing necessary to enjoy outdoor life.

Icelandic Woolens: The lightweight luxury of icewool is available at **Islands** (Jarntorget 83, in the Old Town) where Bibi

Gudmundsdottir Bjornsson will show you reversible jackets, ladies' jackets, coats, hats, mittens, sweaters, and children's fashions (for the 2–12-year-old group).

Jewelry: **Hallbergs** (Drottninggatan 59) is the lodestone for the Finnish Lapponia line. **W. A. Bolin** (Sturegatan 12 and Biblioteksgatan 10) is of the highest order. The firm, started in Russia in the 1830s, produced opulent pieces for a succession of tsars. With the Revolution it returned to Sweden (birthplace of the family) and has maintained its enormous prestige. Its second-hand jewelry auctions, held in March and October, are of special interest.

Lappwear and Crafts: **Nordkalott Shopen** (Norrbackagatan 48) starts with a full range fashioned from reindeer skin—hats, rugs, purses, dolls, boots, and more. Added to these are colorful fabric clothing, jewelry, silver, and wood articles. The pantsuits and boots are strikingly attractive, exotic, useful and real conversation pieces. If you aren't going as far north as the Arctic Circle, you'll find most of its best products here. The only hitch is that it does not have a midtown location. If you don't take a taxi, then it's the T-bahn to St. Eriksplan or Bus #47 to Karlbergsvagen. Maybe a mush up to Lapland would be easier. But, if time is short, then in the Old Town, at **Sameslojden** (Sjalagardsgatan 19) look for the Sami Duodji trademark that insures the origin of these unique creations.

Leather: Aside from the usual bags, briefcases and luggage, venerable **Palmgren's** (Sibyllegatan 7 and Drottninggatan 31) has the world's handiest traveling ''pharmacies'' for liquor. The 2-crystal-bottle size is around $68 and the 3-bottle size is $85.

Music: **Walles Musik** (Stora Nygatan 22) stocks folk culture records and tapes.

Prints and Lithographs: Try the same **Hemlin's Bokhandel** (Vasterlanggatan 6).

Shopping Centers: The 5-block **Gallerian** (off the Hamngatan), and the 3-tiered **PK** across the street, are the most important. **Hotorgscity** ("Haymarket") is near the Concert Hall. Architecture of tomorrow; central patio for refreshments; some (not all) top merchants represented here.

Swedish Silver and Gold in All Price Ranges: **Atelier Borgila AB Lars Fleming** (Sturegatan 24) focuses chiefly on the legendary handcrafted silver that has made Scandinavia famous for these designs and skills. Both antique and new pieces are available, plus some paintings, graphics, and gift items. The **Society of Contemporary Swedish Silver** (Arsenalsgatan 3) has exhibition and sales facilities. **Claes Giertta** (Drottninggatan 77) greets you at his own workshop; closed from early July for a month. **Liljedahls Silversmedja** (Birger Jarlsgatan 35) joins the talents of several masters in this medium. At **Metallum** (Hornsgatan 30), they work with copper, brass and iron as well.

Textiles, Art Weaving, and Embroidery: **Handarbetets Vanner** (Djurgardsslatten 82-84, well out of the center; open Mon.–Fri., 11 a.m.–3 p.m.; closed July) has been fast-dying wools in a rainbow of solid colors for over a century. **Jobs Handtryck** (Stora Nygatan 19) designs and handprints its textiles in Dalecarlia. Many of them are lovely. These are sold by the meter or made up into bags, purses, pillows, tea cozies, place mats, wall hangings, children's dresses, and other carry-home items. **Textilarna** (Osterlanggatan 25), **Textilgruppen** (Hornsgatan 6) and **10-Gruppen** (Gotgatan 25) are highly regarded, too.

Wood Carvings: **Sven Gunnarsson** (Drottninggatan 77) is alive with vitality and color. You can sample its aura by standing outside and, through the window, watching one of its artisans whittling away at his work. Models of well-known political figures are among the denizens here. Prices start as low as $10.

Wool and Yarn: **Svarta Faret HB** (Hornsgatan 29D) is a mecca for those versed in the homely arts that need spindles and spinningwheels. Extra special skeins from small artisan factories. Quite unique.

NOTE · · · Don't try to bargain in Sweden (save in Stockholm's trashy Municipal Antique Market—see our comment above on this). It isn't local custom and the merchants stick steadfastly to their fixed prices.

Jensen silver and Royal Copenhagen porcelain are heavily represented locally, but they sell for less in Denmark.

GOTEBORG

Antiques: **Antikhallarna** (V. Hamngatan 6) is the largest permanent antique and collector's market in Scandinavia with 30 shops for furniture, coins, weapons, glass, chinaware, art, books, stamps, brass objects, tin, silver, and gold.

Department Store: **NK** (Ostra Hamngatan 42) ought to be one of your first stops.

English Lifestyle: **Mulberry** (Sodra Hammgatan 2) is another demonstration of the Swedish hunger for British products of distinctive taste. See under "Stockholm" for further descriptions.

Fashions: **Gillblads** and **Tinna** (both along Kungsgatan) and **Bistro Elle** (Vasagatan) have ladies' wear of noteworthy quality. **Stroms'** specializes in menswear. And don't forget **Silvander and Tornsten.**

Glass, Ceramics, and Gift Items: **Josephsson Glas och Porslin** (Korsgatan 12) leads the pack in its quality, but **Atrium** (Avenyn 31–35) also has beautiful gifts; crystal is a specialty.

Handicrafts: **Bohusslojd** (Avenyn 25) presents the most interesting handicrafts from this part of the country. **Konsthantverkshuset** (Slussgatan 1) is where 40 artists exhibit and sell their textiles, pottery, and wood creations. The **Kronhusbodarna** (Kronhusgatan) originally was used as stores for the city's Artillery. Now it contains shops in turn-of-the-century style. One offers candy and snuff. You will also find a goldsmith, watchmaker, ceramicist, coppersmith, glassmaker, and lithographer. Coffee bar too.

NOTE · · · For other establishments, take your pick from the sample showcases in the Park Avenue Hotel; all the finest ones display here.

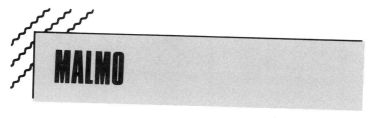

MALMO

SHOPPING AREAS:

A pedestrian mall called the Stroget (the same name as its illustrious predecessor in Copenhagen) is now fully operative. At last many of the Big Guns have moved in. It's an attractive asset to the city.

Department Stores: NK (Stora Nygatan 50) is a branch of the mother company from *Stockholm*. **Caroli City** (Ostergatan 10) is a large shopping center.

Dolls and Children's Items: **Charlotte Weibull** (Gustav Adolfstorg 45) is a delight for gifts for infants and small fry. While there, also have a look at her cunning mini-size Swedish regional costumes.

Furs: **Mattssons Pels** (Norra Vallgatan 98) is an excellent furrier with a sterling reputation—but Copenhagen's aforementioned Birger Christensen is still our runaway choice in Scandinavia and the world.

Glassware, Furniture, and Gifts: Famous **Silverbergs** (Baltzarsgatan 31) is extra-fine, a distinctive and distinguished establishment. For many years it has had broad experience in shipping all over the world.

Souvenirs: **Brokiga Boden** (in nearby Falsterbo) offers interesting smatterings of pottery, glass, pewter, wood-carvings, jewelry, textiles, and lots more. Most of the merchandise is good, and the prices are right. Well above average for its type. **Malmohus Lans Hemslojdsforening** (Kalendegatan 9) and **Roda Traden–"The Main Thread"** (Adelgatan 5) have satisfactory inventories too.

NOTE · · · If you should visit the world-famous resort province of Dalarna (Dalecarlia) be SURE not to miss **Pysse and Thomas Hellstrom** at the latter's studio in *Bleckogarden, Rattvik.* You'll find brilliantly conceived mobiles, paintings, wrought iron, paper designs, salt and pepper shakers, candlesticks, many other articles, all of which have sprung from the nimble brain and gifted fingers of this genius. Extraordinarily original and interesting display.

Watch out for perfumes, cigarettes, or similar imports (heavy duties make them prohibitively expensive).

SWITZERLAND

SHOPPING HOURS

During the tourist influx, so varied that there's no good rule-of-thumb. Stores open anywhere from 8–8:30 a.m.; some fold up for lunch anywhere from 12 or 12:30 p.m.–1:30 or 2 p.m., while some stay open all day; most (not all) close at 6:30 p.m. on weekdays and midday or 5 p.m. on Sat.; some are open evenings and Sun. mornings in summer; large department stores as well as many other merchants remain closed on Mon. until 1:30 p.m. In winter many of the small non-midtown merchants pack up between noon and 2 p.m. on Sat.

PUBLIC HOLIDAYS

Jan. 1, Jan. 2, Good Fri., Easter Mon., May 1 (only Zurich and Basel), Ascension, Whit Monday, Corpus Christi (only Lucern and Lugano), Aug. 1 (Independence Day), Assumption (Aug. 15; only Lucern with mid-day closings), All Saints Day (Nov. 1) and Immaculate Conception (Dec. 8; only Lucern and Lugano), Dec. 25–26, (Geneva celebrates the second Thurs. in Sept. as *Jeune Genevois* and Dec. 31 as *Restoration Day*. Zurich has a special *fete* the second Mon. in Sept., Lucern venerates its patron saint on Oct. 2; and Bern has its *Zibelemarit* (Onion Market) on the last Mon. in Nov.

SAVINGS ON PURCHASES

There is a 6.2% federal tax levied on numerous luxury goods that is refundable if you've spent a minimum of 500 S.Fr. The store where you have made your purchase will be able to inform you about the method for obtaining a rebate.

MAIL ORDERS

In this oldest and historically most stable major Republic on the planet, mail-order queries or transactions are an everyday affair. Its centuries as a host to foreigners have given it virtually unparalleled experience in every conceivable aspect of touristic reception and administration; its people are of course legendary for their honesty, correctness, and dependability.

NEVER fall for any "bargain" mail-order campaign mounted by North American watch peddlers not well known by you. Turn, instead, to a top institution where the integrity is as solid as the core of the Matterhorn. **Bucherer,** famed for its jewelry but much better known for its timepieces, is the largest retailer of watches in the world. A highly substantial portion of its stock—name your type, and 50 gets a 1 that they have it—start at about $30 with $60 to $100 the average range. Bucherer's Service Center and over 100 agents in the U.S.A. take care of the guarantee. While it maintains 18 branches, it's best to request its glossy free color catalog from the *Lucerne* Mail Order Department.

The fabled hand-embroideries of **Ebneter & Biel** of St. Moritz can grace your table or your bedroom by just dropping them a line. They don't have printed catalogs, but handle all requests on a very personal basis. **Edy Rominger,** the master furniture builder from Pontresina, does produce an excellent brochure with large, clear, detailed photographs that show room settings.

Should exclusive, superlatively finished leather goods happen to be the pot of gold in your postal rainbow, **Madler AG** might easily key you into its possession. Our suggestions: (1) Communicate your wish or wishes straightaway to Ms. Stephanie Madler in *Zurich,* and (2) again, detail it or them as fully as possible. Because their goods are of such an individualistic character catalogs and price-lists are not available.

BUYING A WATCH

There has been a tremendous revolution in the industry and before you invest it is worth a brief description of what you are likely to find.

- First, it would be best to save your buying until the end of your Swiss holiday. In so doing you will see many more models and can compare prices. The old system of buying early and checking the watch while you are there so that you can take advantage of a guarantee is of almost negligible value today because the products are generally so accurate.
- Most of the industry is turning toward quartz and other forms of electronic power. Mechanical watches today are usually reserved for the cheapest end of the line or ''souvenir'' category; or they are devoted to collectors of extremely fine mechanisms that range into thousands of dollars. Basically these are artistic creations for those who want fine examples of the ancient watchmakers' art. If what you are looking for primarily is a timepiece for accuracy, the quartz can be inexpensive and extremely precise. As one example, the Swiss are producing the Swatch—made of plastic, useful up to 90 feet in water, less than 20 grams in weight, and 8 millimeters thick. It comes in a variety of colors and costs between $30 and $35. It is becoming a symbol of reverse snobbism. The similar, but slightly more expensive ($40),

Sweetzerland brand is another hot item. In addition, the ubiquitous Migros supermarket chain has stepped into the fray and is handling its own line called Mondaine or "M" watch.

■ There is a difference between the term "Chronometer" and "Chronograph." The former refers to certified accuracy by the Swiss Institute for Official Chronometer Tests. The latter (many of them cheap and inferior) refers to special-purpose timepieces generally utilized to measure sports events. The versatility and accuracy of digitals has almost made the Chronograph an endangered species.

■ Shock-resistance is a useful feature. When so labeled it means it can withstand a 1-meter drop on a hardwood surface.

■ The term "water resistant" means that the watch will resist a water pressure of 30 meters (98 feet). Some professional divers' watches can go down even further. The exact depth is noted by the number of atmospheres engraved somewhere on the watch and in the documentation. **Note:** Controlling authorities in most English-speaking nations no longer accept the term "waterproof."

■ Ultrathin watches, usually favored for dresswear, have been perfected to the point that many now have sporting capacity as well as delicacy. This means that you can have both qualities in the same watch and not have to change from day to evening.

■ At the same time that a slim-line wristwatch can be both tough and ornamental, designers have combined both steel and gold so that your timepiece has greater fashion flexibility. The addition of steel also brings down the price of the instrument considerably because today the quartz movements represent a relatively small part of the overall cost.

■ Among the electronics several choices exist: (1) the Analog Display with the standard dial and hands for the hours, minutes, and seconds, (2) the digital "LED," meaning Light Emitting Diodes, which is better viewed under poor light conditions and (3) the "LCD," which refers to Liquid Crystal Display and is most visible in sunlight. Often the displays are not bright enough.

▪ Some manufacturers produce the same basic design in 2 or 3 sizes that may appeal to people with large, medium, or small frames. This also permits couples to match with "his" or "her" versions of the same brand. In many cases these same options come in both steel or gold, or even with gems added.

▪ Think ahead about what you want your Swiss watch or watches to do, because today you have a multitude of possibilities ranging from seconds, minutes, hours, date, and day—even to such conveniences as built-in minicomputers, alarms, and sock washers.

One thing you can be sure of, if it's Swiss it will have endless experience behind it and a guarantee of integrity that has given that nation such prestige throughout time.

WHERE TO BUY A WATCH

With the widest variety, from dependable, low-cost to precision luxury timepieces in existence and a globewide guarantee service, **Bucherer** is the largest and best-known watch retailer in the world. Any visitor to Switzerland—particularly the first-timer—who misses a look-see here loses a 1-and-only shopping experience. The headquarters is in *Lucerne*, where you will find 3 separate escalatored sales floors with a choice of more than 50 thousand different items. There are 3 branches in the *Zurich* area, 2 in *Geneva*, plus others in *Lausanne, Basel, Locarno, Lugano, Interlaken, Burgenstock, St. Moritz, Davos, Berne, Zermatt, St. Gallen,* and *Vienna, Austria.* One of the primary reasons they give such enormous values is that they manufacture their own watches. Sample rounded-out prices, all subject to small changes: Men's water-protected Quartz wrist models from $60; ladies' gold-filled bracelet watches from $60; travel or musical alarms from $20; cuckoo clocks from $50; 400-day clocks with quartz movement from $50. In their expensive line, you'll see (1) jeweled pieces from $900 to $20,000; (2) the celebrated Rolex gallery, including the famous Day-Date, the "Cellini" series, the sensational new Day-Date Oyster Quartz in 18-karat gold; (3) for the 21st-Century Man and For the Purple Only, Piaget dazzlers styled with faces of precious stones, the most ingenious of which are the quartz men's and ladies' wristwatches. Outstanding here is the patrician swimproof Polo group and "Dancer" line. Baume & Mercier shows selections of stunners, especially the scratchproof "Avant-Garde" in 18-kt. gold, "Riviera," "Monte Carlo," and "Le Roy" lines. Unique timepieces include the Rock Watch, and the Clipwatch as well as the Rado—a futuristic, scratchproof timepiece—and the internationally popular Swatch. Grand selection for specialists in sport, in the sky, on the earth, and on-or-under water. Lots, lots, lots more, too! The Gift and Souvenir Department, on the vastly spacious 3rd floor, is now one of the country's largest. Don't miss the excellent selection of 18-kt. gold jewelry at very competitive prices on the second floor. The collection range spans from Charms Department to all price categories in their yellow and white gold articles (traditional and boutique). New styles are constantly being added by their own design group, who specialize in jewelry set with diamonds and gems such as emeralds, sapphires, and rubies. In the *Lucerne* center (the best bet because of its mammoth inventory), you will find a multilingual sales staff of over 100 people. Tops for the budget, normal, and fatter-than-normal pocketbook.

In conclusion, there is this to be noted: A Swiss watch is more than a timepiece, it is traditionally surrounded by a magic prestige. Because in all categories across the board standards are so high and costs are comparatively low, the traveler who goes home without a good Swiss timepiece on his wrist and 2 or 3 inexpensive ones in his bag for gifts hasn't made the most of his fine opportunity. The U.S. Customs has no limit on the number of watches you may bring in for personal use, but there are restrictions on the *number of certain brand names* allowable. So check before stocking up.

NOTE · · · Don't bargain. Prices are rigid.

Experts say that your watch will Live Longer and Stay Younger if you'll (1) rest it on the bedside table while you're sleeping, and (2) wind it in the morning instead of at night—if you still have such a model. (Getting-up time is fairly constant with most people, but bedtime is apt to vary—and results are happier if it's wound at the same hour.) Self-winders are best worn 24 hours a day, in order to maintain a constant level of tension on the mainspring.

OTHER THINGS TO BUY

Swiss chocolates (but remember, *no candies containing alcohol are passed by U.S. Customs*), carved wooden furniture, hand embroideries, high-fashion specialties, Tidstrand blankets and stylings, Swiss army knives, cameras, photo supplies, handicrafts, leather goods, jewelry, minerals, ski pants and other winter-weather sporting goods, antiques.

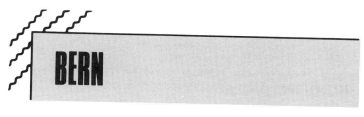

BERN

Embroidery: **Langenthal** (Marktgasse 15) is the inevitable choice for any householder wishing to glorify the table, the bedroom or the bath. Many gift items also on hand, so ask Ms. Niederhauser to help you in your selections.

Glass: **Vitrine** (Gerechtigkeitsgasse 73) offers a refined show-case for the table or for decorative purposes. The **Rathaus Galerie** (a neighbor at number 79 on the same street) also should be included in your shopping excursion.

Handicrafts: **Heimatwerk** (Kramgasse 61) has some distinctive pieces from the Brienz woodcarvers, known the world over for their whittling and other paraphernalia of Alpine charm.

Toys: **Irma Suter** (Gerechtigkeitsgasse 15) has a merry innovative sense in her creation and handling of these wonders. The previously mentioned **Heimatwerk** similarly carries these items in its cellar.

Watches and Jewelry: **Bucherer** (described in the ''Where to Buy a Watch'' seciton above) should be able to meet all your requirements.

SHOPPING AREAS

(1) **Rue du Mont-Blanc** (heading up toward the Central Station at place Cornavin); (2) the streets running along either side of the Rhone; (3) on the Old Town side, the **rue du Rhone** (stretching from place Bel-Air to place Eaux-Vives); (4) the next street parallel to it which changes its name 5 times before it reaches the **Carrefour de Rive** (rue de la Confederation, rue

Marche, rue Croix-d'Or, rue de Rive, Cours de Rive); (5) up in the Old Town, from the place Bel-Air to the place du Bourg-de-Four (rue de la Cite, Grand-Rue, and rue Hotel-de-Ville).

NOTE · · · The **Centre Confederation** has fast become the lodestone for some of this town's most stylish boutiques. The complex also boasts the Stock Exchange.

Accessories and Fashion for Ladies, Men and Children: **Bon Genie** (Place du Molard), the main link of the specialty chain which markets close to 100,000 different luxury items annually, stocks original high-fashion creations, and harbors glamorous boutiques or departments where you will find the latest styles from Europe's top designers.

Antiques: Up in the Old Town, along the rue de la Cite, there are numerous dealers.

Auction Houses: **Sotheby's** (Hotel Beau Rivage), **Christie's** (Hotel Richemond) and **Phillips** (Hotel des Bergues) hold jewelry auctions in May and November; these three are the shakers and movers of the industry.

Chocolate: Aside from the ubiquitous **Lindt & Sprungli** with a vast selection, there are several independent local *chocolatiers* of great repute who will dash any hope you may have of dieting. **Bonbonniere** (11 rue de Rive), **Chocolaterie du Rhone** (3 rue de la Confedertion and Intercontinental Hotel), **Zeller** (13 Place Longemalle) and **Pierre Moreau** (12 rue du Marche) shouldn't be missed.

Cigars: **Davidoff's** stores 1-million brown beauties in both their *Geneva* and *Basel* establishments, kept in caves at constant temperatures as tenderly as vintage wines. Developed under his personal supervision, you may buy here the one-and-only highest quality cigar in the world, banded as "Davidoff Especial." Please remember that all Havanas are still confiscated by U.S. Customs if they find them. **J.-P. Grisel** (2–4 Place Longemalle) opened this shop bearing his name. His experience is vast and his stocks are choice. He is the sole Swiss distributor for the Le Richemond brand cigar—a Dominican Republic effort that is out to rival those of Cuba.

Cutlery: **Coutellerie du Mont-Blanc S.A.** (rue du Mont-Blanc 7, opposite the English Church). The Victorinox Swiss Army knife is probably as well known as the Matterhorn and as well respected as the Swiss watch. Here you will find every possible model from the one actually used by the Swiss foot soldier (without corkscrew) to the mammoth "Swiss Champ" which is probably capable of everything from brain surgery to tank repairs; it even comes with a ballpoint pen. Moreover, if their engraver is available, they will carve your initials on it free of charge while you wait. Beyond these is a virtual armory of knives for the kitchen, the hunt, decoration, and self defense. Stocks also include beautiful flatware by Christofle, fondue sets, chafing dishes and dozens of easily carried low-cost presents. Especially intriguing are the cantonal pewter pitchers and the commemorative cups which will one day be collector's items and which are perfect to celebrate your alpine holiday. Additional branches at Centre Balexert and Cointrin Airport (open every day including Sun. for last minute purchases).

Department Store: **Au Grand Passage** (rue du Rhone 50) is excellent. It has a go-go management team; definitely worth a browse.

Drugstore: **The Pharmacie Principale** (rue du Marche 11) is probably one of the biggest in the world. There's an impressive array of cosmetics, mod-style boutique wearables, and gift items, plus household goods, a maternity and infants department, and an Elizabeth Arden salon. Everything is here from dried pimpernel flowers to turtle oil to bikinis to miniature chamois. If you look hard enough, you'll even find medicines.

Embroidery: **Langenthal** (Rue du Rhone 13) is not only the fountainhead of fine linens and embroidery but it is also a river of quality that runs through the entire nation, boasting 13 tributaries in the most important Swiss cities and resorts. Now over a century old, it still has the vitality of the day it was born, renowned for its tablewear, luxurious textiles for the boudoir, bathcloths, kitchen specialties and other house creations made of linen, half-linen and cotton. Celebrities, embassies, royalty and tastemakers from all over the globe form its patronage; but don't be frightened because the prices are incredible considering what such items cost in the United States (even if they were available). You will certainly be enchanted by the guest towels, potholders, perfumed sachets and handkerchiefs. A unique gift is the calendar with Alpine scenes and flowers for decoration. Ask Ms. Baron to show you around. Locations in *Basle* (Gerbergasse 826), *Davos* (Promenade 52), *Grindelwald* (Main Street; speak with Ms. Sylvia Burger), *Lausanne* (Rue de Bourg 8), *Lugano* (Via Soave 5) and *Montreux* (Av. du Casino 53) as well as other centers. If you have any special orders address them to any of the branch managers or to Ms. E. Schweizer, Secretariat of LWL Leinen Langenthal AG, Headquarters, P.O. Box 346, 4900 Langenthal (Tel: 063–220881).

Flea Market: At Plaine de Plainpalais—Wed. and Sat. mornings are prime time.

Gifts: Try **L'Ile au Tresor** (rue du Purgatoire 3) for a constellation of sunburst pill boxes, antique *objets d'art,* tiny treasures (therefore easily carried or shipped), and a host of goodies that should dazzle back-home friends. **La Verandah** (rue du Rhone 104) is a charmer started by Doris Brynner. There are enchanting present ideas, choice antiques and a complete home furnishing service. Locals are already flocking here and loving it.

Haute Couture Ready-to-Wear Boutiques: The shop in **Geneva's Hotel du Rhone** has high-quality temptations. Even more interesting is **Anita Smaga** (rue du Rhone 51), who stocks Saint Laurent, Nina Ricci and Karl Lagerfeld, Valentino and Ungaro and Fendi. **Pierre Weyeneth** (across from the Richemond) carries Chanel. At **Low** (rue du Rhone 80) you'll find an Italian connection—the flair of Genny, Missoni, Basile and Soprani. **Arode** (no. 31) has garnered the likes of Armani, Lagerfeld, Krizia, Givenchy and Jean-Louis Scherrer. **Gianfranco Ferre** (no. 15), **Dior** (no. 60) and **Lanvin** (no. 68) have their own addresses, as does **Versace** (rue Ceard 3).

Music Boxes: *What* a collection awaits you at **La Boite a Musique** (7 rue des Alpes)! Ask for Messrs. Bernhard.

Shoes: **Bally** (**Capitole,** rue du Marche 18 and **Scheurer,** rue du Rhone 62). Turn to "Zurich" for further description.

Sporting Goods and Clothing: **Charles** (Quai des Bergues 23) and **Delacroixriche** (near the Metropole Hotel on the rue du Rhone 57) will give you a fit—in apparel and equipment. They are tops. **Hofstetter** (Corraterie 12) and **Pierre Ausoni** (rue du Marche 2) are also excellent.

LUCERNE

SHOPPING AREAS

Here's a good walking tour that will afford you an opportunity to see this colorful city and go on a buying spree at the same time. Start strolling up the **Schweizerhofquai** to the Schwanenplatz, follow **Grendel** and **Weggisgasse** around to **Weinmarkt,** then **Kornmarkt** and come down **Kappelgasse.** Cross either Chapel Bridge (the world-famous covered bridge of a jillion photos) or the Seebrucke and head straight for the station. Wander up **Pilatusstrasse** to Pilatusplatz, turn right and follow **Hirschengraben** until you reach Kasernenplatz and the Mill Bridge. Cross this delightful span and continue along **Lowengraben** and **Grabenstrasse** until you come back out along Grendel.

Department Stores: **Jelmoli** (Pilatusstrasse 4) and **Nordmann** (Weggisgasse 5) offer a general assortment of merchandise.

Embroideries: **Langenthal** (Weinmarkt 19) is the unquestioned front-runner in this area and for linens. Ask for Ms. Schmidt who will guide you in your selections.

Florist: **Aux arts des fleures** (Kappellplatz) has beautiful blooms.

Gifts: **Inspiration** (Kappellplatz) is a small, cozy corner with a particularly good selection of decorative candles. **Aux arts du feu** (Kappellplatz 12) offers silver, crystal, and porcelain from Europe's finest manufacturers, but naturally, prices are high.

Handicrafts: **Innerschweizer Heimatwerk** (Franziskanerplatz 14/Burgerstrasse) is bursting with hand woven textiles, toys, wooden figures, copper molds, butter and cookie molds, glassware, pottery, embroidered edgings, wooden bowls, and colorful Swiss-style over-blouses. Many of the articles are made by handicapped people.

Health Foods: **Reformhaus im Bahnhof** (inside station) will keep you fighting fit.

High Fashion Clothing: **Grieder and Danaya** (both along the Schweizerhofquai) dress the local cognoscenti.

Markets: The **Craftmarket** (Pfistergasse) is active on Sat. mornings during the height of the tourist season. There is another one at the **Kornmarkt** (in the Old Town) which is busy year round also on Sat. mornings.

Perfumes and Cosmetics: **Kramer** (Kapellplatz) carries a wide range of beauty products.

Pewter: The best quality we found is at **Bucherer** (Schwanenplatz 5, on the third floor) but **Boutique Presentas** (Haldenstrasse 3, across from the Grand National Hotel) is the runner-up.

Prints and Drawings: **Demenga** (Hirschmattstrasse 6) mounts an especially interesting collection of scenes of old Lucerne as well as other Swiss areas—some dating back 400 years. They are the unchallenged experts in this field. Framed prints start around $120 and climb to $3000, unframed ones begin at about $50.

Records and Musical Instruments:
Musik Hug (Kapellplatz 5) can satisfy your fancy for anything from an alpen horn to yodeling selections on disc or cassette if you want to take those back to amuse friends.

Shoes:
Bally Capitol (Grendelstr. 8). Turn to ''Zurich'' for further description.

Souvenirs:
Casagrande (Kapellgasse 24, branches at Hertensteinstrasse 35 and Schwanenplatz) lives up to its noble Spanish name. In fact, it is a wonderland for the gift seeker. So often the traveler is bombarded by or steered to souvenir shops that stock shoddy products at grossly inflated prices. This is the antonym of that kind of house; many of the items are truly folkloric and some can properly be classified as artistic. The embroidery, as one example, is composed of the finest thread and dyed in fast hues which are so durable they will be prides and joys for decades. And, in addition, there are the special embroidered lace pictures created by talented Mrs. Westphal. The Hummel figurines are now famous all over the world and the Casy Boys are typical Helvetic models created right in Casagrande's ateliers. The carved nativity scenes are constantly in demand. Of course, there are always the predictable souvenirs, too—11,500 different music boxes (that don't break after one wind), cuckoo clocks that work (for a change), beer steins, porcelains (even the revered Lladro brand, the largest collection in Switzerland with more than 500 distinct examples) and, naturally, enough Swiss army knives to send shivers of thrills through every Boy Scout on earth. Swiss dresses for lasses up to 12 years of age are surprising bargains, well below hometown levels and unique in design and trim. Now they carry the unique Noblesse Crystal whose

figurines are so sought after. All three stores ship to anywhere in the world and insure all packages. Moreover, these fine people charge exactly the same exchange rate as the banks do on any given day. Store hours from April to Oct. are daily 8 a.m.– 6:30 p.m. and Sun. 10 a.m.–noon and 2–6 p.m. Nov. to Mar. openings daily from 9 a.m.–noon and 1:30–6:30 p.m. Ask for Mrs. Casagrande, her son Robert, Eiko, or Veronika, all of whom speak English. And as a postscript to their open hearts and kindness, if you show them this book you will receive a gift—on the *casa*.

Watches and Jewelry: **Bader House** (also called *Bader Huus*) is not only a monument in this city—dating back to 1523—but it is also a landmark to the most skillful of Swiss traditions. The building here is a *must* for sightseers, standing on the historic *Kornmarkt* in the Old Town and facing the glorious Town Hall. Mr. and Mrs. Peter Bader follow the parade of generations who have served customers from all over the world. Here you will find some of the finest examples of Bader's platinum specialty— the design creations which have become so celebrated globally. There's also a radiant treasury of precious jewels set in gold for a wide range of prices. Apart from the locally inspired works there are the Scandinavian styles of Bjorn Weckstrom, Zoltan Popovits and Poul Havgaard. Loose cut diamonds naturally are in the lineup of temptations, starting with ½ carat stones sold at highly favorably conditions. The settings, which you can choose, run from classic to contemporary. Then how about the Chopard timepieces with those whimsical ''Happy Diamonds'' dancing with such dazzle inside the dial to the rhythm of your body movements? Corum is here with its distinctive face. Names of such renown as the handmade Blancpain, the sportsman's rich-looking Hublot, the rugged TAG-Heuer, fashionable Gucci and Pierre Cardin, Tissot, the funloving and inexpensive Swatch, and many more.

A second Bader establishment is located on Pilatusstrasse which carries additional watches as well as dashing modern jewelry in gold and silver. The layout here permits the customer to browse leisurely among the numerous showcases without sales staff to disturb your reverie. Assistants are on hand for any explanations, but the atmosphere is relaxed and you may even be invited to have coffee while chatting. Mr. Daniel Rey is the man to ask for at Pilatusstrasse; Mr. Peter Bader will help you at the Kornmarkt address. On Thurs. both stores stay open till 9 p.m. and on Sat. and in summer they do not close at lunchtime. Of course you'll get the tax free benefits and when home you'll be gratified to learn that Bader can arrange for mail order purchases for the gifts you forget to buy in Lucern.

ST. MORITZ

Arms: **Haus des Jagers** (Via dal Bagn 53) means "House of the Hunters" and here is where a discerning huntsman can sight down the barrels of some of the most beautiful stock- or custommade weapons on this planet. Gunsmithery traditionally has been a high form of art in Europe. It is alive and well here. And it comes at a price—a big one!

Cashmeres: **Lamm** (Via Maistra 15) is your golden fleece in sweaters (many exclusively designed for them), vests, tams, and casual sportswear. You'll also find shetlands and, if you'll pardon the pun, Lamm's wool.

Chocolates: **Hanselmann** (Hauptstrasse) is where calorie-and-status-seeking hikers and *apres-ski* types wind up after a hard day on the slopes. It's a *confiserie* where the service is punk and the pastry seems to be following suit. Nevertheless, it is so famous that you might still want a boxful of house-wrought candies to take to the homefolks.

Embroidery and Linens: **Ebneter & Biel** (Hauptstrasse, the main shopping street) has set the tables of Europe's most elegant private homes, palaces, and distinguished addresses. Filmdom's lovelies regularly slumber in its dainty personal wear. And you and I can afford to purchase quite a wide range of glorious hand-made or machine-finished items for our own use or as top-quality gifts—even with some products priced low enough to be included in the "afterthought" category.

Fashions: The brightest lights of Europe's ready-to-wear industry shine in the **Palace-Arcade** and **Gallaria Caspar Badrutt.** Both are lined with boutiques that will eviscerate wallet or purse. In the former, have a look at **Ritzino** and ask Ms. Sidler to show you the latest.

Furs: **Victor Goldfarb** (Palace-Arcade) cuddles snowbunnies in his smartly styled pelts. **Linder** (Chesa Tuor Pitschna) similarly shows a profusion of sporting cuts on its racks. If you are looking for more formal townwear, do your shopping in the valley cities.

Jewelry and Antique Pieces: **La Serlas,** like the gem that it is, appropriately is located in a rich and beautiful setting—just opposite one of Europe's most prestigious hotels, the Palace. Naturally, luminaries from all over the globe are drawn to this exclusive boutique where they find truly masterful creations. The collections are especially strong in Art Deco, pieces from the forties, and settings of the fifties. The interested and friendly *patrons,* Heini Schmid and Paul Helbling will be on hand to reveal the select items you may be shopping for; they can explain how to save you significant sums on the sales tax deductions. The season here generally follows that of winter sport and the summer vacation period: Dec. until after Easter and July 1 until the end of Sept.; closed on most Sundays. Excellent and very, very special.

Gifts and Handicrafts: **Edy Rominger** (Via Maistra 1 plus factory showroom at Pontresina) has creations, worth a trip to Europe, if interior decoration, architecture, or distinctive gift items are your interest. Artisans even will carve the entire inside of an Alpine chalet for you in every detail, then crate and send to you for easy reassembly in your home or vacation hideaway. The prices are incredibly low for such skills. **The Engadiner Werkstube** is crammed with pewter, ceramics, textiles and the like. **Wega** is best for its selection of books and postcards.

Photo and Optics: **Rutz** is superb and it seems to have everything.

Sporting Goods: **Corviglia Sport** will dress you up for upland pastimes; choices are contemporary and stylish. **Testa Sport** is also outdoorsy in a rougher-shod version, especially for climbers.

Watches and Jewelry: **Bucherer** has a branch here that will answer every caprice.

SHOPPING HOURS

As this is a seasonal resort hours differ somewhat from more urban climes. Winter: weekdays 8 a.m.–noon and 2–7 p.m., Sun. 8–9:30 a.m. and 4–7 p.m. Summer: weekdays 8 a.m.–7 p.m., Sun. 8–9:30 a.m. and 3:30–6:30 p.m. Off-season: weekdays 8 a.m.–12:30 p.m. and 2–6:30 p.m., closed on Sun.

SHOPPING AREAS

Right up the center of the town from the station to the church square along the **Bahnhofstrasse.**

THINGS TO BUY

Skiing equipment, mountaineering gear, sportswear for all types of activities, regional souvenirs, cheese, beauty products, gifts, and mineral objects.

Boutiques: **Glacier Sport** is a wonderland of outerwear and equipment for climbing, skiing, tennis or resorting to anything. **La Cabane** is also fashionable. **Bayard** has 2 excellent locations. All of these are on the main lane of town.

Cheese and Cheese Related Gifts: **Chas Josi** (a few doors from the Nicoletta Hotel) is such a cheese-lover's paradise—

you'll forget your cholesterol count. They have at least seven different kinds from the Valais (for raclette) plus a myriad selection of other types from France and Italy. There are accessories such as rustic bags (for the boiled potatoes served with raclette) made out of sacking with colorful printed linings, baskets for the spuds, too; cheese boards in wood, glass, and stonewear; butter molds and stamps and lots of teas, jams, and honey.

Embroidery: **Langenthal,** on the main street at Bahnhofstrasse 35, is the nation's leader in this Swiss specialty. The linens for dining room and boudoir as well as novelty items for gifts and to take home are extraordinary. The kind Ms. Truffer will help you with your choices.

Gifts: **Haus der Geschenke** (also across from the Hotel Schweizerhof) has a wonderful choice of carved Aosta coffeepots which make a happy way to end an evening. (We'll say no more.) You can watch a whittler at work in the rear. **Geschenke Boutique** (near the Church) is brimming over with candles, glasswear, brass items, and other present ideas.

Mineral Objects: **Etoile des Pierres** (past the Church and a few doors along over the bridge) has one of the most creative displays of semi-precious stones we've ever seen. Set on tables faced in rock, the large, rough "befores" are side-by-side with the shining "afters." Rings, pins, necklaces, ashtrays, keyrings—they abound.

Pharmacy-Parfumerie: **Testa Grigia,** on the main walking street, is *the* spot in town you should know about if you ski, hike, or simply expose your city hide to the severe Alpine sun and high-mountain climate. For burns, bumps, bruises, sniffles, or sore anythings, the kindhearted English-speaking pharmacists are endless founts of knowledge and sympathy. For beauty products from the great European houses, gifts, accessories, and pampering items by Dior, YSL (in stunning black opaline packaging), Carven, Trussardi, Jil Sander, Paloma Picasso, Gucci, plus an Alp of other prestige lines, this is a treasure trove. Whether its lipstick from Charles of the Ritz, a chapstick from the drug counter, a sumptuous velour bathrobe, a Boucheron fragrance, a sporty, colorful wristwatch cleverly integrated into a sweatband (by SWEET-zerland, about $40), a frivolity from Versace, Christian Lacroix or Lauge, or a not-so-frivolous Cartier bauble (their newest scent is Panthere encased in an art deco bottle), here is the place to begin your search and enhance your visit. They have the full La Prairie line by Niehans, the newest Swiss cellular cosmetics Cellcosmet and Cellman, the botanical skin care products of Sisley which are based on natural plant extracts, a wide range of homeopathic medicines and you'll see the exquisitely packaged products of Montana in amazing blue, plus the Morabito and Kanebo brands. In addition, there's custom jewelry by Valentino, Celine and Dior. Ask for our friend, Pharmacist Christine Gentinetta, the proprietress, or if you are at the sister branch, Pharmacy Gentinetta, get your advice from Mrs. Claudine Petrig.

Souvenirs: In Zermatt that's spelled **WEGA** (Shopping-Center am Bahnhof, Schweizerhof Hotal Arcade and facing the Post Office—"PTT"). They carry dolls in regional dress, postcards, packets of Alpine flower seeds, cow bells, Alpen horns, a wide selection of foreign language books and specialized volumes on skiing and mountaineering, Swiss army knives, and any other gadget or gimmick that you can think of.

Trachten: **Alex Boutique** (in the Hotel Alex) *Trachten* is the generic word for the ethnic dress seen in Alpine districts, Bavaria and the Salzburg region—and here are some of the best examples to be found from any of those sectors. They are perfect for evening (a smash-hit in the best circles today) as well as for sports- and daywear. Names such as Helene Strasser, Ludwig Lust and Brigitte Hernuss may not mean much to you in America, but they are stars of the European pageant. Blouses run from $200 and full outfits are about $700. There are also quite a number of items for children.

NOTE · · · **Connoisseur's special!** In addition, Gisela Perren, the Austrian wife of Alex Perren of the famed Hotel Alex (mentioned above), will show (by appointment) her exquisite collection of antique jewelry. These are rare pieces of impeccable quality reaching back to the early Victorian era and through the period of Art Nouveau. The number to call is 671726.

SHOPPING AREAS

Bahnhofstrasse is the heart, but there are some good pickings along the arteries that fan off from it. Browse in among the web of lanes in the old section of town behind the **Limmatquai** near the Grossmunster Church.

NOTE · · · As an incentive for would-be shoppers the Zurich Tourist Office is offering a Shopping Pass obtainable through them or at participating stores. For 5 SFr. (roughly $3) you'll get vouchers for price reductions (these will depend upon individual purchases) or gifts at top addresses around town. In addition, this go-getting organization is selling a souvenir line that they created depicting some of the most famous city sites.

Antiques: **Schlusselgasse** (around St. Peter's Church) is a good starting point.

Books: **Buchhandlung Friedrich Daeniker** (In Gassen 11) specializes in English and American publications—if you have any spare time to read, that is.

Chocolates: **Confiserie Sprungli** (Bahnhofstrasse 21 at the Paradeplatz) is for chocophiles what a trip to Mecca is for the devoutly religious—but don't make your visit an only once-in-a-lifetime one. **Teuscher** (Storchengasse 9, Globus Department Store, Transit Shop of Airport) is heavenly, too. They specialize in truffles with the Champagne variety as a real *tour de force*.

Electric Razors: **S. Ritschard** (Storchengasse 14) is the only shop we know in Europe totally dedicated to this specialization. All the top European, Japanese, and American brands are here: traveling types, battery powered, multivoltage—everything. My husband bought an Austrian Porsche-designed Payer and says it's the best he's ever owned. Consult with Mrs. Ritschard, who knows her whiskers.

Embroidery: **Langenthal** (Strehlgasse 29) is tops for linens and superb handwork to brighten any bedroom, dining salon, kitchen or bath. (See under *"Geneva"* for details.) Mrs. Rossi will show you the stock at this location.

Flea Market: There is a modest one at Burkliplatz (lake end of Bahnhofstrasse) on Sat. Go around 7 a.m. for the best buys.

Greek Gold Jewelry: Legendary tastemaker Ilias Lalaounis offers a dazzling display of his masterpieces at **Grieder** (Paradeplatz). Please turn back to "Greece" for details which should make your mouth water.

Handicrafts: If you're as sick of souvenir-stand junk as we are, and if you'd like to see some honest-to-goodness regional craftsmanship instead of mish-mash, the 13 **Schweizer Heimatwerk** shops might delight your soul. There are 7 of them in Zurich. The headquarters is at Rudolf Brun-Brucke—and if you have any trouble with your taxi driver, tell him that it is the former "Urania-Brucke." The branches are in the National Bank Building (Bahnhofst. 2), in Rennweg Street 14 where there's a gallery for contemporary craft (only a few steps away), in the National Gallery, near the main station (open mid-May–end-Sept.), in Transit Halls A and B at *Zurich Airport,* in the Glatt shopping center in *Wallisellen,* at Hinterlauben 10 in *St. Gall,* and at Understadt 38 in *Stein am Rhein.* In all you will encounter only the finest handwrought products from Alpine farm families and small artisans all over the national map. Original costumes of the Swiss cantons, for both children and children-at-heart, range between $30 and $100; colorful Toggenburger wooden articles are $5 to $25; handpainted provincial ceramics start at $6; woodcarvings run from $15 to $60. Dolls in at least 30 different styles of national dress are tagged from $4 to $30. Handloomed textiles in gay patterns are stocked in profusion for about $15 per meter, or in ready-cut Hasli sets or Hasli aprons, from $9 to $30. Fondue dishes, Swiss army knives, music boxes, all kinds of doilies, leather-belted-and-decorated cow bells, carved wooden masks from the Alps, carved cookie-forms, Swiss semiprecious stones set in silver or gold and other jewelry as well, minerals for collectors, peasant toys, basketware—this is only the beginning. We'd suggest that you try the Rudolf Brun-Brucke center first, and then skip over to the neighboring Bank Building shop for what you might have missed. Ask for Manageress Miss Kaser in the former and Manageress Mrs. Butler in the latter. Assembled here, without question, is the most exciting harvest of exclusively Swiss rural treasures in existence. One of the best of its type in the world.

High Fashion and All Accessories: The **Zurich-based Grieder department-specialty stores** (Paradeplatz and Zurich Airport) have often been called "The Neiman-Marcus of Europe." They are indisputably a pervasive traditional arbiter of high fashion throughout Switzerland. Grieder designs are so exclusive that, even with their fine ready-mades, there is almost no chance of ever running across a duplicate. In this league as well are **Weinberg** (Bahnhofstrasse 10/11 and 13) and **Gassmann** (Poststrasse 7 off Paradeplatz).

Leather Goods: **Madler AG** (Bahnhofstrasse 26, at Paradeplatz) is an illustrious, historic, and widely renowned firm. This fine old house, launched in Leipzig by gifted patriarch Moritz Madler in 1850, evacuated itself from East Germany after World War II. In the process, the Government stripped all but 3 of its then-bulging assets: its priceless name, its priceless traditions, and its priceless skill. The new venture was re-formed here in Zurich, headed and owned by charming, competent, and most elegant Miss Stephanie Madler, the only descendant of five generations still in this fine and artistic trade. Awaiting you in these precincts is a sumptuous scope of stylish suitcases, small luggage, carry-on bags, handbags, vanity cases, briefcases, similar articles, and scores of strikingly beautiful, hard-to-find gift items. The workmanship is exquisite; the modes have a special cachet; the quality is superlative; the cost range is appealing. Ask anyone of the well-trained staff if you have any queries; let them also show you the unusual articles in materials ranging from exotic leathers to horse manes. Travelers from all over the world who know this shop would not dream of leaving town without having paid a visit to it. Miss Stephanie Madler would bring geysers of pride to Founder Herr Moritz. Superb!

Pewter and Gift Items: **Zinngiekerei Eugen Braumandl** (Zahringerstrasse 20), founded in 1904, is known for its excellent collections and selections. Among visitors, the most popular choice is the handsome and characteristic pewter Swiss wine pourer.

Photo Art Gallery: **Zur Stockeregg** (Stockerstrasse 33) Here is probably the most advanced and comprehensive assemblage of important photographs to be found anywhere in Europe—books as well as prints.

Shoes: **Bally** (**Doelker** at Bahnhofstrasse 32 and **Capitol** on the same main street at No. 66) has been the finest name in European shoes and bootery since the middle of the last century. Stylings, while basically classic, spring with a sprightly gait into contemporary moods as well. The whole field is covered: men, women, and children, plus extensive lines in ladies bags, richly crafted accessories and honey-smooth outerwear for both genders. Today you'll find Bally affiliates in approximately 120 Swiss locations; stores with a particular selection are located in the main streets in *Geneva, Lausanne, Basel, Berne, St. Gallen, Lucerne, Lugano,* and *Locarno;* look under individual cities for street addresses. Except for local holidays which may cause the times to vary slightly, the operating hours generally run from 9 a.m.–6:30 p.m. on weekdays and from 8 a.m.–4 p.m. on Sat. All major credit cards are honored; Bally features a shipping facility and a repair service which render the same attention to detail as you might expect from one of Switzerland's most prestigious houses.

Watches and Jewelry: **Meister** (Bahnhofstrasse 33) carries the most prestige in the city and its stock comprises the finest names in timepieces. In this homeland of bankers (and depositors) you can imagine that the jewelry creations are nothing short of splendid. **Meister** (Bahnhofstrasse 28) specializes in silver. There's a similar level of gleaming quality here. Best of all, both shops believe strongly in personal service and customer attention.

ELSEWHERE IN SWITZERLAND

Antiques: Traditional hunting grounds are **Cheneau-de-Bourg** in *Lausanne,* and **Kramgasse** in *Berne.* **Antiquities Moinat** in *Rolle* is perhaps the nation's best-known dealer. Buy in Off Season, because his prices seem to skyrocket when the tourists swarm. Closed Sun. and Mon.

Brass Ornaments: *Appenzell* has gone global with its fashionable belts bearing the moo-cow symbol. They also adorn dog collars, keyrings and purses. The master craftsman copied by everyone is **Kurstgewerbe Hans Fuchs,** a grubby workshop, one block behind the Krone Hotel in the center of Appenzell.

Gold Coins: Be especially wary of $20 U.S. gold pieces, because Italian craftsmen are minting nice new ones—with plastic cores!

Textiles: For embroidery we've already mentioned **Lagenthal** under "Geneva," but you won't want to miss the shops in other Swiss towns: Grindelwald has a new one on the main street, with others Montreux, Davos, Lugano, Basle, and Lausanne.

Since 1896 prodigious **Tidstrand** (originally Swedish) has been unchallenged as the greatest designer and manufacturer of blankets and allied products in existence, with worldwide distribution limited to only the most illustrious specialty shops and department stores. When they moved to Switzerland they added an exclusive fashion line. The only full retail outlets to date are **Boutique Tidstrand** at *Verbier* and **Boutique Tidstrand** at Rue de Leman 33 in *Martigny,* a 45-minute drive from *Lausanne.* The visiting hours here are from 9 a.m.–noon and 2–6 p.m. Production of blankets, throws, shawls, skirts, coats, capes, jackets, and accessories at the latter. Unrivaled.

Record of Purchases

Date Purchased	Item	Quantity	Store	Value	Method of Payment	Shipped/ Taken	VAT Refund